Mountain Arbiters

Village of Liglig, northern Kalinga

Mountain Arbiters

The Changing Life of a Philippine Hill People

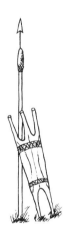

Edward P. Dozier

THE UNIVERSITY OF ARIZONA PRESS
Tucson, Arizona

About the Author . . .

EDWARD P. DOZIER lived among the Kalinga under
a National Science Foundation grant in 1959–60,
to prepare the present study. A member of the
Anthropology faculty at the University of Arizona,
Professor Dozier received his Ph.D. from UCLA,
and taught formerly at the University of Oregon
and Northwestern University. He is a native of
Santa Clara Pueblo, New Mexico, and a recognized
authority on the Southwest. Among his other publications are *Hopi Tewa* (University of California
Press), and *Hano — a Tewa Indian Community in
Arizona* (Holt, Rinehart, and Winston, 1965). He
is a member of the board of directors for the Association on American Indian Affairs, and a Fellow of
the American Anthropological Association.

Contents

Illustrations

(All photographs by the Author)

Photographs

Maps

Population Tables

Figures

Preface

A GENUINELY INDIVIDUALISTIC PEOPLE, cultivators of dry and wet rice, the Kalinga of northern Luzon have the reputation of being relentless headhunters. Today, through Western influence and acculturation, these people have exchanged headhunting for a system of peace pacts and a consequent concern over legal matters. Although the social and cultural characteristics of the Kalinga provide the broad material for this study, the preoccupation of the group with custom law has led to use of the title, *Mountain Arbiters*. For in arbiting regional disputes, matching oratorical wits, and vying for local or municipal position in the structure of modern Philippine politics, the Kalinga seem to be satisfying the same drive for individual distinction that made them take to spear and headaxe.

This volume will be difficult to place in any of the usual rubrics of anthropological studies, for I have tried to do a number of different things. My first objective has been to describe as fully as possible the social and cultural characteristics of the Kalinga, drawing from my own research as well as from that of others. A second objective has been to compare two different Kalinga areas, the southern, where the growth of irrigated rice on terraces has been practiced for perhaps a century, and the northern, where rice terraces have come in the memory of living men. The social and cultural differences exhibited by the Kalinga in these two areas have been explained as due partly to historical and partly to environmental circumstances. I have not always stayed within the limits of these explanations, however, but have ventured other interpretations which seemed more plausible in specific instances. Also I have often found it helpful to range beyond the two groups of Kalinga to consider other Mountain

Province peoples in attempting to explain certain items of Kalinga behavior or certain social institutions. The result has been the erection of a number of problems, some of which have been analyzed with greater rigor and with more and better supporting data than others. A year was too brief a time to do full justice to the analysis of the many intriguing and challenging problems that emerged, but rather than have these problems molding in my notes, I decided to include them in this study. Some of these problems I hope to investigate with further research; others may simply serve as leads for other investigators.

Many institutions and people have assisted in bringing about this study. My indebtedness is first of all to the National Science Foundation for making possible field research in the Philippines through the grant of a Senior Post-Doctoral Fellowship. Before leaving for the Philippines, I was fortunate enough to spend a year (1958–59) at the Stanford Center for Advanced Studies in the Behavioral Sciences. The informal seminars and discussions were valuable preparation for field work, and I am grateful to Dr. Ralph W. Tyler, director, and to my colleagues at the Center. Writing and organization of the manuscript was fostered by a grant-in-aid from the American Philosophical Society, and by The University of Arizona. My appreciation goes to both institutions. Finally, I am indebted to the faculty and staff of the Department of Anthropology and the Arizona State Museum for the use of facilities and many other courtesies during the preparation of the manuscript.

Many people were helpful to me and my family before we left the United States and while we were in the Philippines. Their names if listed would fill several pages of this study. Here I include only those people who directly facilitated my anthropological investigations.

My debt to Professor and Mrs. Fred Eggan is immeasurable. They first aroused my interest in the peoples of the Mountain Province and assisted in many ways in making our field work in the Philippines a pleasant experience. Professor Eggan followed my work in the field and has read this study critically in final draft. I am grateful to the late Professor Felix Keesing and his wife who gave me the benefit of their own travels and studies in the Philippines in a number of informal meetings. In addition, Professor Keesing received my notes from the field, read them carefully, and made discerning and critical comments.

Others who have read the whole or parts of the initial draft are the following: Dr. Harold C. Conklin, Reverend Father Jules De Raedt, Reverend Carl Lutz, Dr. George Peter Murdock, and Mr. William H. Scott. While the critical comments of these readers have been immensely helpful to me and they have undoubtedly contributed to whatever merit this study may have, none of these people are to be held responsible for the shortcomings of this book. I have not always followed suggestions, but have often stubbornly held on to an original form or an idea at variance with those of my readers.

In acknowledging my gratitude to people in the Philippines, I shall proceed geographically from south to north, from Manila to the heart of the north Kalinga country.

Upon our arrival in Manila, Professor H. Otley Beyer and Dr. Robert B. Fox provided me with much valuable information about the Mountain Province and the area in which I was to conduct my field investigations. Dr. John Province helped us through customs and provided transportation to Baguio. In Baguio the number of people to whom I am indebted is large, but a few stand out. Father Alfred R. Griffiths, headmaster of Brent School, and his wife, were most generous and hospitable, and we benefited from their intimate knowledge of the Balbalasang Kalinga. The late Lawrence L. Wilson made his library on anthropology available to me, and generously shared his vast storehouse of Philippine experiences with me. Dr. and Mrs. Danao provided health services to the whole family and made us feel the warmth of a typical Philippine family. Mrs. Cecile Afable introduced me to the first Kalinga I met. In numerous informal discussions she gave liberally of her rich and extensive knowledge of the Mountain Province and performed many services which facilitated my field work.

Mr. William H. Scott, principal of St. Mary's High School, Sagada, Bontoc subprovince, assisted me in many ways. His own field notes on the Kalinga and other Mountain Province peoples provided checks and comparative materials, and in addition he was a genial host; he fed me and housed me on several occasions.

For generous hospitality and delightful conversation, I am grateful to Father and Mrs. Richard Over in Bontoc. Theirs was a pleasant halfway station in my travels to and from the Kalinga country — a welcome rest from the jars and bounces of the Dangwa truck.

In Lubuagan it was a pleasure to discuss Kalinga behavior and customs with the Belgian Fathers. I am especially grateful to Father Francisco Billiet who gave me the benefit of his fifty years of experiences and observations among the Kalinga.

Juanito Suyam, his brother, Bomacas, and a host of his relatives in Lubuagan provided a home with the generous hospitality so characteristic of the Kalinga. My information about the Southern Kalinga came primarily from Juanito's kinship circle which I was privileged to observe and experience in its daily round of activities.

In Salegseg I met another group of Belgian priests: Father Jules De Raedt, Father Miguel Seys, and Father Juan Hanssens. They contributed immensely to my education in the behavior and customs of the Northern Kalinga, and provided, in addition, delightful company.

It will be impossible to list the many Kalinga from the northern regions who welcomed me in their homes and permitted me to observe freely, always ready to inform and explain Kalinga behavior and customs. The following are those who come most readily to mind: Mr. Julian Ande, head teacher, Salegseg Central School; Mr. Matias Calumnag, teacher, Pantikian; Mr. and Mrs. Lino Taway, Tappo, Mabaca; Mr. and Mrs. Ponciano Daquiwag, teachers, Mabaca School; Mr. Thomas Dayag, Poswoy; Mr. Francisco Dasayon, Apata, Pinokpok; Mr. and Mrs. Augustin Salingbay, Balala, Mabaca.

Mr. Juanito Baguingan of Poswoy deserves special mention. He has worked constantly with me, has acted as a guide and interpreter and has contributed substantially to this study.

Since I cannot acknowledge by name the many Kalinga who have in one way or another contributed to this study, I express my thanks and appreciation to all of them — a more generous and hospitable people would be difficult to find.

A final important acknowledgment: Only the encouragement and support of my wife, Marianne Fink Dozier, have made possible the research and the preparation of the manuscript for publication. I have drawn liberally from her own field notes on Kalinga child-rearing practices and have discussed all phases of the research material with her; and the interpretations of the study are essentially joint contributions.

Field Methods

I established residence for my family in Baguio, and our house there functioned as research headquarters for the year. The materials I gathered in the Kalinga hamlets were organized and typed in Baguio. Early in the research period I enlisted the help of a number of Kalinga college students from Lubuagan and the northern Kalinga area, who shared our house in Baguio and performed a variety of research tasks. My initial contacts in the hamlets were made through these young men who introduced me to their relatives in the isolated villages. In the field three young men from Lubuagan, Poswoy, and Salegseg, respectively, regularly secured information of a statistical nature for me: house lists, population figures, genealogical charts, and the like. On two occasions when I returned from the northern Kalinga country to Baguio, I brought back older Kalinga informants with me so that I could continue the collection of data while my field notes and the information collected by my young Kalinga assistants were being organized and typed.

I lived in Lubuagan with one Kalinga family for one month, and my family joined me later in the hamlet of Alingag (northern Kalinga) for another steady residence of a month. Aside from these periods, I did not maintain prolonged residence in other hamlets. My visits to the regional populations consisted of a week in one hamlet, two weeks in another, and so on. The scattered residence pattern which disperses families of a kindred into different hamlets brings about considerable mobility of the regional population. Individuals and families frequently visit one another and attend feasts associated with the life cycle. During the dry season, mobility is accentuated and travel is extended inter-regionally; anywhere from three to ten peace-pact celebrations might be visited over a period of three months. I became a part of this pattern of mobility, for to share as much as possible in northern Kalinga life, one must go along with the Kalinga to regional festivals and the popular interregional peace-pact celebrations.

English is widely spoken in Lubuagan and the northern Kalinga areas. I conducted all my interviews in English. With some informants I used interpreters, but even older Kalinga frequently spoke English so that communication was not a problem at any time.

So many Kalinga have contributed to the information comprising the primary sources of data for this study, that it would be impossible to mention them all. Nevertheless, some individuals supplied more information than others, and I list here a number of my main informants. In Lubuagan, members of the immediate family of Juanito Suyam, one of my collegiate assistants, provided most of the information, but other members of his large kinship circle also contributed materials either through formal sessions or informally in social contacts. Juanito's kindred was distributed over a number of towns or wards in Lubuagan proper, but I most frequently visited those in Tangadan, Kimatan, Linas, and Mabilong. Juanito's father, the elder Suyam, age about sixty-five, furnished excellent information on the peace-pact system. Suyam held four peace pacts, more than any other pact-holder in Lubuagan. Dakiwas, a man about fifty-five years old, from Kimatan, brother-in-law of the elder Suyam, provided most of the information on agriculture. The bulk of the religious information came from Juanito's paternal grandmother, a medium, with Juanito, his brother, Bomacas, and the latter's wife, Manuela, acting as interpreters. At all times during my stay in Lubuagan I supplemented recorded materials obtained from informants with observation of actual behavior.

Information in the north was also gathered in the context of a family group. In Bolo (Salegseg region) the Agnas family furnished especially detailed information on economic patterns and social organization. Carolina Agnas Daquiwag, a woman about thirty years old whose own children had passed through the various stages of the *Kontad,* was an excellent informant for this important phase of the Kalinga life cycle.

In Tappo, Mabaca, Mr. and Mrs. Lino Taway, a couple in their mid-forties, provided information particularly on the peace-pact system; Marcelo Banatao, a man of about sixty years old, also from Tappo, supplied materials on agriculture, hunting, and inheritance patterns. I worked most intensively in Mabaca with Mr. Augustin Salingbay of Balala, a man of about sixty-five. Mr. Salingbay provided information on all areas of Mabaca life.

My materials from Poswoy are especially rich. Here, as in Lubuagan, the kinship circle and family of another student (Juanito Baguingan), provided a convenient context where formally recorded information was constantly reinforced by observation of actual behavior. In both cases, the genealogical relations had been charted, and thus the genealogical positions of specific individuals were known. Juanito's maternal aunt, Kalingwan Wanason, an intelligent and cooperative medium, permitted me to tape-record her chants of the *dawak* curing ceremony described in the chapter on religion, and furnished additional information on ceremonies and religious practices.

All information obtained through formal interviews was checked with other informants and confirmed by "participant observation." In social gatherings, festivals, peace-pact meetings and the like, someone was always by my side explaining what was going on. I carried a note pad at all times and was able to use it continually. This was a delightful experience after my work among the Pueblo Indians of the southwestern United States where the ethnographer is always suspect, and note-taking is taboo except when the complete confidence of an informant has been gained, and then only in a place where the ethnographer is alone with his informant.

Much of the information was obtained, not by formal interviewing, but in casual conversations, or else the information was simply "absorbed" by observation. I did not need to assume a "false role"; I told everyone that I was a college professor interested in obtaining information on all aspects of Kalinga life. While most Kalinga never quite understood my role, they accepted me as an individual who indeed wanted to collect all sorts of information. I received complete cooperation in my work, and regional leaders even assigned informants to help me write a "history" of the Kalinga. I accepted such aid in all cases, but I also sought out additional informants of my own. Very early I became aware that the Kalinga, like most people, wanted a favorable and embroidered picture of their way of life, and I had to be constantly on guard not to be sold "a bill of goods." In my work with informants and in my observations, I tried at all times to remain objective and critical. It is possible, therefore, that this study may not be completely acceptable to the Kalinga, for what have emerged, as in any objective study of a human society, are both favorable and unfavorable aspects. On the other hand, no study is completely free of the biases of the investigator, despite precautions to the contrary. I enjoyed my field work and I frankly like the Kalinga, hence I may have inadvertently emphasized the positive aspects of Kalinga culture.

Except for the college students who obtained rather specific types of information for me, I did not pay my informants, although I compensated them with gifts. I also took numerous black and white photographs of my informants and their families and gave them copies. Another type of service may be considered compensation: I obliged regional leaders by speaking at festivals and peace-pact celebrations, and on two occasions, served as "commencement speaker," once at the elementary school in Mabaca and again at the central elementary school in Salegseg. Such occasions were gratifying to me, however, and, like the Kalinga, I enjoyed the flowery introductions and a chance to be the object of attention and applause.

I have made comparisons of many aspects of Kalinga culture with those of other mountain peoples in northern Luzon. The data for such comparisons have been abstracted from published literature or from unpublished manuscripts made available to me by my colleagues. I have tried in every case to credit these sources, but in the desire to present an integrated account, I may have in some instances failed to acknowledge properly my indebtedness to other investigators. Hence I want to express here my gratitude to all scholars, past and present, whose contributions I have used in the hope of presenting a comprehensive and scientifically valid study.

Language and Orthography

This is only a brief statement of the Kalinga language and a description of its sound system. I am concerned here primarily with the task of providing an orthography adequate to record terms and texts which must be presented in a general description of Kalinga culture. The phonetic variations are those which have come to my attention; undoubtedly a more systematic study of the various dialects will reveal more significant aspects of the language. Such investigations have already been initiated by the Summer Institute of Linguistics (see Gieser, 1958). Studies of this kind will eventually reveal the nature of the dialectical variations throughout the Kalinga area.

In a lexicostatistical study of Philippine languages, Thomas and Healey (1962: 22–23) propose a tentative Philippine "family tree" in which Kalinga is placed in one of three branches of the Northern Philippine Family of the Philippine Stock. The Philippine Stock itself is derived from a Philippine Superstock.

Kalinga informants report that dialects in all Kalinga regions are mutually intelligible. Such regions are not confined to the Kalinga subprovince, but extend over the borders of the subprovince into parts of the provinces of Abra and Cagayan; northward into the subprovince of Apayao and southeastward into Bontoc subprovince. All Kalinga are aware of the phonetic substitutions that must be made when speaking with Kalinga from other regions. Today Kalinga who have traveled extensively also employ a phonetically modified or simplified Kalinga when speaking with Kalinga from distant regions. This modified Kalinga consists of a simplified phonetics where affricates are rendered as stops and *l* is pronounced as [l] in all environments (see description of sounds). The orthography adopted for this paper represents essentially the modified Kalinga speech, although I have attempted also to indicate some of the distributional sound changes. The modified Kalinga is undoubtedly influenced by Ilocano phonetics since the phonetic changes involved are toward an approximation of the Ilocano pronunciation. The linguistic changes noted for Kalinga have also been observed for other Mountain Province languages; that is, all these languages appear to be adjusting to Ilocano phonetics. Ilocano is the accepted lingua franca over most of Northern Luzon and its influence is most profound. Earlier, Spanish influenced all of the Mountain Province languages, and the vocabulary of virtually all Philippine languages contains many Spanish loan words. While English is now widely spoken over the Mountain Province, its influence on the sound systems of these languages is not. yet clear, although it has contributed to the vocabulary of Mountain Province languages.

All of the Kalinga dialect regions visited speak of their language as *Kinalingga* (Salegseg: [Kinalinggha]) but refer to the people as *Kalingga* (not *Kaling-a* but *Kalingga*). The meaning or origin of the word Kalingga is obscure. One informant thought it derived from *kaling-a* which he translated as "warrior" or "enemy warrior." In this paper, *Kalinga* (pronounced *Kalingga*) is used without italics, both as a designation for the people and their language.

The fact that Kalinga dialects are mutually intelligible indicates that vocabulary differences are not extreme or that speakers are cognizant of the phonetic correspondences between distant geographical sectors even though dialectical variations might be fairly extreme. If indeed vocabulary differences are slight, then the evidence for recent Kalinga expansion is strengthened; a fact also supported by non-linguistic evidence to be discussed in some detail in this study.

The following symbols have been adopted for this paper:

Stops: voiceless *p, t, k;* glottal –; voiced *b, d, g.*
Continuants: *l, s, m, n, ng;* voiced semivowels *y,* and *w;* voiced vowels *i, o, a.*

Only a brief and tentative analysis of Kalinga sounds was made, hence our units may not have the full status of phonemes. Nevertheless, we believe the classification describes fairly well the modified or simplified Kalinga sound system to which adjustments are being made among the dialects considered, and this orthography may even be appropriate for a wider area of Kalinga dialect regions.

Within recent times, population increases and other factors of acculturation have brought about migrations from formerly geographically restricted regions. Thus Uma, a colony of Lubuagan about six kilometers away, has grown into one large village and a number of small satellite communities. While Uma has acquired political independence (by making its own peace pacts) from its parent region, dialectically it is still considered Lubuagan. The migrations out of Salegseg, Mabaca, Poswoy, and adjacent regions have been to more distant places: Pinokpok District, eastern Abra, and Southern Apayao. These areas are beginning to make their own separate peace pacts with other regions, but are still dialectically related to their home regions. Thus Kalinga dialects are becoming dispersed over wide areas of Kalinga subprovince and spilling over into adjacent provinces and subprovinces. This dispersal has made for familiarity of regional dialects; thus one hears such remarks as: "They are fond of 'r' in Buaya." "In Poswoy they have so much 'xwoi' in their speech." etc. Out of this interaction, and with Ilocano phonetics as a model, has grown the modified or simplified Kalinga which may eventually replace the local dialects. This modified Kalinga is being used increasingly by educated Kalinga who feel that speaking a local dialect stamps one as provincial and unsophisticated. Indeed, even in soliciting linguistic information from educated Kalinga, the investigator encounters resistance in obtaining dialect pronunciation. Invariably, the educated informant responds with the modified Kalinga sounds, although in his own dialect region he employs his dialect speech (cf. Gieser, 1958, p. 23).

Phonetic Symbols

> (In the text terms and sounds phonetically recorded are enclosed in brackets []; other non-English designations and sounds are italicized.)

STOPS

p, t, k These are bilabial, dental, and velar respectively. All are voiceless and only slightly aspirated. They occur essentially as described in all positions. Because of the lightly aspirated quality of these stops, non-Kalinga speakers may have difficulty in distinguishing them from the voiced counterparts.

b, d These two sounds show variation across all the dialects surveyed, but are rendered by Kalinga speakers as voiced bilabial and voiced dental stops respectively in all positions when speaking with Kalinga from distant regions.

In my preliminary and tentative survey, I have observed the following distributional pattern: [b], voiced bilabial unaspirated stop, occurs initially and finally in Lubuagan syllables; most frequently as syllable initial in Poswoy and Mabaca and only rarely in final position. In Salegseg [b] of other dialects is absent completely, the distribution of this tentative phoneme appears to be as follows: A bilabial voiced affricate [ph] before *i, o,* (u) (see examples); preceding *a* (ə), it becomes [phy], e.g. [phy-ato], "stone" [bato] of other dialects. Some speakers render [ph] as a strongly articulated voiced bilabial palatalized stop [by] before *a* (ə).

[ph] is heard occasionally among speakers from Poswoy, Mabaca, Buaya, and even Lubuagan dialect regions, but [ph] and [phy] are most characteristic of the dialect regions of Salegseg, Balbalasan, Ginaang, and adjacent barrios (cf. Scheerer, 1921, pp. 175–207 and Gieser, 1958, pp. 10–23).

d Dental and voiced and because of its lightly aspirated quality difficult for non-Kalinga ears to distinguish from *t.* In initial and final positions in a word, *d* is sometimes rendered as a voiced or unvoiced alveo-palatal affricate [ǰ] or [č] by Lubuagan speakers, but also occasionally by Kalinga from other dialect regions.

g Velar and voiced. Again non-Kalinga speakers will have difficulty distinguishing *g* from lightly aspirated *k.* In Salegseg, especially, the distinction is difficult because of an aspirated *g* in certain positions, e.g. Kalinggha.

(glottal stop)

All vowels are preceded by the glottal stop which is unmarked in this position. Intervocalically the glottal stop is not very pronounced and within the word the glottal check can hardly be detected. The glottal stop appears to be insignificant in final position.

CONTINUANTS

l   Alveolar voiced lateral. This sound appears to have the following variants: [ʎ], a central voiced oral, typical in Salegseg, Mabaca and Poswoy regions; and a retroflex [r] most characteristic of Lubuagan and Buaya. In all dialects [l] appears to be the norm in initial position, but in certain medial positions within a word (the exact environments not yet determined [ʎ] occurs in Salegseg, Mabaca and Poswoy; while in Lubuagan and Buaya, in apparently the same positions, the retroflex [r] is found.

It seems safe to use the symbol [l] for all of these phonetic variants since Kalinga speakers in using the simplified phonetic system render all variants by [l]. These sounds also appear to be in complementary distribution, but a larger corpus of phonetic data is needed to establish definitely such a distribution.

s   Voiceless, grooved dental fricative. Occasionally heard as alveo-palatal voiceless [s], e.g. [siko] "elbow." Frequently in the Salegseg dialect, *s* occurs as a voiceless glottal fricative [h] (i.e. in place of [s]. Example: [həʎoghog] for [səʎogsog] "Salegseg."

m, n, ng These are voiced bilabial, dental and velar nasals respectively. No distinctive variations were noted within or across the sampled dialects.

y   Palatal voiced semi-vowel. In Poswoy, *y* is commonly pronounced as a voiced alveo-palatal affricate [ǰ]. *y* has not been observed to occur initially in a word or finally in a syllable.

w   Bilabial voiced semi-vowel. In Poswoy, *w* is preceded by a lightly articulated velar fricative, e.g. [Pos*xw*oi]. *w* has not been observed initially in a word or finally in a syllable.

VOWELS–ALL VOICED

i   Lower high front unrounded [ɪ] to upper mid unrounded [e].

o   Back upper mid rounded, varying freely with back lower high rounded [u]. While *o* and *u* may contrast in certain words and therefore constitute separate phonemes, such cases are rare and for our simplified orthography it has been thought best to indicate them with a single symbol.

a   Low front unrounded [a] to a central, upper mid, unrounded [ə]. [ə] is most characteristic of the Salegseg dialect, but found occasionally also among certain speakers in Mabaca, Poswoy, and Buaya. In the modified Kalinga, [ə] is replaced by *a,* as well as in dialects that do not have [ə].

             Stress has not been studied, but it is important in a few forms, along with length, to differentiate meaning, e.g.: apó: "grandparents"; á: po "grandchildren."

DIPHTHONGS

             These are combinations of ei, oi, ao, oa, yu. The semi-vowels *y* and *w* are used to represent diphthongs.

Upper case letters of the above symbols have the same value as those of equivalent lower case. For names of people, place names, and the like, spelling ordinarily used in such cases has been retained.

Kalinga terms for ceremonies, the names for steps in ritualistic performances and many other designations vary from one region to another, indeed from one town to another. It was obviously impossible to obtain all of these·variant terms; I have therefore attempted to indicate in each case the place from which my information was obtained and the terms and names employed apply specifically to such regions or towns, unless otherwise indicated. Kalinga and non-English words are *underlined* on first occurrence and defined or identified. When the origin of non-English words other than Kalinga is known, the source language is identified in parentheses immediately after the first occurrence of the term. The native terms included in this study are those which were supplied by informants without prompting. I hope in this way that I have obtained designations which the Kalinga themselves consider significant in their own culture. My objective, however, was not to establish "cognitive domains" of the Kalinga, although such a task could be a fruitful and significant endeavor in a study specifically designed for that purpose.

EDWARD P. DOZIER

Mountain Arbiters

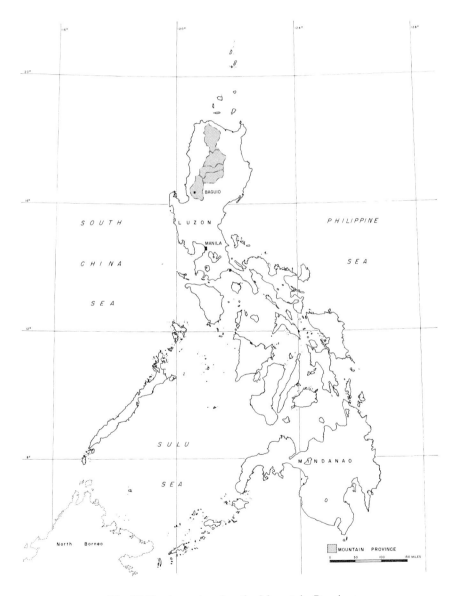

The Philippines, showing the Mountain Province

Introduction

SINCE THE BEGINNING OF THIS CENTURY the mountain peoples of northern Luzon have been studied by a number of scholars. There is some information, therefore, on all of the major groups: Bontoc, Ibaloy, Ifugao, Ilongot, Isneg (Apayao), Kalinga, Kankanay, Negrito, and Tinguian. The most adequately described are the central peoples of the Mountain Province, the Bontoc and Ifugao; for many of the others the information is sparse or on specialized topics. The Kalinga fall in the latter category. Virtually the only study of these people is the report by Barton (1949) on Kalinga custom law. While Barton's study is excellent, it is on a specialized subject and of a group (Lubuagan) who have long practiced irrigated rice farming. The bulk of the Kalinga population is, or was until recently, engaged in dry rice cultivation, and hence a study focused on a group who are still predominantly dry rice farmers is needed to give us a broader knowledge of Kalinga social and cultural institutions.

The present study is an attempt to provide this knowledge and to record the nature of social and cultural differences between those Kalinga who subsist primarily on wet rice and those who are predominantly dry rice cultivators. In order to add to the investigations of Barton, several weeks were spent in Lubuagan, while the remainder of the research time was devoted to the Northern Kalinga who still subsist largely on rice grown on hill and mountain sides by slash and burn techniques.

Unless otherwise indicated, references to the Southern Kalinga are specifically to the Lubuagan *region,* Lubuagan Municipal District.[1] Field investigations of the Northern Kalinga focused on the regions of Mabaca, Salegseg, and Poswoy in the Balbalan Municipal District (see maps).

The recency of irrigated rice terraces among the Kalinga has been demonstrated by Scott (1958:87–92). It is also common knowledge among old Kalinga, in Lubuagan and northward, that rice terraces have

[3]

diffused into the area in recent times from the south. Nonetheless it is not possible in the Lubuagan region to ascertain precisely when the first fields were constructed, although it is possible for example, in the Salegseg, Mabaca, and Poswoy regions in the north. The Southern Kalinga appear to have grown rice in irrigated rice terraces for some hundred years. The Northern Kalinga, on the other hand, report that the first

TABLE 1

Population of Lubuagan Municipal District

(Obtained from the 1960 census filed in the municipal office)

Region or barrio	*Population*
1. Lubugan	3,616
2. Uma	1,124
3. Tanglag	673
4. Kagalwan	583
5. Dalupa-Ableg, Magsilay*	864
6. Guina-ang	668
7. Dangtalan	972
8. Mabongtot	570
9. Balatoc, Kolayo,** Batong Buhay (mines)#	1,196
Total	10,266

* Usually a separate region in peace pacts.
** Colony of Tinglayan and included in its peace pacts.
\# Mixed population (lowlanders, other mountain peoples, and Kalinga from different regions).

irrigated rice fields were built when they were children, and, of course, the construction of rice terraces is an important activity of these Kalinga at present.

The knowledge that irrigated terraces are fairly well established among Southern Kalinga, but new in the north prompted the working hypothesis of my research. I wanted to find out if significant social and cultural differences might be correlated with this difference. It is important to note at this point that my research did not propose to investigate the nature of the ecological environment. I had neither the time nor the competence to attempt such a study, but did include a section on agricultural practices to add information to the historical and socio-cultural emphasis of my study. An exhaustive study of ecology, focused on the Ifugao, has been recently completed by Harold Conklin of Yale University. Conklin's report will fill an important gap in our knowledge of ecological conditions in the Mountain Province (see also Conklin 1957, 1961). The focus of my own study was on historical processes and social and cultural manifestations.

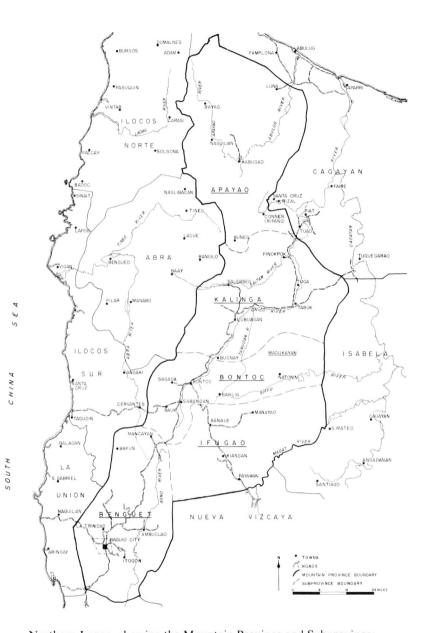

Northern Luzon, showing the Mountain Province and Subprovinces

In Obal, Salegseg region of northern Kalinga, a plaited bamboo dwelling stands next to an Ilocano-type plank house, exemplifying the diversity in house types that exists in some Kalinga communities.

The original hypothesis postulated that important social and cultural differences would be correlated with differences in the basic economy. Field work has demonstrated the validity of this hypothesis, but with certain reservations. Investigations of past conditions by questioning informants and examining historical documents revealed that differences between the two groups of Kalinga were also profoundly affected by historical circumstances. The Northern Kalinga were influenced by Spanish penetration in the Abra and the Ilocos lowlands to the west. This influence came indirectly by contact with such groups as the Tinguian and Ilocano, particularly the latter, who directly experienced the modification of their culture by Spanish civil and religious administration. On the other hand, proximity to and contact with the complex irrigated rice cultivators of the Bontoc and Ifugao influenced the Southern Kalinga

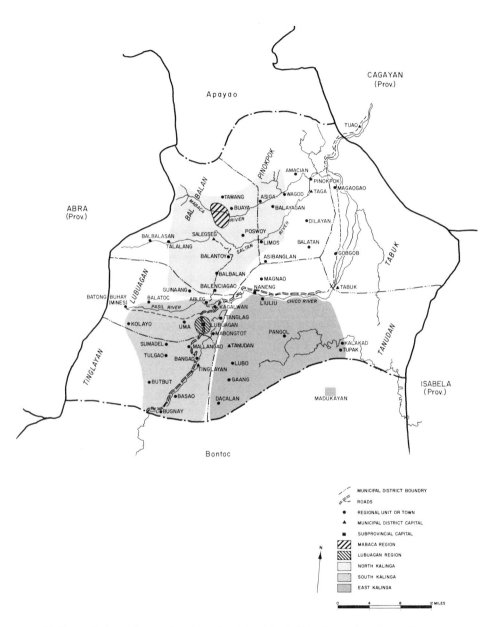

Kalinga Subprovince, showing the Municipal Districts, the three Kalinga culture areas, and all important towns

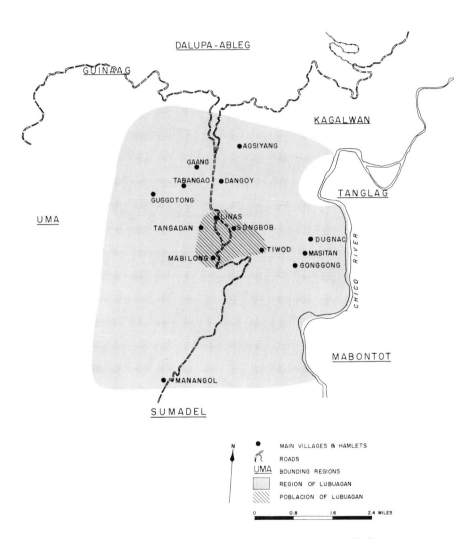

Lubuagan Region, environs of the Southern Kalinga

in another direction. It has been impossible, therefore, to isolate completely the economic from the historic variables, in accounting for differences between the two groups. Both of these factors, economic and historical, are intricately involved, and both may be considered as causal agents in explaining the differences between the Southern and Northern Kalinga.

Since the American period, cultural differences between the two groups have diminished. The construction of roads and trails, the development of trade, and the opportunities for wage-work have made the Kalinga and, indeed, all mountain peoples, highly mobile. The prospects indicate that the process of cultural leveling will continue, and that the Kalinga, together with other mountain peoples, will enter into full participation with the general national population of the Philippines.

Southern Kalinga country is bordered on the north by an east-west river, the Pacil. There is no clear physical demarcation line on the south, but an irregular area devoid of settlements separates Kalinga and Bontoc villages. The western and eastern boundaries are clearly defined by the high ridges on either side of the Chico River rising to heights of five and six thousand feet. Characteristic vegetation cover on the tops of the ridges is pine, *cogon* (Ilocano) grass on the steep slopes, and semi-tropical and tropical growth in the river valleys where groves of coconut trees mark the settlements. The lower levels, where most of the villages are located, vary between 1,500 and 2,000 feet in elevation. The Chico River swings

TABLE 2

Population of Balbalan Municipal District
(Obtained from the 1960 census filed in the municipal office)

Region or barrio	Population
1. Salegseg	1,813
2. Balenciagao	517
3. Balbalan	491
4. Banao	
Pantikian	718
Talalang	285
Balbalasang	600
5. Buaya	
Buaya	483
Tawang	427
6. Mabaca	613
7. Poswoy	
Poswoy	650
Daoangan	715
Ababaan	217
Total	7,529

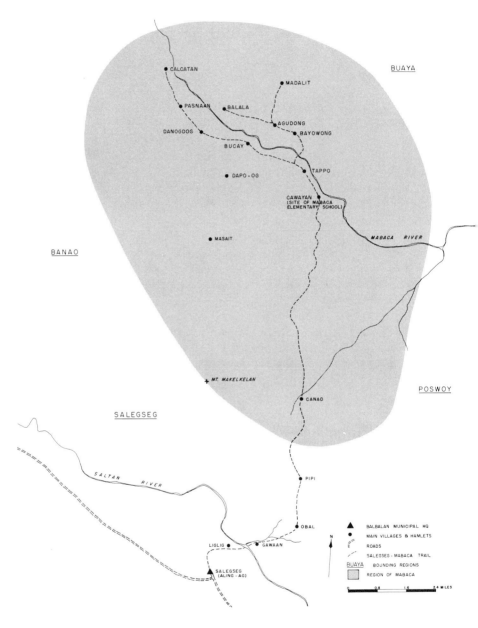

BUAYA

● CALCATAN

● MADALIT

● PASNAAN   ● BALALA

● DANOGDOG   ● AGUDONG
                              ● BAYOWONG
        BUCAY ●

● DAPO - OG   ● TAPPO

                    CAWAYAN
                    (SITE OF MABACA
                    ELEMENTARY SCHOOL)

BANAO

● MASAIT   MABACA   RIVER

POSWOY

+ MT. MAKELKELAN

                              ● CANAO

SALEGSEG

SALTAN   RIVER

                                        ● PIPI

                                        ● OBAL

LIGLIG ●   ● GAWAAN

        ▲ SALEGSEG
          (ALING - AG)

▲   BALBALAN MUNICIPAL HQ

●   MAIN VILLAGES & HAMLETS

    ROADS

    SALEGSEG - MABACA TRAIL

BUAYA   BOUNDING REGIONS

        REGION OF MABACA

0   0.8   1.6   2.4 MILES

Mabaca Region, environs of the Northern Kalinga

in wide arcs in this area before turning sharply northeastward toward the Cagayan Valley. The arcs of the river and the rapid lateral streams have formed slopes which are gentler than those of the Bontoc country further south. Here the Kalinga have terraced the slopes into rich rice fields, but the terraces do not achieve the engineering excellence of the Bontoc and Ifugao ones. Kalinga terraces are not held back by vertical retaining walls but slope gently at an angle.

The northern Kalinga area is also mountainous — not so high as the southern portion of the Mountain Province, but characteristically an area of high sierras, steep mountain sides, and deep canyons. Numerous rapid streams run down to join the two large rivers of the Saltan and Mabaca which flow northeastward into the Chico. The typical vegetation is a tropical or subtropical rain-forest, thick in the narrow valleys, but often bare on the mountain slopes where the people have burned the verdant growth to cultivate upland rice and sugar cane. Irrigated rice fields are new in the area and appear only where the topography lends itself easily to terracing.

The most densely populated area of the Kalinga Subprovince is the Lubuagan Municipal District where the 1960 census figures gave a total figure of 10,266. The *barrio* (Spanish) or region of Lubuagan, however, consisting of some fifteen closely clustered towns and *sitios* (Spanish) contains about 4,000 people, almost half of the total municipal population.[2] The 1960 population of the Balbalan municipal district indicated 7,529 inhabitants scattered in small hamlets of which the largest settlement, Alingag, listed only 147 people. The other municipal districts of Kalinga Subprovince indicated populations as follows in the 1960 census: Tinglayan, 9,120; Tanudan, 4,595; Pinokpok, 7,037; and Tabuk, 21,235. The increase in Kalinga population from figures given by the Keesings (1934:88) and the 1960 census is remarkable. In 1934 the population of the Kalinga municipal districts was as follows: Tinglayan, 6,769; Lubuagan, 6,490; Tanudan, 3,286; Pinokpok, 3,786; Tabuk, 2,417. Pinokpok and Tabuk municipal districts have experienced a large influx of Ilocano and Ibanag immigrants in recent years, and what proportion of the population is specifically Kalinga would be difficult to determine. The total Kalinga population of the subprovince of Kalinga and the populations of the neighboring areas considered to be Kalinga are generally estimated at around 40,000. The 1960 population figures for the barrios of Lubuagan and Balbalan municipal districts are provided in Tables 1 and 2. Town and hamlet populations and numbers of houses for the region of Lubuagan (Table 3) are based on 1959 figures obtained in the municipal office; similar data for Mabaca is based on an actual house and population count made in 1959

TABLE 3

Population of Lubuagan Region

(Based on 1959 figures obtained in the municipal office)

Town or hamlet	Houses	Population
Lubuagan población (contiguous villages or wards)		
Linas	122	625
Kimatan	47	229
Balili	54	303
Tiwod	33	172
Botgotong	13	56
Mabilong (contiguous villages or wards)		
Mabilong proper	254	1,248
Gongogong	31	124
Dugnac	70	320
Manangol	20	105
Doyaas	23	134
Dang-oy (contiguous villages or wards)		
Upper Dang-oy	47	261
Lower Dang-oy	33	154
Ga-ang	54	141
Tabangao	18	77
Agsiang	10	51
Totals	839	4,000

Persons per house 4.8

Settlement patterns in the northern Kalinga area differ markedly from those in the south. In the north the clustering of houses are small hamlets consisting of a half-dozen to no more than thirty houses. Undoubtedly as a safety precaution, such settlements are located in deep canyons or in small terraced areas on the slopes of steep mountain sides. In the south, particularly in Lubuagan, Tinglayan, and Bangad regions, the settlements are considerably larger and may be properly called towns. The town of Mabilong in the Lubuagan region, for example, consists of 254 houses with a population of 1,248. Moreover, Mabilong is contiguous with several other towns forming the municipal center of Lubuagan, with a population of almost 4,000. This is also true of settlements in the Tinglayan Municipal District where, for example, Bangad and Tinglayan proper have several hundred houses each, and each town contains more than 1,000 inhabitants.

Although dwellings differ considerably even within one village, and even more radically among distant sectors of the Kalinga country, we may hazard a few general statements about them. All houses are raised above the ground on posts, with steps or a ladder leading up to a single entrance. The majority of the houses are square or rectangular, single-room dwellings. The walls are commonly made either of split and plaited bamboo or handhewn planks. In the more traditional homes the floors are of split bamboo mats which rest on a grating of small beams. The mats are removable and are taken to a nearby stream two or three times a week and thoroughly washed before being returned to the house. Each dwelling has a fire pit set a little off center and toward the back of the floor. This is a square box about a yard wide and four to six inches high, filled with sand and accumulated ash. Above it is a rack for drying wood, food, or wearing apparel. Roofs are pitched, made of *runo* (Ilocano) reeds, and thatched with cagon grass.

In every sitio or town there are one or several houses with galvanized pitched roofs and floors and walls of handhewn boards. Occasionally such homes have a second house of traditional construction, either connected to the main house or situated nearby, which is used as a kitchen. Predominant in some towns and sitios, these houses will undoubtedly replace the typical native thatched-roofed houses of traditional construction in the near future.

In the south there are a few octagonal-shaped houses which Barton (1949:10) reported were the homes of the wealthy and influential men at Lubuagan, although my informants denied that this was the case anywhere among the Kalinga. Well-to-do families usually live in houses hav-

TABLE 4

Population of Mabaca Region

(Based on a house and population count made in 1959)

Hamlet		Houses	Population
Canao		41	224
Cawayan (site of school house) Tappo Bocay Dapoog Masait		19	102
Danogdog Pasnaan Calcatan		9	48
Balala		12	88
Madalit		13	71
Agodong Bayowong		18	79
	Totals	112	612

Persons per house: 5.5

The elaborate Kalinga dwellings are often made of handhewn planks, such as this one in Obal, Salegseg; but the elevation and the thatched roof are still maintained, as in this octagonal plank house, a type common to southern Kalinga.

ing pitched roofs of galvanized iron. Such houses are typically large, containing one large room or occasionally two or more small rooms, plank walls, and floors, windows, and doors of modern construction.[3]

Community life is similar in all the Kalinga areas I have visited. Women and children are most in evidence around the village. Babies, rarely put down, are carried by mother, father, aunts, or sisters in blanket slings. The blanket is passed over one shoulder and tied in front, while the baby rides on the back or on either hip, comfortably supported by the blanket. For a mother with a nursing child, the baby is simply slung around to the front when it wishes to suckle. A woman carrying a baby in a blanket sling goes about her work seemingly unhampered, transporting heavy loads poised on her head, winnowing rice, cooking, and performing a myriad of other household tasks while the baby observes the world about it or naps peacefully under the rocking motion.

Children under six or seven years of age are characteristically seen playing around houses and nearby small streams without any clothing. Their play, as elsewhere among children, consists of an imitation of

Both of these southern Kalinga dwellings, one small and one large, exemplify features common to houses throughout Kalinga country. Both are raised above ground and made of split or plaited bamboo, with pitched roof of reeds, thatched with grass. Below in right foreground rice is spread out on a carabao hide, ready to be threshed and pounded.

This man wears the traditional dress of the Northern Kalinga, and has betel nut ingredients in the bag *(tay-ay)* suspended around his neck.

adult activities. Girls assume adult tasks early; by the age of ten or so they are tending babies, carrying loads and taking on responsibilities almost equal to those of adult women. The lot of Kalinga boys of comparable age, and even up to the time they are married, is much less demanding. They rarely tend children or perform work essential to the Kalinga household. Their primary task seems to be gathering fuel and transporting it home on their shoulders.

Dogs, pigs, and chickens roam at will about the village. The barking of dogs at night may be disturbing to an unaccustomed visitor, but if he is to spend any time in a Kalinga village, he must adjust or get no sleep. The visitor who is offended by roaming pigs should keep away from Kalinga towns and sitios. From the new born to huge brutes, pigs are everywhere. A grunting sow with suckling young lying contentedly beneath a house or somewhere near the playing, naked children is a typical village sight. The *carabao,* or water buffalo, rarely seen in the village, is commonly in the outskirts of the settlement or in rice fields, either at work or wallowing happily in a pool of water or puddle of mud.

The dress of the Kalinga in the upper Saltan and Mabaca river valleys differs in many respects from the Kalinga of the Chico Valley.[4] Differences were more pronounced early in this century, but there are still some significant differences. Formerly, in what is now the northern Balbalan district and the whole of Pinokpok district, the Kalinga dressed themselves in brightly colored cotton fabrics. Worcester (1913:1213) describes the dress of these Kalinga as follows:

> The men wear regulation clouts, but they are not seldom ornamented with beads, buttons, etc. Their short jackets of gaudily colored cloth are also often adorned with beads and tassels. Gay turbans are commonly worn, and their hair, banged across the forehead and left long behind, is frequently stuck full of scarlet hibiscus, marigolds, and other gay flowers and of really gorgeous feather ornaments. Handsome blankets worn over one shoulder and under the opposite arm, and ornamental bags for carrying small personal belongings complete the usual costume of the male, except for the ear plugs, which are fashioned with especial care and are often inserted in such a way as to project backward against the sides of the neck and turn the lobes of the ears directly forward. Their front ends are covered with embroidered cloth or adorned with highly polished coins, bits of looking-glass, or other bright objects. In some instances the ear plugs are made of rolls of brightly colored worsted.
>
> The women wear gaily colored upper garments and skirts. The wealthier ones have enormous necklaces of agate beads, while heavy and peculiarly shaped ear ornaments of brass and of mother-of-pearl are almost invariably in evidence. Their heads are adorned not only with abundant natural locks, but with switches made from the tresses of departed female ancestors or of relatives having long hair. Into the masses of hair thus built up are thrust gay scarlet and yellow feather plumes.

The traditional dress of women among the Northern Kalinga features a shell ear plug as ornamentation.

The dress of the Southern Kalinga in the present municipal districts of Lubuagan and Tinglayan was more simple and subdued in color. Men wore their hair long in back and banged in front as the Northern Kalinga, but decorations and garments were at a minimum. The gee string was like that of the Kalinga of the northern regions, but commonly the upper body was bare although tatooed if the man had participated in a killing. A choker of agate beads was also worn, and sometimes a basket hat like that of the Bontocs but decorated with beads. Women wore simply the wraparound skirt (*ka-in* or *tapis* (Ilocano)) while the upper part of the body was left bare. Occasionally a sort of bustle made of woven rattan was worn under the skirt, apparently to enhance the charms of the wearer. The arms were tatooed from just below the elbow to the shoulders and some times an area just above the breasts. Some women, especially unmarried, post-adolescent girls, also painted their faces with a red pigment. Strands of agate bead necklaces and occasionally bead wristlets completed the costume.

Changes have taken place in these Kalinga costumes. The coming of Ilocanos and Christian influences has modified traditional dress, more in the north than in the south, but in general throughout Kalinga land. The colorful costume of the Northern Kalinga has been replaced for women by the American-style cotton dress, a garment which as Barton (1949:11) has appropriately remarked "is worn until it falls into tatters, with launderings few and far between." Men wear trousers or trousers cut into shorts and either nothing above the waist or an old shirt. Gee strings for men and tapis for women are seldom in evidence any more among the Northern Kalinga.

Perhaps because Ilocano influence is less strong in the Lubuagan and Tinglayan districts and Christianity less effective, these Kalinga adhere to traditional costumes much more faithfully.[5] Women are more often bare above the waist and perhaps the majority prefer the native wrap-around skirt. Men, too, are more frequently seen wearing the traditional gee string. Agate necklace beads are also more consistently worn by the Kalinga women of the south, although the men in both areas wear the agate bead chokers only in native dances or to have their pictures taken.

Feuds and occasional killings characterize the Kalinga in the south (especially in the Tinglayan District) and hence men who travel away from their barrios are well armed with headaxes and spears. Weapons are rarely seen in the north where the feuding pattern has virtually disappeared. Adherence to traditional dress is undoubtedly part of a complex of cultural conservatism among the Southern Kalinga and feuds and

Not only food and water, but many heavier items, are commonly transported on the heads of women throughout the subprovinces of the Kalinga.

revenge killings are important ingredients in this complex. We will discuss this topic in greater detail later on.

Activities are always in evidence revolving around the principal crop, rice. The rhythmic sound of pounding rice is heard from early morning until late evening.

Notes to Introduction

1. The term *region* (not italicized hereafter) in this study will be used to indicate a number of related aspects: 1) a quasi-political unit whose geographical limits are definitely known to its members and by those Kalinga from adjacent regions; 2) an endogamous area whose members are all related within varying degrees; 3) a dialect region; and 4) a peace-pact area. (*See* detailed discussion of the "region" in Chapter II.)

2. The term *barrio* is used interchangeably with "region" since the Kalinga themselves usually designate these territorial units as barrios. Elsewhere in the Philippines the term barrio is used simply to designate a large community or a series of settlements without the specific aspects associated with the term as employed in this study. A *sitio* is synonymous with "hamlet" and is so used here.

   The division between the Northern and Southern Kalinga in the manner delineated here was first made by Vanoverbergh (1929: 182–184). Vanoverbergh in a footnote of this article also noted the distinctiveness of the Eastern Kalinga without actually setting an eastern Kalinga areal division: "A small section of the eastern part of both Bontoc [the Mandukayan] and Kalinga Sub-provinces is inhabited by people who form a connecting link between the Northern Kalinga on one hand, and the Southern Kalinga and Bontoc Igorot on the other."

3. For other descriptions of Kalinga house types, see Barton 1949: 9–12; Scott 1958a: 327–329; Scott 1962a.

4. Compare Vanoverbergh (1929: 181–242).

5. Insofar as missionaries have objected to the scanty dress of Mountain Province natives, we may say that where natives still go about scantily dressed, missionary influence has not been very effective.

1. History and Background of the Kalinga

A HISTORICAL RESUME of what is known of the people now designated as the Kalinga helps to shed light on the central problem of this study: the causal factors involved in the differences between the social and cultural characteristics of the Northern and Southern Kalinga. Immediately apparent even to a casual visitor is the difference in the subsistence economy; the Southern Kalinga are predominantly wet rice cultivators, the Northern primarily dry rice farmers. Review of the historical events reveals, in addition, that each area has been subject to different kinds of influences and that each area has developed independently in a different direction. While both areas apparently shared an essentially similar history prior to Spanish intervention, subsequently the north received more Spanish influence while the south remained relatively isolated. This differential effect on the two areas needs to be considered along with economic factors in attempting to indicate the factors which underlie Southern and Northern Kalinga cultural differences.

In reviewing early accounts it is not possible to isolate the Kalinga specifically from other mountain peoples of Northern Luzon. In this presentation, therefore, the early period is discussed in terms of the mountain peoples generally. Only with the beginning of the Spanish period and the work of the Catholic missionaries are there references to a people who can be clearly identified as Kalinga. The identity of the Kalinga becomes clearer still in the accounts of early American writers. With the establishment of American rule and on to the present under Philippine sovereignty, the historical record of the Kalinga and their relations with other peoples is as reliable as the history of any people in a literate, historically conscious nation.

[*21*]

Early History

In an unpublished manuscript, Keesing (n.d.) appropriately summed up the historical reconstruction schemes attempting to explain the derivation of Northern Philippine populations and cultures as falling mainly into two major categories: 1) [Those which] "may be interpreted as representing separate migrations into the area, as a result of which variant customs were introduced from different zones of Southeast and East Asia . . ."; 2) [Those which] "may be interpreted, in part at least, as a result of the dynamics of differential change among regional and local groups from earlier more uniform heritages."[1]

The derivation of Philippine populations from Southeastern or Eastern Asia is not seriously questioned by scholars. The archaeological evidence appears to support such an origin, although there is considerable controversy as to the times and places from which the different migrant groups are purported to have come. Most discussions among historical reconstructionists, however, revolve around the derivation of contemporary indigenous Philippine cultures. In explaining the variant cultures of the mountain peoples of northern Luzon (as well as the derivation of the peoples themselves), most scholars in the past have employed the first reconstruction scheme noted by Keesing above. Thus Beyer (1921) and the Keesings (1934) hypothesized that the Negritos came first, the dry rice cultivators next, and the wet rice cultivators as a third and later group.[2] Each of these groups was associated with a distinct set of social traits. Cole (1922:236), on the other hand, postulated that Tinguians, Western Kalinga, and Apayaos as inland extensions of the Hispanized Ilocanos, came later into the area (than the rice terrace farmers) and from a "somewhat different region of Southeast Asia."

A more recent approach is the explanation of cultural differences among the mountain peoples of northern Luzon primarily as the result of development and change *in situ*. Eggan (1941, 1954, 1960), Scott (1958b) and Keesing (1962:319) have used this explanation in accounting for cultural differences among such peoples as the Ibaloy, Sagada, Bontoc, Ifugao, and Kalinga.

The historical reconstruction scheme which conceives of the importation of a complex set of social institutions from the outside, places too much emphasis on the conservatism of culture and ignores the influences of the environment and subsistence economy on the development of social institutions. Eggan (1954) has argued well against the notion of migrants bringing with them complex social institutions from distant Assam (where some parallels exist with peoples living in the more densely populated region of the Mountain Province). Moreover, in the mountains of Assam the language of the Tibeto-Burman group belongs to Sino-Tibetan or Sinitic, a completely different stock from the Malayo-Polynesian languages of the Philippines. It is also unlikely that these migrants, reportedly coming as early as 1500 B.C., could have come in very large numbers, and small boatloads of migrants are not likely to maintain large-scale community patterns in a new land under pioneer conditions.[3]

After reviewing the institutions of the peoples in the more densely populated area of the Mountain Province, Eggan (*op. cit.*) concludes:

> This brief review of certain Mountain Province institutions suggests that while various elements may be old, and in certain cases brought to Northern Luzon by ancestral migrants, their organization and integration to the complex village structures of the central Mountain Province is a relatively recent process. In studies of diffusion it is essential to discriminate between technology and material culture on the one hand, and forms of social organization on the other. Social structures have jobs to do and they build on what is available often with considerable remodelling. Under the conditions that existed in early times, so far as we know them from archaeology and from comparative observation, it is difficult to assume that a complex and specialized social system could have been carried and maintained in the Mountain Province environment.

Recent studies of social institutions have brought about explanations which emphasize factors other than migration in attempting to explain the social and cultural peculiarities of Mountain Province peoples. Keesing (1949) significantly draws attention to a correlation between size of village and water supply in the Lepanto region. Eggan, in the paper quoted above, stresses the importance of local ecological conditions and the density of population in explaining the greater complexity of social and religious institutions in the central Bontoc-Lepanto area. Scott (1958b:93) notes that certain religious and social patterns are associated with those groups growing root crops in *swiddens* which differ from those associated with groups subsisting on rice grown in swiddens.[4] The first group would include all Ifugaos, Bontocs, and Benguets, the latter Isnegs and Kalinga. The cultural differences I have found between Northern and Southern Kalinga appear to be associated with differences in population density and economic activities, predominantly wet rice for the former and dry rice for the latter. As we will see, however, historical factors also appear to be important in explaining these differences.

Contemporary writers are pointing to such key factors as the form of subsistence economy, water supply, population density, and ecological conditions as influential in molding social and religious organization. I am sure that none of these writers would deny, however, that present Mountain Province religious and social institutions were built on a former more simple, wider, and more generalized base. Such a base may have been brought to the mountains of north Luzon by the original migrants to the Philippines.

The importance of yams and sweet potatoes in the central and southern portions of the Mountain Province suggests that a root crop, perhaps taro, formerly served as the basic food in these areas.[5] In the north among the Kalinga and Isneg, wild fruits and plants are extremely important in the diet. Undoubtedly in all areas, gathering as well as hunting played a much greater role in the early economy of the people. Very likely, refugee groups fleeing from Spanish oppression in the seventeenth century also subsisted for long periods on the flora and fauna of the mountains. It is also reasonable to suppose that swidden cultivation preceded irrigated farming. It is significant, for example, that the same variety of rice is grown in the swiddens as in the irrigated paddies.

At present and in the recent past in the Mountain Province, densely populated regions can be correlated with irrigated rice cultivation, and conversely, those areas having sparse populations can be correlated with dry rice farming. Complex social and religious organizations go along with peoples practicing wet rice farming. Even in the Kalinga area, the Southern Kalinga show greater complexity in social and religious organization than their linguistic neighbors in the north who have adopted irrigated rice farming more recently. Indeed, both groups of Kalinga still raise rice in swiddens but more so in the north than in the south. The Northern Kalinga are also more dependent on gathering coconuts, guavas, and other fruits in season (cf. Keesing 1949).

It is interesting that Philippine scholars apparently never employed the culture-area concept and the age-area hypothesis to explain the development of culture among the Mountain Province peoples.[6] Wissler's (1923) statement of a culture center with diffused material, social, and cultural traits going out to the margins like the ripples in a pool would have applied in a general way in the Mountain Province. In line with the age-area hypothesis, the oldest traits would be sought in the margins, and new ones would be expected to be present and to emerge from the center. The central Bontoc-Ifugao irrigated rice growing area would, in Wissler's terms, be considered the culture center, while the dry rice agriculturalists like the Isneg, Northern Kalinga, and pagan Gaddang would be marginal groups, characterized by older material, social, and cultural traits. The concepts developed by Wissler do not provide complete answers, but as alternative explanations for cultural development, it is surprising that scholars did not use them in accounting for the indigenous cultures in Northern Luzon. The culture-area concept and age-area hypothesis, together with studies of diffusion (within a restricted area) characterized

American anthropology for the first three decades of this century at the same time that migration theories were being employed by Philippine scholars.

Assuming that terraced, irrigated rice farming was introduced or developed in the Mountain Province in comparatively recent times, some approximate time must be offered for this introduction or development. We have suggested above that the mountain peoples progressed in situ through an earlier stage of primary dependence on taro, and later on sweet potatoes and yams in the south and central region, and previous to wet rice, swidden farming in all areas.[7] Finally, the shift to irrigated terraced farming is still going on, diffusing from the center outward (cf. Scott 1958b). How long the mountain people have been in their present environment is highly speculative, but it is clear that the dialect-culture groups have not been isolated from one another for a long period of time. The languages spoken are closely related; a glottochronological count gives only about 1,000 years separation time for Ifugao and Kankanay-Bontoc (Eggan 1954:331), while in the borders of most of the cultural groups, the languages are mutually intelligible. The development of terraced rice farming in the central region is undoubtedly old, but to be calculated in centuries rather than in millennia, in view of language similarities and the continuing spread of terraced farming.[8] While the elaborate terraces of Ifugao and Bontoc suggest several centuries of construction, it is remarkable how quickly steep mountain sides can be terraced. Thus in the Salegseg region whole sides of mountains have been terraced, not as spectacularly as among the Ifugao, yet they are still formidable achievements when we realize they are less than a century old. All informants agree that the first rice terraces in most of the Northern Kalinga area were begun in the memory of old men, still living, and of course new terraces are still being constructed. The development of terraced farming, as other material and social elements, appears definitely to have taken place in the central Bontoc-Ifugao area and then moved outward to the margins, a process still going on.[9]

How old the rice terraces are in the Bontoc-Ifugao area can only be determined by intensive archeological and ecological investigations. For Ifugao an ecological study by Professor Harold Conklin has just been completed, and his work may help to determine the age of these terraces.

Recent History

The early historical penetrations which have influenced the cultures of the Indies profoundly in the south appear to have reached the mountain peoples of Northern Luzon in weak currents only. For a time, beginning approximately in the third century A.D., sporadic control of the Southern Islands of Sulu, Mindanao, the Bisayas, and Southern Luzon was maintained successively by the Indo-Malayan empire of Srivijaya and the later Javanese empire of Madjapahit. Only faint suggestions of these influences are evident among the Mountain Province peoples. The bamboo instruments of the Kalinga are reminiscent of some Javanese instruments (Barton 1949:27). Barton (1956:3) characterizes the Ifugao *Hudhud* epics as "remotely suggestive of the Ramayana or Mahabharata."

Moslem penetration strongly affected the Southern Islands of the Philippines, but the imprint of Islamic culture in Northern Luzon is only suggestive. The Keesings (1934:60) and others have suggested the extensive use of red and yellow colors among the Kalinga and Gaddang as a possible recent influence from Mohammedan Moros or peoples from the south who may have come in contact with Moros. In the same category may be placed a number of dress styles and ornamentations such as the short jackets and turbans made of red and yellow cloth formerly worn by the Northern Kalinga and by the Tinguians of Abra and Apayao. The brass rings worn by Northern Kalinga women on the lower arm from elbow to wrist also suggest Moro influence. But the pre-Spanish invasion of Mindanao and other Southern Islands which converted so many of these people into "Moros" apparently never reached the Mountain Province peoples.

From India, China, or Japan must have come knowledge of metal working. Copper and gold were known and a number of methods for extracting, smelting, and casting had been locally developed by methods known on the Asiatic mainland. Gold was mined especially in the southern part of the Mountain Province among the Kankanay and Ibaloy. The mining and processing of gold, particularly, may have been stimulated by Chinese pirates and merchants from the third century A.D. Spears, head-axes, and other similar tools apparently were made in the past from Chinese cast-iron kettles (Barton 1956:19 and 133). Today the Kalinga make spears out of discarded automobile springs. The region of Balbalasan, Kalinga is well known throughout the Mountain Province for the manufacture of excellent spears and headaxes. Iron was apparently never mined, the mountain peoples fashioning the metal from other forms into steel implements and utensils by well-developed smithing procedures. At present, intricate bellows are made from wooden boxes or bamboo cylinders and carabao hide. The iron is heated in a charcoal fire kept burning by forced air draft provided by the bellows. Soot with high carbon content is worked into the iron and the metal shaped by alternately pounding with a stone hammer and plunging into water.

Huge bamboo cylinders form the bellows for blacksmithing in the Salegseg region. The Kalinga have never mined iron, but are competent in fashioning implements and utensils from already existing forms of the metal.

Chinese jars and plates and brass gongs as well as agate beads were obviously brought in by Chinese traders. These are valued heirlooms throughout the Mountain Province and handed down from generation to generation. While contact with the Chinese in the early periods was perhaps rarely direct, the mountain peoples secured a wide variety of Chinese manufactured items from lowland peoples over a period of many centuries. Fox (1959:325) reports that the "porcelain and stoneware collections made in the Philippines, notably those of Professor H. Otley Beyer and E. D. Hester, demonstrate that trade with the mainland began as early as the tenth century A.D. during the T'ang Period (618–907 A.D.) reaching a climax in the fifteenth century during the reign of the early Ming emperors." Fox (*op. cit.*) also reports that "extensive trade was carried on [in the Calatagan area of South-central Luzon] in the late fourteenth and early mid-fifteenth centuries with pottery which was made in Siam [Thailand], notably at Sawankhalok, and Annam (Indo-China)."

Trade in the items which form the heirloom collections of the Kalinga and other mountain peoples apparently stopped with the establishment of Spanish colonial rule. Prior to Spanish intervention there must have been an extensive trade in plates, jars, vases, and ornamental beads. These items are numerous and varied indicating complex trade relations with lowland traders who had contact with Chinese merchants. Undoubtedly with the termination of trade in these articles of Chinese manufacture, the items already accumulated acquired special significance and value far out of proportion to their value in the world market. Chinese plates, jars, gongs, and beads largely determine the wealth of Kalinga families at present, and together with rice fields form the most valued possessions to be passed on to the children.

The Spanish Period

Spanish colonists and Catholic missionaries entered the Philippines in the late sixteenth century. In a fashion reminiscent of Mexico, Spanish civil and religious authorities quickly began the task of civilizing and Christianizing the Philippine population. In a remarkably short period of time a uniform culture emerged among lowland Filipinos. Except for the "Moros" or Moslem groups of Mindanao and other islands in the south, and among the peoples of the rugged mountain areas, the bulk of the population became Christian and adopted a Hispanicized mode of life.

The collection of tribute and the construction of missions characterized Spanish colonial policy here as elsewhere in Spain's colonial possessions. Scattered hamlets and towns were congregated into larger settlements or barrios to facilitate civil administration and the Catholic missionary program. The Spanish language became the official language, although it was not widely taught and disseminated. Yet Spanish loan words quickly diffused into the various native languages and dialects even of those in remote and isolated areas.

Spanish activity in the mountainous regions was primarily a missionary program and was complicated by a number of problems. Rough mountain terrain and hostility of the natives were primary obstacles, but the malarial mosquito, found only in the foothills, helped to isolate mountain populations. The mountains also became refuge areas for peoples in lower elevations who fled from the militant Spanish civil and missionary program. These people preferred a primitive mode of existence to Spanish subjugation.

The mountain fastness of Northern Luzon, the area of the present Mountain Province, contained a population which effectively resisted Spanish colonizing efforts and has remained until recent times relatively uninfluenced by Christianity and Western European domination. The area of the present Kalinga is perhaps the most isolated of all and it became a refuge area for lowland populations resistant to Spanish

Bugnay, on the Bontok-Kalinga border, is the first village recognizable as Kalinga, and marks the beginning of the Tinglayan Municipal District which is located in the middle Chico River Valley.

advances as well. Indeed much of the population of Kalinga may represent the descendants of ethnic groups formerly in lower elevations, primarily from the Cagayan Valley, but perhaps also from Abra and the Ilocos areas.

Early Spanish efforts to Christianize the natives of the Kalinga area were in the hands of Dominican missionaries.[10] These missionaries worked from the Cagayan Valley along the lower Chico River. Missions were established in 1604 at Tabang and Piat along the banks of the Chico in present-day Cagayan Province. In 1612 another mission was founded at Tuao, higher on the Chico. The natives in this area were known in the seventeenth century as Itaves, Itavi, Itawis, or Tawish. It is not clear which historic ethnic groups were designated by these terms, but these people are probably the ancestors of the present Ibanag, Isneg, and Kalinga. While the languages spoken by these people differ today, they are closely related and may have been mutually intelligible during the early period of Spanish contact. The Ibanag have been Christians for a long time, and their language serves as a lingua franca in the Cagayan Valley at present.

The three missionary posts were concentrated settlements of peoples who previously lived in hamlets and were undoubtedly dry rice cultivators. This is evident from Aduarte's "history" (Blair and Roberts 1903–09) written in 1640 (quoted in Keesing 1962:225):

> After the religious went among them, they were gathered into large villages that they might be more easily instructed in the faith, having been previously scattered among many small ones, like so many farmsteads. There were three villages thus formed: one of about five hundred tributes, named Taban [Tabang] . . . and the other two of more than a thousand tributes each . . . Pia [Piat] . . . [and] Tuao. . . . Thus all the people were brought together and united, to reduce them to settlements, and to a civilized mode of life and government: and to the church . . . [with] all the fields around [the villages].

While the more rugged terrain of the Upper Chico and its tributaries of the Malatag, the Saltan, and the Mabaca may have been occupied at this time, these populations were augmented by refugees from the oppressive missionary program in the lower elevations. In 1693, the front of mission work was moved still higher on the Malatag to Santa Cruz de Gumpat, in an attempt to reach populations in the more remote regions. Shortly before, (in 1688) a mission outpost was also established at Tuga on the Chico some sixteen miles south of Tuao. This mission was to serve the southern and western "heathens"; hence specifically the natives in the heart of the Kalinga country. Tuao was the main establishment of the missionary program for the mountain populations in the north. It remained the headquarters of missionary work throughout the eighteenth and nineteenth centuries, and was able to resist effectively the raids of the mountain folk and to quell uprisings because it was strongly fortified and maintained a garrison of soldiers. Tuao also became an agricultural center where rice, maize, and cacao were grown, and it became particularly important during the eighteenth century as the producer of tobacco. Santa Cruz and Tuga were frontier posts whose existence was precarious.

In 1718 there was a revolt among the newly converted Christians of the Cagayan Valley and the populations of the new missions fled into the mountains. The missions of Santa Cruz and Tuga were moved to locations nearer Tuao, and finally these missions were abandoned. The entire missionary program suffered a decline soon after the Cagayan revolt, and the outpost missions fell into ruins. There is no evidence that Spanish missionaries ever got closer to the mountain populations from the north and east than the missions of Santa Cruz and Tuga (cf. Keesing 1962:224–235).

The missionary program from the west, that is, from the Ilocos and Abra areas, was under the direction of the Augustinian order. These missionaries converted the lowland populations but they did not succeed in converting the Tinguians of Abra (Cole 1922:243–246; Eggan 1941: 17). It is, therefore, inconceivable that they could have carried on extensive missionary work among the Northern Kalinga east of the mountain range. The work of these missionaries and the civil authorities who accompanied them did, however, pave the way for a lively trade among the Northern Kalinga, the Tinguian, and the Ilocano beginning in the first half of the nineteenth century. Tobacco was the primary crop although a number of forest products were also traded for cotton cloth, salt, iron, and a variety of manufactured goods. Keesing (1962:235) cites from Buzet's historical survey (1850–51) to indicate the importance of these tobacco plantations and trading activities between the Cagayan Valley and the Ilocas lowlands:

> They have a peaceful nature and live as tranquil and harmonious families. They cultivate rice and other vegetables. They have large tobacco plantations which they cultivate by means of a simple and natural system inherited from their forebears. The tobacco ... is considered the best of the Cagayan province ... [some is] taken in canoes on the Abra river to the province of Ilocos Sur.

The "natural" system mentioned in the report apparently indicates the dry cultivation techniques used by the Kalinga and applied as well to the growing of tobacco.

During the latter half of the nineteenth century, Spanish authorities created a number of political-military jurisdictions or *comandancías* under those provinces extending into the mountains (Keesing 1962:235). The Kalinga were first included in the "Comandancia of Saltan" established in 1859 under the newly created province of Isabela. Later in 1889, the Kalinga came under the Comandancia of Itaves, established as a part of the Cagayan Province. The purpose of these jurisdictions was to control the uprisings of the mountain peoples and protect the settled Christianized communities in the lowland areas adjacent to the hostile populations (Keesing 1962:235). Beyond the stated purpose of political control and the establishment of a number of military posts, the creation of these comandancias brought about the construction of new trails and the improvement of old ones. A particularly wide trail referred to as a military "road" was built from Ilocos Sur through Abra and across the mountains into the heart of the North Kalinga country (cf. Keesing 1962:235 and 328).

The exact number of the military posts established in the Kalinga country is unknown. Schadenberg (1887) reports a military post at Balbalasang on the upper Saltan River and another at Balitokan in the region of Guinaang on the Pacil River. Of the one at Balbalasan, Schadenberg remarked: "Balbalassan is the name of the cuartel of the *Guardia Civil,* inhabited by a lieutenant and ten men, who are not very beloved by the inhabitants of the ranchería of the same name, distant about 20 minutes."

Old Kalinga residents remember these military or civil guard stations or have heard about them from older generations. They tell of the oppressive demands made by the Spaniards for foodstuffs and labor services and the maltreatment of their womenfolk by Spanish officers and lowland soldiers. But the Kalinga as a whole were never conquered and subjugated by the Spanish. The military stations were in a precarious situation, and Spanish authorities were able to maintain them only by the possession of superior arms. At best there was an uneasy truce between the military posts and the hostile populations. In the Kalinga country and other remote places, headhunting, killings, and the old feuds went on unabated. The military posts maintained themselves and kept the trails open, but they were unable to pacify or control the mountain people.

Trade and Spanish activities in the mid–1850's brought about fairly frequent and intimate relations between Tinguians and Northern Kalinga. As the result of these relationships, or perhaps because of a common heritage, the Northern Kalinga and the Tinguian of Abra appear to be as close culturally to one another as the former are to the Southern Kalinga. Indeed, some of the early travelers and American administrators did not differentiate the Northern Kalinga area from the Tinguian country, but consistently separated the Kalinga population south of the Pacil River from that north of the river (e.g. Schadenberg, below; Folkmar 1906). Mountain Province Governor John C. Early made a three-fold division of the Kalinga area in essentially the same manner as we have delimited them in this study (*see* map of Kalinga Subprovince, p. 7) and did not differentiate between the Northern Kalinga and the Tinguian. Governor Early (Worcester and Hayden 1930:810) reported as follows in his annual report of 1925:

... Kalinga holds three pretty distinct cultural groups. On the Bontoc border the people (Lubuagan) resemble those of Tinglayan who are first cousins of the Bontocs. In the west in the Saltan and Mabaca valleys the people are Itnegs or Tinguianes, quite recently immigrants from Abra and in the eastern foot-hills are Kalingas, a strange nomadic people ...

Among these groups the Itnegs are the most prosperous and forward looking, the Lubuagan people next, and the Kalingas least ...

The statement that the Northern Kalinga (Itnegs) are recent immigrants from Abra alone is debatable. The Northern Kalinga, like the Kalinga population generally, are probably the descendants of a number of different peoples not only from the Abra area but from the Cagayan Valley as well. As we have suggested there was very probably an original small population of mountaineers. To this population were added refugees from the lowlands fleeing from Spanish oppression.

Language relationships between Kalinga and Tinguian are close. Salegseg informants report that if their own region is used as a reference point, dialectical differentiation grades off gradually to the south and to the west, adjacent populations having no difficulty communicating with one another in Kalinga, but having to resort to Ilocano, the lingua franca, in order to speak to distant groups, whether Kalinga or lowland Tinguian.

Northern Kalinga and Tinguian contacts necessitated the development of mechanisms for getting along with one another and the two peoples effected peaceful relations by the mid-nineteenth century. The initial device was probably the friendship pact which was widespread in the Philippines, but these pacts, we believe, soon developed into the important and specialized peace-pact institution of the Kalinga (*see* section on the peace pact). In addition, a number of intermarriages were effected between the two areas to bind kinship groups together and thus insure peaceful relations. Headhunting disappeared among the Tinguian and has only occurred sporadically among the Northern Kalinga since the American period. This is in direct contrast to the Southern and Eastern Kalinga areas where killings and "wars" are still of occasional occurrence. The peaceful disposition of the Tinguians and the Northern Kalinga was noted by Buzeta (1850:1:52–53) who characterized the "Guinaanes" [Southern Kalinga] as "cruel and fearless" as compared to the peaceful Calauas [North Kalinga] and the Tinguian.

Schadenberg (1887) referred to the people in the western portion of Northern Kalinga as the Banao people (*see* map of northern Kalinga "regions" above page), and delimited the area by listing the settlements:

... The natives of Balbalassan belong to the Banao people, and they inhabit the following rancherías: Inalangan, Balbalassan, Talalang, Linguaan, Sogsogan, Detaboman, Tapas, Bulao, Buot, Ambituan, Dangassan, Tagpago, Salegseg, besides several smaller groups of houses which may be considered as outposts of the rancherías enumerated. *Banao* therefore is, according to the old division of the natives, which today still retains its full value and will retain it still for a long time, equal to *Province of Banao.*

Schadenberg (1887) was also impressed by the cultural and physical differences between the Northern Kalinga and Tinguian on the one hand and the Southern Kalinga on the other. After noting some material cultural differences between the Northern Kalinga and the Tinguians, Schadenberg remarked:

> For the rest, my attention was not called by any special habits or usages amongst the Banao people (Northern Kalinga) as they accord in that respect wholly with the Tinguianes of Abra and Ilokos.

As for the physical characteristics of the Southern Kalinga as compared to the other two groups, Schadenberg reported:

> The Guinanes are a finer type of men than the people of Banao. The men are taller, their appearance prouder and more self-possessed; the thick and bulby nose that defaces the people of Abra and Ilokos is seldom seen amongst them; they have it straight and well formed, often even aquiline.

The physical type referred to by Schadenberg is a type considered East Indian or "Dravidian" by Barton (1949:13–14). Barton reports that about 10 per cent of the Lubuagan Kalinga population is of this type. Most characteristic feature is the nose which occurs straight or convex in profile and high and narrow as compared to other types. The body build is slender and the individuals exhibiting this type are usually taller. The skin color of the "Dravidian" type also tends to be darker than other groups in the Mountain Province. While the "Dravidian" type is most prevalent in the Southern Kalinga populations, it occurs in all Kalinga areas. The Kalinga are aware of this special physical type among themselves and call it the "Indonesian type" apparently from reading the writings of H. O. Beyer *(see* especially Beyer 1921).

In the paper referred to above, Schadenberg lists a number of characteristics which he believes to be unique to the "Guinanes." It is clear from the description of the territory of these people that he is including both the Southern and Eastern Kalinga under the term "Guinanes."

> Guinan must be apprehended as a province which reaches as far as the mountains of Cagayan, borders with Banao (Northern Kalinga) Bontok and Isabela and whose principal river is the Rio Basil (Pacil).

The information Schadenberg presents is, however, derived from the region of Guinaan and hence would not apply to all areas of southern Kalinga. Indeed, our knowledge of present Kalinga cultural differences would necessitate setting up an Eastern Kalinga division separate from both the southern and northern Kalinga. Then too there are differences

A woman with decidedly East Indian features, and another with "Polynesian" cast of countenance illustrate the diversity of physical types in the population of Lubuagan, southern Kalinga. Both women are from the village of Tangadan.

from region to region and those regions most distant from one another are the most divergent. Schadenberg's paper is important nevertheless for indicating a similarity of Northern Kalinga and Tinguian cultures, and the distinction of these two from the Southern Kalinga. It would not be amiss, therefore, to consider the Tinguian another subarea of the Kalinga, or in reverse, to consider the Northern Kalinga simply as a variant of Tinguian culture.

Until the construction of trails and roads from the south during the American period, the main entry into the mountainous interior was from the north. There were two routes up the Chico or over the Cordillera Central from Abra, thence down the Saltan to the Chico and up again into the heart of the mountains. The Southern Kalinga, Bontoc, and Ifugao were thus more isolated from lowland influences than the Northern Kalinga. This isolation gave the Southern Kalinga a different cultural direction (if we assume that both groups stemmed from the same cultural base). The Southern Kalinga also borrowed irrigated rice cultivation from the central area long before the Northern Kalinga. Indeed, as we have noted, irrigated rice terraces are still being constructed in the north. Along with irrigated rice terraces other social and cultural traits (primarily of Ifugao and Bontoc provenience) also diffused. These have been taken over by the Southern Kalinga, but have only begun to penetrate into the northern areas. Hence a Southern Kalinga cultural variant influenced by cultures south of it, but only minimally affected by Spanish and lowland cultures, is understandable.

There is no evidence that the Spanish system of municipal government, operating through appointed or elected *presidente, concejal,* and *teniente* was actually instituted in the Kalinga country before the American period.[11] This system of local government was, however, established in Abra and the Ilocos areas and Kalinga traders were familiar with it. It was therefore understandable that the municipal form of government was adopted without apparent resistence when the mountain people came under American administration and has been adjusted to traditional governmental patterns on the local level throughout the Mountain Province.

The changes brought about by Spanish activities among the Kalinga in the late nineteenth century, particularly in conjunction with the establishment of comandancias and the associated military stations, were indirect. The construction of trails or the improvement of existing trails to maintain the military posts opened up trade, and this in turn brought about friendly relations between Tinguians, Kalinga and Ilocanos. Among a headhunting and feuding people, the establishment of friendly relations necessitated the development of mechanisms to remove old interregional hostilities. Such hostilities appear to have disappeared or at least to have become minimized as peace pacts were instituted and as intermarriages took place between formerly endogamous Kalinga regions and the Tinguians of Abra.

The Revolutionary Period[12]

Dissatisfaction with the Spanish regime was general throughout the Philippines, and while the mountain peoples did not have as intensive contact as the lowlanders with Spanish authorities, they detested the military establishments. The maltreatment they received at the hands of the officials at these posts, the constant demand for tribute and labor services, as well as the occasional punitive expeditions sent against them, prompted the mountain people to destroy these posts and massacre the inhabitants of Spanish garrisons as soon as the Filipino revolution began in 1896. The revolutionary forces which moved into the mountain area to drive out the Spaniards received complete support initially from the inhabitants. The military system of government was replaced by a civil system, but the insurgent government had its hands full attempting to organize the lowland areas and could devote no time to setting up an effective government in the mountain areas. In the main centers they did station troops who unfortunately followed the same if not more harsh methods than the earlier Spanish authorities. As a result there was widespread disorganization and economic devastation. Roads and trails were neglected, and the lively trade which had opened up toward the end of the Spanish period came to a standstill. The missionary groups withdrew with the Spaniards, and those areas that had become Christian returned to paganism. Headtaking was resumed, and internal warfare broke out throughout all groups in the mountains. In fear of hostile neighbors, rice fields and swiddens were abandoned while the inhabitants fortified themselves in villages or went into hiding. The general disorganization became intensified when the Americans drove out the revolutionary forces in 1900. It was not until 1902 that the Americans were able to provide control over the remote parts of the Philippines.

The American Period

An influential member of the first commission established in 1899 by President McKinley to guide the governmental affairs of the newly acquired Philippine Islands was Dean C. Worcester. Worcester, more than any other individual, determined the political destiny of the mountain peoples of northern Luzon. He was made Secretary of the Interior for the Philippines and was given the administrative control of all the non-Christian tribes except the Moros. When the mountain area of northern Luzon was organized in 1908 into the Mountain Province, Worcester was charged with the official duty of visiting and inspecting the area at least once during each fiscal year. He welcomed the opportunity to become intimately acquainted with its people.

The construction of a road into Baguio in 1905 opened the land of the *Igorots* to government officials.[13] Vehicle roads were begun shortly after the turn of the century to other parts of the Mountain Province while horse-trails, bridges, ferries, and a network of telephone lines were appearing in previously remote areas.

The establishment of the Mountain Province provided for a governor and a lieutenant governor for each of the six subprovinces: Benguet, Bontoc, Lepanto-Amburayan, Ifugao, Kalinga, and Apayao. In 1920 the subprovince of Lepanto-Amburayan was reorganized; a part of it was transferred to Ilocos Sur and La Union, and other portions added to Bontoc, thus making the five subprovinces as they still exist today: Benguet, Bontoc, Ifugao, Kalinga, and Apayao. The area from Bugnay to near Lubuagan which had been a part of Bontoc subprovince was also later placed within the subprovince of Kalinga. The latter reorganization fitted the territorial concept of the native inhabitants, as the peoples of Bugnay and northward to the Mabaca River consider themselves Kalinga and not Bontoc.

Administration of the Mountain Province came under the central jurisdiction of the Bureau of Non-Christian Tribes in Manila which was a unit under the Department of the Interior. In the Province itself there were the provincial government with the capital at Bontoc, the five subprovincial centers, and on the local level, the municipal district governments. During the early years of the American period, the governor was appointed by the governor-general of the Philippines, and he in turn appointed the lieutenant governors of the subprovinces. Governmental units on the local level were variously interpreted by the mountain peoples, and the lieutenant governors had exceptional powers. During the first and second decades of the American period, the lieutenant governors were carefully chosen for courage and administrative ability. While the provincial governor had the authority to appoint these men, Dean Worcester as Secretary of the Interior played a prominent part in their selection and indeed in the selection of the provincial governors as well. Such men as Pack, Hunt, Dinwiddie, Echman, Folkmar, Gallman, Hale, Kane, and Early are remembered fondly by the mountain peoples. They were forceful men who ruled their areas with a stern hand and as a consequence, received the respect and admiration of the former headhunters. Worcester (Worcester and Hayden 1930:452–458) pays this high tribute:

> As a result of . . . just, firm and kindly treatment [the] governors and lieutenant governors soon find themselves endowed by their people with powers far in excess of those conferred on them by law. They are *ex officio* justices of the peace, but are just as apt to be asked to settle a headhunting feud between towns, which has caused a dozen bloody murders, as a quarrel growing out of the joint ownership of a pig. They are the law and the prophets, and no appeals are taken from any just decisions which they may make, nor is their authority questioned. On the contrary, their people usually object when sent to the courts, as is of course often necessary.
>   These officers are always on the watch for opportunities to get the people of hostile towns to swap head-axes, or dance together, and so become friends. When one town has been in the very act of raiding another the timely appearance of an unarmed *Apo* [respectable term of reference to a highly esteemed and influential person] has sufficed to shame the culprits into laying down their arms and going home without them. No one who has not seen for himself can appreciate the courage, tact, and patience of the handful of Americans who have not only brought under control the wildest tribes of the Philippines, but have established the most friendly relations with them.

A few remarks about the activities of the first lieutenant governor of Kalinga (1907–1915), Walter Franklin Hale, are in order here.[14] Hale is remembered affectionately as "Sapao," a name given to him according to Barton (1949:220) because he once accompanied a group of Igorots against the Ifugao region of Sapao.[15] Kalinga credit Hale for bringing down the incidence of headhunting, and establishing law and order throughout the subprovince. Hale began his work among the Kalinga by visiting all the villages under his jurisdiction. Later he established his headquarters at Lubuagan which has remained until the present time the subprovincial headquarters. In the early days of his administration, Hale had a standing invitation for all Kalinga to come and discuss their problems with him. When there was trouble, he went himself to investigate it and settled the problem by inflicting fines on those responsible, or by putting the offenders in a jail at Lubuagan, or sending them to the provincial prison in Bontoc. Later, Hale relied more on carefully selected native policemen and instructed all Kalinga that such policemen or their relatives were not responsible for their actions while on official duty. Formerly, Kalinga applied the traditional custom of revenge on native policemen, and Kalinga were reluctant to serve in these positions.

In all matters that did not conflict seriously with governmental regulations, Hale modified rules to fit existing traditional practices. He encouraged the peace-pact institutions which were developed by Kalinga initiative to bring down the incidence of crime and feuds. Early in his administration, Hale recognized the existence of regional units where certain influential leaders or *pangngats* exercised authority and received the respect of the local population. Such units were asked to name their most influential pangngat to represent them. Each regional unit then had a spokesman upon whom Hale conferred the title of *presidente* [with Spanish spelling and pronunciation]. The presidente was given an army coat and a small salary to establish his authority. When trouble developed in such a region, Hale immediately sent for its presidente to discuss the problem and instructed the latter about its resolution. Hale realized that the Kalinga were not yet prepared to function in terms of the larger municipal districts, and he reinforced the traditional Kalinga consciousness of territorial regions. It was not until toward the end of the American period that the larger municipal districts began to have a meaning for the Kalinga, and even today peace pacts are made between the traditional territorial units. Important municipal officers are now elected, yet the old local units tend to support their own candidates.

Secretary of the Interior Worcester (Worcester and Hayden: 1930) had great admiration for Hale and paid him the following tribute:

> Although a constabulary garrison was early stationed at the town of Lubuagan, comparatively little progress was made in bringing the Kalingas under effective control until their territory was made a separate subprovince of the Mountain Province and Lieutenant-Governor Walter F. Hale, of Amburayan, was transferred to it as its lieutenant-governor.

Lieutenant-Governor Hale has now [1913] been in the special government service longer than any other man who remains in it, and has an admirable record for quiet efficiency. Like Gallman [former lieutenant-governor of Ifugao] he is a man with chilled-steel nerve, and he needed it in the early days in Kalinga where the people, who had been allowed to run wild too long, did not take as kindly to the establishment of governmental control as had the Bontoc Igorots and the Ifugaos. The Kalingas are a fine lot of headhunting savages, physically magnificently developed, mentally acute, but naturally very wild. Hale soon made friends with many of the local chiefs, and thereafter when he received invitations from outlying *rancherías* to come over and have his head taken, would quietly accept to the extent of setting out accompanied by a few soldiers, or none at all, and talking the matter over with the people who made the threat! In the end they always decided that he was too good a man to kill.

The lieutenant governors had a variety of duties and responsibilities. They were required to make monthly inspection tours of the entire subprovinces to determine the needs of the various areas as to trails, jails, health, and sanitation measures, among others. They had to make spot decisions, call on native leaders, explain the task to be performed, and call for workers. They were also to determine the feasibility of establishing schools and to advise the provincial governor accordingly. The early work of the lieutenant governors was, however, largely concerned with the building of trails and the maintenance of law and order. These were the things given first priority by Worcester as Secretary of the Interior, but they also accorded with the needs of the country. The entries in a diary kept by Hale during the early years as lieutenant governor of Kalinga Subprovince show that he implemented these priorities. But Hale did not always follow regulations; if he felt that a job needed to be done, he did it or had it done whether the task was authorized or not. Hale believed that trails and roads must be built to open up the country and he raised the fixed annual "public improvement tax." The provincial government authorized the collection of two pesos annually from every able-bodied adult male between the ages of eighteen and fifty-five. The mountain peoples preferred to work this out and were given permission to do so by rendering ten days of work on trails and roads. Hale doubled the number of days and frequently had as many as five hundred Kalinga working on a single stretch of road or trail. The result was an excellent system of roads and trails well constructed and maintained in fine condition. Unfortunately in succeeding years many of the trails constructed during the early American period have been permitted to fall into ruin.

The work of the early lieutenant governors was almost completely involved with the establishment of law and order and with the building of roads and trails. Little attention was given to other matters such as education and health which also needed attention in the Mountain

Province. During the second decade of the American period, however, efforts were made to establish schools and to improve health and sanitary conditions.

The objectives for schooling among the mountain peoples were established by the first director of education, David P. Barrows: First, to teach English, and second, to provide vocational training to meet the special needs of the people (Barrows in Taft Commission Report 1900: 684). The first schools were boarding schools, in Baguio, Cervantes, Lagangilang (Abra), Bua, and Bontoc. As with schools for American Indians in the United States, the primary objection to the boarding schools was that they drew away from the homes young people sorely needed for work in the villages. In addition, pupils became homesick far from home and in unfamiliar surroundings; as a result, many returned home, and attendance could be maintained only by forceful means with the cooperation of the constabulary.

As the first groups of educated natives returned, further difficulties arose. The students objected to traditional life in the villages and to working in the fields. Yet there were no other jobs for them to do. As dissatisfied, displaced individuals they were a disappointment to relatives and to themselves. Negative reaction against the boarding schools began to mount up. In 1907 (Annual Report of the Philippine Commission 1908, Vol. 2, p. 828) as a result largely of dissatisfactions with boarding schools, a series of village schools was begun. These were elementary schools to be taught and staffed where possible by native teachers trained in the boarding schools. At the same time the boarding schools were converted into higher grades where American teachers were retained. A high school with emphasis on agricultural and vocational training was also established at this time at La Trinidad in Benguet.

The government's educational program was boosted during the early years by missionary groups. Of primary importance were the elementary and high schools established by the Belgian order of the Congregation of the Immaculate Heart of Mary (Roman Catholic), the American Episcopal Mission (Protestant), and later the United Brethren (Protestant). By tacit agreement in the early years the American Episcopal and Belgian Roman Catholic missions staked out different areas of the Mountain Province for missionary work. In more recent years, however, as other missionaries entered the field, considerable overlapping among the various missionary groups has occurred.

The first schools were necessarily established in areas closer to principal governmental centers, especially in Benguet and Lepanto. Bontoc and Ifugao lagged behind in school facilities, and it was not until the second decade of the century that schools began in Kalinga and

Apayao. These latter subprovinces demonstrated an immediate favorable reaction to schooling, however. Thus, in 1932, the school district of Balbalan in Kalinga led with ninety-eight out of every one hundred children of school age in attendance, while Lubuagan, also Kalinga, was second with ninety-one. The enrollment of girls by schooling districts, which is also indicative of the popularity of schools, revealed a similar trend. Of every one hundred pupils, Balbalan was highest with forty-three; Apayao, second with forty; and Lubuagan, third with thirty-five (Keesings 1934:246–247).

Health and sanitary matters received attention coincident with the establishment of schools. The conditions under which the Kalinga live tend to eliminate all but the exceptionally fit. As a result, the adult populations are of magnificent physique, but the toll of those who do not make it into adult life is great. Infants and young children are subject to a variety of ailments, and while many children are born, not many of them survive. Among the most prevalent illnesses fatal to children are intestinal diseases of various kinds. These ailments are the result of contaminated sources of water supply and congested living conditions. Other common illnesses affecting both children and adults are respiratory ailments, bronchopneumonia and tuberculosis being especially prevalent. These ailments are undoubtedly brought about by low temperatures in the high humid mountains and the absence of adequate heating facilities. Malaria is common among the Kalinga living in lower elevations in the more tropical forested regions, but not in the higher elevations where the malarial mosquito is absent. Indeed, malaria may be more common at present when the Kalinga are able to travel freely to lowland areas than formerly when populations were restricted to the highlands. Smallpox was perhaps the greatest killer until vaccinations stemmed the tide of epidemics. Skin diseases are also common; infected cuts and scratches quickly become festering sores which when healed leave ugly scars. Almost everyone suffers from some form of eye infection — undoubtedly the result of ill-ventilated, smoky rooms, and a poor diet which lowers resistance to diseases of all sorts. Goitre in various stages of development is most common among women, but also occurs in men and children and is evidence of iodine deficiency in water or food.

Illness among Mountain Province peoples is attributed to the work of malevolent spirits and especially to the spirits of departed relatives. Kalinga reaction to sickness is met by sacrifices of chickens, pigs, and carabaos to appease these spirits. Such practices in families where there is considerable illness tend to impoverish them and are extremely time-consuming. A practice most disturbing to early American administrators was mourning for the dead by exhibiting the corpse in a bamboo chair

A potter of Salegseg region in northern Kalinga, this woman is suffering from goitre, a common affliction among the Kalinga because of iodine deficiency in water and food.

for ten days or more, depending upon the wealth and influence of the deceased. In other areas of Kalinga, the body of the deceased was simply placed on a scaffold outside the village until the flesh and inner organs had rotted away and then the bones were buried. The government passed a law to compel burial within forty-eight hours, but such regulations could not be enforced in the remote areas of Kalinga. At present, the corpse is exposed for long periods of time only by a few families. The influence of schools and missionaries has brought about changed attitudes and beliefs which have been more effective than government regulations in discouraging this practice.

By the second decade of the present century, health measures had become well established. Vaccinations for smallpox slowly gained acceptance, and medicines distributed by government officials and missionaries were welcomed; indeed, in some areas the demand for medication could not be met. Hygiene was introduced as a subject in the schools, and most important of all, hospitals were established in the main centers of population. By 1932, there were three government hospitals: Bontoc, Kiangan (Ifugao) and Lubuagan (Kalinga). Also by 1932, thirty-seven government dispensaries had been established at strategic points throughout the Mountain Province. In isolated areas, missionaries, constabulary officers and school teachers dispensed medicines and administered medical aid (Keesing 1934:235–236).

For a people whose notions of the causes of illness differed so greatly from Western European concepts, an entire change of attitudes and beliefs had to take place. In bringing about such changes, school teachers and missionaries were most effective. By changing their belief that illness is brought about by malevolent or ancestral spirits, the natives became receptive to the acceptance of modern medicine and medical practices. This change in attitudes and beliefs has been gradual, however, and has not completely displaced traditional notions about illness even at the present time.

Missionaries entered the Mountain Province early in the American period. We have noted that the Spanish Dominicans and Augustinians did not really penetrate the mountain areas and the appellation "non-Christian" was appropriate to characterize these peoples in the initial stages of American rule. Missionary work progressed rapidly, however, and the term was no longer applicable by the end of the second decade. This did not mean that the mountain peoples had all been converted into devout Christians and had discarded pagan beliefs and customs. Far from it; they were still strongly attached to their indigenous religious faith and practices, but they had also accepted Christianity in varying degrees. To most non-literate, non-Christian peoples, religion is an additive process, and the mountain peoples simply added what Christian concepts and practices seemed important to them. The deeper values of Christianity were not internalized; only the more obvious external elements were taken over. Most of the mountain peoples reckoned being a Christian a prestige factor and hence wanted to be considered Christian even though they did not understand Christianity and were still essentially pagan in their religious orientation.

Three Christian denominations were especially important in the initial period of missionary work in the Mountain Province: Roman Catholic, American Episcopalian (Protestant), and United Brethren (Protestant).

Roman Catholic missionization in the Mountain Province was entrusted to one Roman Catholic order, the Belgian Fathers of the

Congregation of the Immaculate Heart of Mary. The Belgian Fathers entered the Mountain Province in 1907 with seven missionaries. The first missions were built in the southern part of the province, but a mission was established among the Kalinga in Lubuagan in 1925 by Father Francisco Billiet. Shortly afterwards the mission at Salegseg (Balbalan District) was opened and another at Tabuk. At present, missionary posts of the Belgian Fathers, besides the ones reported, are located in the following places in Kalinga Subprovince: Allaguia, Pinokpok Municipal District; Tinglayan, Tinglayan Municipal District; and Naneng, Tabuk Municipal District. Another mission at Natonin in the eastern part of Bontoc Subprovince serves natives who consider themselves Kalinga and are so considered by other Mountain Province natives. In all, there are thirteen Belgian Fathers serving the Kalinga. Schools are also associated with most of the missions, and medical dispensary units are an important feature of every mission post. At Lubuagan, instruction is offered on the elementary, high school, and junior college levels, and at Tabuk there is a kindergarten, an elementary, and a high school. The instruction in these schools is conducted by Missionary Sisters of Saint Augustine. At Salegseg and Natonin, high schools are under the direction of the Belgian Father in charge with lay teachers. There is also an elementary school at Tinglayan taught by lay teachers with a Belgian Father in charge.[16]

The Protestant Episcopal Church in the United States of America began missionary activities in Bontoc in 1903. The mission was established by Bishop Charles Henry Brent and Reverend Walter C. Clapp, and consisted of a school and a medical dispensary. Later missions and schools were established at Sagada and Baguio. In 1925 Deaconess Charlotte Massy opened a mission at Balbalasan, Kalinga. The latter mission is in the western margins of the Northern Kalinga.[17]

The Belgian Fathers and the Episcopal missionaries operate a number of stations outside of the main missionary centers. The work is extremely difficult and young energetic priests are needed to visit the isolated towns and hamlets under their jurisdiction. In recent years the Episcopal Church has ordained a number of native priests. One in Sagada, Father Longid, is now an auxiliary bishop. The first native of the Apostolic Vicariate of the Mountain Province was ordained in 1940. There are about eight such priests now. In addition to ordained priests, both Episcopalians and the Belgian Fathers have a number of native catechists who receive a small compensation for their work. These men visit the remote towns and hamlets and instruct the populations about church doctrine in the native dialects.

The United Brethren Church (Protestant) is a member of the

Evangelical Union of Protestant Churches founded in Manila on April 26, 1901 (Wilson 1956:53). Its missions are located in Ilocos Sur, Ilocos Norte, and the Mountain Province. Among the Kalinga, the United Brethren Church has a high school at Lubuagan (the Kalinga Academy) and another at Tabuk. The missionary activities of this church cover a large area of the Kalinga Subprovince, and additional stations were being planned in 1960. An American nurse maintains a dispensary at the mission in Lubuagan and travels extensively in neighboring towns and hamlets to administer medical aid.

The Philippine Lutheran Mission group began work among the Kalinga in 1960 with a mission station at Basao, Tinglayan Municipal District. The Reverend Carl Lutz is in charge of the mission.

Except for the few native priests ordained in recent years by the Episcopalians and the Belgian Fathers, and the catechists and other native lay missionary workers, the missionary workers in the Mountain Province are foreign. The priests of the Congregation of the Immaculate Heart of Mary are Belgians, while the Protestant missionaries are American.

The Present and Prospects for the Future

The direction of change described in the final portion of this historical sketch has continued to the present except for the interlude during the Japanese occupation from December, 1941 to April, 1945. This was a period of economic deprivation, and educational programs and missionary activities came almost to a complete standstill. The Mountain Province natives remained consistently loyal to the American cause. Kalinga harbored Americans and served as feared guerrilla warriors. A number of Kalinga proudly exhibit tattooed chests acquired as the result of killing Japanese soldiers. When the Philippines again came briefly under the American regime, the Mountain Province quickly recovered itself, and educational, health, and missionary activities were resumed.

The Philippines received independence on July 4, 1946, and a new Republic of the Philippines was born. The transfer of governmental responsibilities from American to Philippine jurisdiction was conducted smoothly. There was actually little change in conditions in the Mountain Province from one sovereign power to the other. Relations with Americans have continued in friendly fashion and many of the Mountain Province people continue to participate in American economic activities through work in the mines, army camps, and other American installations. Missionary activities are expanding and educational facilities have been enlarged to reach a considerably larger proportion of the population.

Tribal wars occasionally flare up in remote areas of the Kalinga territory, but for the most part the peace-pact institution and the constabulary have been successful in coping with these difficulties.

The construction of roads and trails has suffered a decline in the Kalinga area. With the exception of the "national roads," trails are poorly maintained and in the remote areas they are badly eroded, steep, and fit only for foot travel. It is impossible to take a horse on most of these trails since bridges over torrential rivers are lacking and the paths frequently climb almost perpendicular walls over slippery rocks. The national roads are kept open primarily because of the rather heavy bus and truck traffic on them. The mountain peoples have become enthusiastic travelers and patronize the "Dangwa" buses or trucks. Bado Dangwa, the present governor of the Mountain Province, himself an Igorot mountaineer from Benguet, has a virtual monopoly of bus and truck service between Baguio and points north to Bauko, Sagada, Bontoc, Kiangan (Ifugao), Lubuagan, Tabuk, Salegseg, and Pinokpok. Dangwa claims that national and provincial funds are not sufficient to maintain these roads, and he has his own equipment and men to keep the roads open. The road between Lubuagan and Salegseg is poorly maintained and Dangwa has threatened on more than one occasion to stop the service on this road or raise the fare. The costs of maintaining this stretch of the national highway undoubtedly are considerable. In its northern extremity the road is simply a wide trail. Landslides frequently close the road for a week or more. Nevertheless the road has not been permanently closed and the fares have not been raised. Undoubtedly the desire to maintain good will has served as a deterrent, for Dangwa realizes that the Northern Kalinga have consistently supported him in his campaigns for governor of the Mountain Province.

At present, there is an increasing awareness of local government in terms of the municipal form of government. Kalinga Subprovince was early divided into six municipal districts: Tinglayan, Lubuagan, Balbalan, Tanudan, Pinokpok, and Tabuk. Hale had recognized the local territorial regions familiar to Kalinga's sense of local government, but the provincial government urged the establishment of large territorial regions. While there are some fifty to sixty regions in Kalinga, the municipal districts have been fitted to a certain extent with a native feeling for a larger but also ethnic factor of identity. All Kalinga recognize the three "cultural" areas defined on the map (above page 7). The six municipal districts partially, at least, recognize these divisions, thus the municipalities of Tinglayan and Lubuagan are in the Southern Kalinga area, Balbalan and Pinokpok in the Northern Kalinga area, and Tabuk and Tanudan in the eastern division. Tabuk, more than any of the other municipal

"Dangwa" buses, operated by the governor of the Mountain Province, provide most transportation over any distance for the Kalinga. A family is shown waiting for the bus from Bugnay to Bontok.

districts, lies outside of the areas considered Kalinga. This municipality is primarily in the lowlands and the bulk of its population, especially in recent years, has become Ilocano by intrusion.

The regional units of the Kalinga have not disappeared as important loci of government, however. They are extremely important in the peace-pact institution discussed in a subsequent chapter. Moreover, the regions have their barrio councils which take up local problems with the municipal government. In the Balbalan Municipal District there are thirteen such barrios, corresponding in every case except one with the traditional territorial regions. The one exception is the region of Salegseg which apparently because of recent population growth is divided into two barrios: Salegseg and Gawan, each with its own barrio council. Also for reasons of population growth a number of the traditional territorial regions of southern Kalinga have been split up into one or more barrios. But the original boundaries of the territorial regions are still recognized and specified in peace pact relations.

The present municipal government elect the following officers: mayor, vice-mayor and six councilors, the latter being elected at-large. The positions of treasurer, secretary, and clerks are appointive, but such individuals must have civil service qualifications. In the barrios or regions are the barrio lieutenants who are elected by their own regional members and are the contact between the barrio or regional unit and the municipal government. The individual hamlets, or perhaps two or three together, have their vice-lieutenants. The barrio lieutenant, vice-lieutenants, a secretary, a treasurer, and three councilmen (each responsible respectively for education, health, and livelihood) form the barrio councils. There are thirteen such councils in the Balbalan Municipal District.

All of the above officials must be qualified voters (i.e., above the

age of eighteen) and both sexes have the right of franchise. To hold municipal positions they must be literate.

Behind the scenes, but still extremely influential, are the old local leaders. Formerly leadership among the Kalinga was acquired by a distinguished head-taking record, oratorical ability, and the power to influence decisions in public gatherings. These individuals were called *mangngol* (courageous warriors), and together with other influential regional individuals formed an unorganized group of leaders usually referred to as pangngat in the south and *lakay* or *capitan* (Spanish) in the north. At present individuals with a war record have almost disappeared, and leadership is most often associated with economic standing and oratorical ability. Literacy requirements prevent some of the older individuals from holding municipal offices, but they can and do hold barrio positions. These individuals are usually peace-pact holders, and their personality and influence is important in maintaining interregional good will and peace. Pangngats or lakays are consulted in all important matters that arise within the region.

The historical sketch we have provided here indicates that the present Kalinga area received immigrants from the Cagayan Valley and possibly from the Abra region during initial contacts with the Spanish. For a period of about two hundred years afterwards, and perhaps extending back before the advent of the Spanish, the people were obviously isolated in the rugged mountainous regions. Here the rough terrain, lack of water transportation, and the practice of headhunting contributed to restricting the populations into small, self-sustaining endogamous groups fearful of other similar groups. This isolation may not have been extended backward much more than two hundred or three hundred years, however. The presence of Chinese pottery and beads indicates a fairly extensive trade with Chinese traders, or more likely with intermediary groups between the high mountains and the lowlands.

Kalinga cultural and linguistic characteristics do not exhibit sharp breaks with those of their neighbors. The Northern Kalinga, particularly those living from Salegseg westward to Balbalasang, bear such a close resemblance to the Tinguian described by Cole (1922:231–489) that we may be justified in considering these people a single cultural group. Cultural similarities between Tinguian and the Kalinga indicate a possible common heritage. On the other hand, interaction between these two peoples was brought about or intensified with the opening of the Spanish military road from the mid-nineteenth century on, and undoubtedly resulted in cultural borrowing. The Kalinga peace pacts which appear to have been developed at this time were subsequently reinforced in the American period as roads and trails were constructed and improved.

Cole's concluding section in his study of the Tinguian (1922:489) of Abra contains the following statement:

> The relationship of the Tinguian and Ilocano has already been shown by the physical data and historical references; but were these lacking, it requires but a little inquiry and the compilation of genealogical tables to show that many Ilocano families are related to the Tinguian. It is a matter of common observation that the chief barrier between the two groups is religion, and, once let the pagan accept Christianity, he and his family are quickly absorbed by the Ilocano.

The Tinguian have gone in the direction predicted by Cole; they are now all essentially Ilocano people. Cole's predictions made for the Tinguian may well hold for the Kalinga at present, particularly the Northern Kalinga. These people have started on the road toward eventual Ilocano absorption, and I predict that in two or three generations an Ilocanoized population will extend essentially unbroken from the Ilocos region through Abra, over the Cordilleran Central through north Kalinga and thence down into the Cagayan Valley.

The breakdown of the formerly endogamous regions appears to have started with a few marriages with the Tinguian, and such unions have slowly increased to the present. While these marriages are not numerous, the fact that they are taking place forecasts important change in the former strictly endogamous character of the regions. Interregional marriages are not only with Tinguian; many of them are with other Kalinga. Such marriages are, of course, the result of considerable mobility in recent years of all the mountain peoples, although the Kalinga appear to be especially enthusiastic about travel. Young Kalinga are eager for education. In Baguio alone there are some three hundred Kalinga students from all areas. Most of these students are attending private colleges and trade schools. A similar number are reported to be attending school in Manila. In addition, there are many Kalinga wage workers in Baguio, Manila, Tabuk, and in the mines of northern Luzon. Kalinga of different regions are therefore coming in contact with one another as well as with other mountain peoples and lowlanders. It is clear that the isolated nature of Kalinga life and the character of Kalinga culture will undergo revolutionary change.

Notes to Chapter 1

1. Keesing's published study on the enthnohistory of northern Luzon did not summarize these schemes so succinctly (cf. Keesing 1962:318).
2. Keesing no longer subscribes to the postulations made in this earlier study (1962:318–319).
3. Beyer's "Type B Indonesians" associated with irrigated terraced rice cultivation. Migration of these people is believed to have started about 1500 B. C. and continued until about 500 B. C. (Beyer and Veyra 1947:2).
4. *Swidden* is a term now generally applied by anthropologists to indicate a field, usually on the slope of a hill or mountain, cleared by burning for planting. Crops raised on such a plot are not watered by man; the maturing of such crops depends on natural rainfall. Such a plot is impermanent and abandoned when the yield is low (*See* Conklin, 1957:3, for different types of swidden farming).
5. Scott (1958b:90) also suggests that taro may have been formerly the staple crop and reports as significant that Sagada begins its agricultural year ritually by planting three taro roots.
6. Vanoverbergh's description of Mountain Province dress and adornment patterns (1929) is suggestive of the culture area approach.
7. It is significant, for example, that the first Spanish expedition to penetrate Ibaloy territory in 1624 made no mention of rice or of terracing techniques, but reported the "usual and natural food" of the "Ygolote" as "yams" [taro] and camote grown on the slopes (Blair and Robertson 20, p. 274).
8. Keesing (1962) and Eggan (1954, 1960) subscribe to a local development of wet terrace agriculture in quite recent times, possibly in the dynamic period of early Spanish contacts.
9. Compare Scott 1958a. Scott (*Ibid:* 90–91) notes that the Bontoc are employed by Northern Kalinga farmers to build rice terraces, a statement I was able to confirm by actual observation. In most cases, however, a Northern Kalinga farmer prefers to employ a Southern Kalinga from Sumadel, Bugnay or Butbut to build his rice terraces. These barrios are on the boundary line between Bontoc and Kalinga. Men from other areas were also occasionally hired in the early days for building rice terraces. One story current in the Salegseg

area is of an Ilocano man brought up from Abra to construct a rice paddy. A group of Kalinga, however, reckoned his head more valuable than a rice field and immediately beheaded the man!

10. The information which follows is extracted mainly from Keesing (1962:221–237).

11. These are the Spanish names for officials of the municipal government system, used in the lowlands and known by the Kalinga.

12. Information on the revolutionary and early American periods is drawn primarily from Worcester and Hayden (1930).

13. Early American writers used the term *Igorot* specifically for the Bontocs, but in Spanish sources the designation refers to all pagan inhabitants of the mountains of northern Luzon. For the derivation of the word and an interesting account of how the people so designated felt about the term, see Scott (1962b).

14. Most of the information on Hale is abstracted from Hale's diary (Wilson 1957).

15. Wilson (1957:1) gives a slightly different version of how Hale received the name of "Sapao." Wilson reports:

    Sapao, which signifies strong but terrible, was the name they gave him and he received it in typical fashion. There was a chief of a recalcitrant (head-hunting) village which was named *Sapao.* Continuous irresponsible head-hunting was against the law, so Hale sent word for this chief to come in, but the chief's return message was: "Come and get me." So Hale strapped on his .45, hiked over the rough country, climbed up the steep hill to *Sapao,* calmly walked in through the hostile village to the house of the chief, and got his man.

16. The information on the Belgian Fathers was secured from the *Catholic Directory of the Philippines, 1960,* and supplemented by talks with priests of the Belgian Order in Lubuagan and Salegseg.

17. I am indebted to Mr. William H. Scott of St. Mary's School, Sagada, Mountain Province, for checking and verifying this information.

2. | Social Organization

THREE SUB-CULTURAL areas are evident to anyone who has visited the Kalinga Subprovince and neighboring subprovinces. These cultural subdivisions are geographical and may be simply designated as the southern, northern, and eastern Kalinga areas. The Kalinga themselves are cognizant of these divisions and frequently refer to the social and cultural characteristics of each subdivision. In a sense, of course, there are as many distinctive subcultures as there are regions, and the Kalinga tend to think of differences in this way. The home region is where one has relatives and where one's loyalties are anchored. The feeling is still strong that people from other regions, whether Kalinga or not, are not to be trusted, and that one has no responsibility toward them. This is of course a reflection of past conditions when anyone from another region was an enemy and hence, fair game. Circumstances have changed and the peace-pact institution protects the life of a member of another region and extends to such a person the same privileges as a regional member. Yet if the peace pact is broken, conditions revert back to the past, and the life of a person from a region with which a pact has been severed is in danger until the pact is reinstituted. Thus the past situation when regional populations were hostile to one another still pervades the thinking of the Kalinga. Yet proximity and formidable geographical barriers have delimited larger sub-cultural units. The populations among a number of neighboring regions, set off from another similar group of regions by large rivers or high mountain ridges, did have some intercourse with one another and hence greater cultural exchange.

While the peace pact is definitely a recent device to overcome inter-regional hostilities, locally other mechanisms existed even in the past

[53]

which occasionally brought together neighboring regional members. A trading partnership between men of two different regions is quite widespread in the Philippines and is obviously an old type of relationship. This relationship protected the traders and members of their families from harm when in one another's region. Occasionally such contacts resulted in interregional marriages and hence provided the basis for considerable social and cultural exchange. It is understandable, therefore, that despite interregional hostilities, those regions that occupied contiguous territories and were bounded by prominent geographical features had greater contact with one another than those regions remote from one another and separated by geographical barriers. The three subcultural divisions of the Kalinga are of this kind — they are sharply delimited geographically from one another while inside each subdivision, geographical barriers are minimal.

We have already noted in the introduction that the northern and southern Kalinga areas are rather sharply divided by a fairly large and swift-flowing river, the Pacil, which runs for a considerable distance of its course in a deep gorge. The cultural differences between these two areas are of course attributable to other than the factor of isolation; one of these factors is economic, the other historical. These factors have been discussed in considerable detail in the last chapter and we need not repeat the discussion here.

The eastern Kalinga area is perhaps the most isolated from a geographical standpoint. The high ridge running north and south, parallel to the Chico River, separates this area from the southern Kalinga. The northern and eastern Kalinga subcultural areas are separated partly by the southern Kalinga area which intervenes between them, and farther north by the Chico River. Since the American period, the Eastern Kalinga along the Tanudan River, across the ridge from the Chico and running parallel to it, have had considerable intercourse with the Southern Kalinga, and a number of marriages have taken place between the two groups. As the result of these circumstances the Tanudan River Kalinga and the Southern Kalinga are perhaps not as distinctively apart culturally as each is from the northern Kalinga area.

An interesting group of nomadic Kalinga is reported in the eastern part of the present Tanudan Municipal District, the Kalakad-Tupak regions. This group may well form a fourth major subcultural area of the Kalinga. Little is known of these people even by other Kalinga. The Kalakad-Tupak Kalinga are in touch with the Eastern Kalinga and have extended peace-pact relations with them; however, not with the Gaddang. The Kalinga of the Kalakad-Tupak regions are reported to exist primarily on wild fruits, hunt and defend themselves with the bow and arrow and live in tree houses. Until more information is gathered about this group, however, we cannot identify them as culturally separate.

It is relevant here also to call attention to another group of Kalinga, the Madukayan. This group of Kalinga was reported to have a population of 359 in the 1948 Philippine census and occupy a barrio of the same name in the municipal district of Natonin, Bontoc. These Kalinga are migrants from the Tanudan Valley, however, and are culturally Eastern Kalinga (cf. Scott 1958b:318-319).

Along the margins of the three major cultural areas delimited here, influences of outside cultural groups are evident. Thus the Isneg in the north, the Bontoc in the south and in the north central portion of the Kalinga Subprovince, Ilocano pressures from Cagayan and Tinguian influence from Abra Provinces have all left their cultural imprint on the Kalinga. Yet each area exhibits internal uniformity in dialects, in dress and adornment, and somewhat in architecture, although house types tend to be rather variable even within a single village (cf. Anderson 1960, Vanoverbergh 1925, Scott 1962c).

The Region

The largest geographical unit recognized by the Kalinga is the region. Northern Kalinga refer to the region in their dialect as *boboloy* or *(bob∧ i)*, but in speaking with outsiders they use the term "barrio" or "tribe." A Kalinga universe roughly coterminous with the boundary lines of the present subprovince is also recognized by the Kalinga. The primary reason for this has been linguistic affinity and the spread of the peace-pact system. The Kalinga as a whole were never a political unit, however. They had no organization beyond the kinship group, except the peace-pact institution which is not an instrument of Kalinga political federation, but simply a treaty between kinship groups and of recent origin. It is quite clear that in the past, region and kinship circle (to be described later) were equated in the thinking of the people. Closely related kin intermarried and occupied a specified area, the region, where they carried on their subsistence economy. Since the formation of the Mountain Province and its subprovinces in 1907, the Kalinga are in fact developing a kind of "tribal" consciousness, but this is not yet strong. (Cf. Scott 1962 b: 243).

The evidence is clear that formerly interregional relationships were much more hostile than at present and that, conversely, there was greater intraregional solidarity. Traditionally the Kalinga were a people who made headtaking an intricate part of their culture; killings and counter-killings between regions were common, and feuds were deeply imbedded throughout the land. Members of a region did not venture outside; beyond the borders of one's own region, one was likely to be killed, for there was always a backlog of unavenged killings between any two regions. In times of calamity, disease epidemic or crop failure, a group of men might leave their region, and, proceeding with caution and stealth, take a head from a neighboring region, believing that the misfortune might thereby be dispelled. While headhunting expeditions most commonly took place after a catastrophe — death, illness, crop failure and the like — the enemy's head, no matter how or when it was taken and brought home, elevated a man's position in his region. The road to status and prestige in the past lay in a series of successful head-taking expeditions. Undoubtedly headhunting as well as the occasional, more organized retaliatory war parties also fulfilled an economic function. Headhunting and warfare discouraged the enemy from encroaching on potential swidden plots, and an aggressive regional group might extend its range of swidden plots at the expense of the enemy.[1]

Until recently, security was within one's region only, and only regional members could be relied upon and trusted. The Kalinga of each region married among themselves, observing only the prohibition of marrying close cousins, and pursued their economic, social, and religious activities within the confines of their own region. It would seem, therefore, that formerly the region was occupied by an endogamous local group and Murdock's term "deme" would be an appropriate designation for the kinship group whose members were bound to one another by common residence and consanguinity (Murdock 1949:62-63).

Regions differ in size and their limitations are imposed by apparently available food sources, population densities, and the strength and prowess of neighboring regions. The Lubuagan region in the more densely populated southern area has a diameter of approximately four miles, whereas in the sparsely populated northern area, Mabaca and Buaya have diameters roughly of seven and eight miles each. The northern regions today most nearly typify past conditions. Here, populations are small and dispersed in hamlets or sitios. In the Mabaca region the settlements are scattered over an area of about sixty square miles. The largest of these, Canao Norte, has only forty-one houses closely clustered together.[2] There were thirteen settlements designated by name in Mabaca at the time of my visit. These ranged from forty-one houses to one (*see* Table 4, page 16). Informants report considerable shifting of the settlements; former sitios have been abandoned, others reduced to a single house or two, while new ones have been founded. The nature of the subsistence economy — swidden agriculture — undoubtedly accounts for frequent changes of habitation, but safety precautions have also brought about relocation of settlements. Dwellings characteristically are located on leveled areas on the slopes of steep mountains where the view is unobstructed, or in isolated pockets in deep canyons. Until recently, villages were stockaded, *gibao,* and along the trails approaching the village were carefully concealed pits at the bottom of which were sharpened bamboos ready to catch and maim or kill the unwary stranger. Deadfalls in the form of an overhanging or leaning heavy log to be tripped by a string across the trail were designed to kill a stranger or warn the village of his approach. Only the members of the region knew the location of such traps and warning devices.

In Kalinga thinking, the kinship group is still equated with an endogamous region. Peace pacts, for example, are thought to be between kinship groups rather than between areas (cf. Barton 1949:174). In the north and in certain isolated areas of the south, regional populations are small; hence, the theory of equating kinship group with region may sometimes accord with fact. Populations of the regions in the north, the region of Salegseg excepted, have about five hundred people; whereas in the south the norm is about 1,000, with the Lubuagan region alone having a population of 4,000 (*see* population figures). It is virtually impossible in the northern Kalinga regions for an individual not to be related, at least within third-cousin degree, with every other individual. At present, the Kalinga still operate in terms of the kinship principle, but it is obvious that in the more densely populated regions, kinship group and region cannot correspond. In recent years, with expanded populations within the region, greater interregional mobility, and increasing marriages with Kalinga of other regions, the native equation of kinship group with region is beginning to be modified. As a result the modern imposed municipal form of government is beginning to have meaning. But the importance of the region as a socio-political unit has not anywhere been displaced in favor of the larger municipal district.

Expanded populations have brought about pressures on cultivable land and accompanying these, migrations out of home regions, and the founding of new colonies. In such cases, the daughter colony for a time remains a political dependency of the parent region. That is, it is considered a part of the parent region and included in all its peace pacts. Uma in 1940 during Barton's study (1949:35) was such a dependency of Lubuagan, but it had already started to break away from the parent region by making a separate peace pact with Balbalasan. At present, Uma is completely independent and makes its own peace pacts with other regions. Other linked parent-daughter regions are the following: *Tinglayan District:* Butbut-Bugnay, Sumadel-Mallango, Sumadel-Kolayo (the daughter colony is in Lubuagan District); *Balbalan District:* Pantikian-Balbalasan (called Banao), Poswoy-Daongan-Ababaan, Mabaca-Amacian (daughter colony in Pinokpok District); *Lubuagan District:* Guinaang-Dalupa-Ableg; *Tanudan District:* Lubo-Gaang.

Daughter colonies eventually do become completely independent politically from the parent regions, although daughter colony members intermarry with members of the parent region, even after political relations have been suspended. Besides the high mobility of the Kalinga this extension of marriage relations to migrant populations is another factor contributing to the breakup of the localized, endogamous regions.

A number of Kalinga migrants from different regions of Balbalan District, i.e. the northern Kalinga area, have also in recent years settled together in various parts of Pinokpok and Tabuk districts, the subprovince of Apayao and the province of Cagayan. Formerly these areas were not occupied by Kalinga for two primary reasons: 1) they were enemy territory, if occupied at all; and 2) the areas were malaria infested. At present, with danger to lives diminished by the peace-pact institution and Philippine law enforcement forces, and the effectiveness of malaria control projects, large numbers of Kalinga and other mountain peoples have migrated into these areas. The Kalinga settlers are for a time protected by the peace pacts of their former home regions but some settlements are now making their own peace pacts with other regions. Some of these new communities are: Amacian in Pinokpok District, mostly Mabaca immigrants (*see* above); Magaogao, straddling Pinokpok and Tabuk districts; Wagud, Pinokpok District; Mawanan in Apayao has a mixed Ilocano-Kalinga population as do Balaknit and Tuao in Cagayan. These communities all have peace pacts of their own, while they remain covered by pacts from home for other regions.

Northern Kalinga inhabitants have also founded settlements in the province of Abra. Two of these communities, Bunig and Lakob, have peace pacts with many of the Kalinga regions of the central area.

Expansion in Kalinga population can be correlated with the adoption of a more stable economy in the form of wet rice agriculture; while modern conditions, particularly contact with Western cultures and Christian missionaries, have brought about mobility and friendly interaction among Kalinga of all regions. Basic to free movement for a people formerly living in small groups and in hostile relations with their neighbors of adjacent regions has been the peace-pact institution. This is a peculiarly Kalinga invention which insures physical safety and generous hospitality for members of regions having a peace pact with one another. This institution will be described in greater detail in another section; it is important here to mention only that the *bodong* (the peace-pact institution) of which all Kalinga are extremely proud, may be properly credited with stopping headhunting and reducing the number of interregional killings.

The region may be considered in relation to the bilaterally extended

family, which we have designated as a kinship circle or personal kindred
(*see* below, page 101 f.f.) In Kalinga conception this unit includes
spouses as well; hence, it is not completely equivalent with kindred or
personal kindred as these terms are usually employed by social anthropologists (cf. Davenport 1959:562–565; Freeman 1961:201; Murdock
1949:60–61; but see Befu 1963:1331; Nadel 1947:17). The Northern
Kalinga, and to a certain extent all Kalinga, conceive of the region as
being inhabited by a single kinship circle or personal kindred and so
operate in defending and avenging the regional population in interregional
conflicts. The peace-pact institution also operates along the same principle at present in assessing fines, collecting indemnities and the like.
Actually, of course, every region has a number of kindreds with considerable overlapping as is the nature of kindreds everywhere, and in
intraregional disputes the kindred is delimited more narrowly to include
second cousins (Lubuagan) or third cousins (Northern Kalinga). Since
northern Kalinga regional populations are small, drawing the boundaries
of the kindred or kinship circle around third cousins may in some cases
actually include the whole regional population. Indeed, because of small
populations the northern Kalinga regions do settle most intraregional
difficulties amicably like a large bilateral kin group. In the southern
Kalinga regions where populations are considerably larger, there is usually
a resort to the vengeance pattern even in intraregional disputes. From
a wider perspective, the territorial principle imposed upon a closely
related bilateral kin group makes the kindred (as among the Northern
Kalinga) a discrete political unit. Or should this unit now be considered
a "deme"? (Murdock 1949:62–63). If so considered, we have a unit
not previously reported in the ethnographic literature for the mountain
peoples. One cannot sidestep the native conception, however, which
considers the regional unit a kindred (with spouses included) and phrases
it in terms of including third cousins; among the Northern Kalinga, at
least, all are conceived to be related within the third-cousin degree of
relationship in a region.

Villages and Hamlets

Within each region are a number of villages and hamlets. The
Northern Kalinga use the term *barrio* (Spanish) for the endogamous
area we call a "region" and *sitio* (Spanish) for the hamlets characteristic
of the northern area. In the south where the settlements are typically
large, the term barrio is variously employed, both for the region and for
the large towns such as Mabilong, Lubuagan, and Bangad proper, which
are towns within a region having populations numbering several hundred
inhabitants. While the region is usually named after its main or largest

settlement, as for example the regions of Lubuagan and Bangad, other regions are designated by a name for which there is no settlement bearing the name. Thus, for example, the regions of Salegseg and Mabaca have no settlements by that name. An individual everywhere among the Kalinga identifies himself as from such-and-such a region, and only when pressed to name the exact place of residence will he designate his town or hamlet specifically. This is because the settlement in which he lives is not an important social unit among the Kalinga. To the Kalinga, the household, extended household, kinship circle or kindred, and the territorial region, are the significant units of his society. An individual's household and extended household are localized in a town or hamlet, but his kinship circle or kindred is dispersed throughout the various settlements in his region. And as we have indicated above, in the north more consistently than in the south, the kinship circle or kindred is often conceived to be the whole regional population.

Among the Northern Kalinga, but undoubtedly characteristic of the Kalinga generally in the past, hamlets are never very permanent, and there are frequent shiftings of the settlements and a reshuffling of the population within the region. Despite such relocations of settlements, kinship ties remain a strong bond, and considerable visiting among close kin goes on. There are numerous occasions on which the members of the kinship circle or kindred come together. In the north where kinship group and region are believed to be co-extensive, regional solidarity is strong; but in the south, swollen populations within a region have given rise to complicated problems. Whereas feuding and vengeance within a region are practically unknown in the north, in the south such conflicts are of common occurrence. Thus, for example, when I asked a boy in Tangadan, Lubuagan region, to accompany me to Mabilong, a barrio of the same region and only about fifty feet from Tangadan, he begged to be excused. His family explained that he might be the victim of revenge for an unsettled fight several weeks before between two youths, one of whom was a first cousin of the boy. Lubuagan informants report many similar instances and Barton (1949) reported a number of serious disputes and even killings involving kindreds within the region of Lubuagan during his period of study there in 1940.

The Household and Extended Household

The household is the residence unit among the Kalinga. It is occupied by a nuclear family and perhaps an aged parent or grandparent of one of the spouses. In a few wealthy households, there may also be a servant *(poyong)* or two. The average size of the households in the Lubuagan Municipal District in 1959 was 4.5 persons, but for the more densely populated Lubuagan region, the average was 4.8. The number of households for the whole of Balbalan District was not available, but a survey of one region, Mabaca, indicated 5.5 persons per household. (*See* Tables 3 and 5, pages 15 and 16.) The genealogies from Lubuagan and Mabaca indicated many children (as many as fifteen in some families, although the mean was about seven) born to a family but only three or four surviving beyond the age of puberty.[3] Mortality below the age of twelve is high, particularly below the age of three. Diarrhea was given as the chief cause of death in early childhood. The generally unsanitary conditions which surround houses and settlements are, of course, breeding places for disease bacteria of all kinds. The purity of drinking water is never strictly maintained, and the inhabitants of a village frequently use the nearest water source which is often polluted. Pigs roam the village and may be seen wallowing in mud near streams from which drinking water is drawn. When disease epidemics hit a village, the whole population is usually infected since dwellings are clustered close together, and usually no precautions are taken to avoid getting the disease.

While the individuals living under one roof are usually restricted to a nuclear family with perhaps an attached dependent relative, economic activities are shared by a larger interacting circle of relatives living in two or more houses located in a common area. This larger unit, varying in size, but involving two or more nuclear families, we may designate as the extended household. The maximum number of interacting households from our Lubuagan sample of extended households was four and the mean three. The range and mean were the same in Mabaca, but there more individuals live under one roof. The number of interacting households, especially in Lubuagan, is partly dictated by the number of married daughters since residence there is predominantly matrilocal or uxorilocal, and the bride's relatives construct a home near the girl's parental home or on land provided by her relatives. Initially a Lubuagan couple may live with the wife's parents while their own house is being built, but as soon as it is ready they move. Informants in Lubuagan report that residences of this type may be broken in two ways: 1) if parents have many daughters and they have already provided dwellings for them, then one of the daughters may be permitted to locate in her husband's household area in a house constructed with the aid of relatives of both bride and groom; 2) if the groom's parents are well-to-do and influential, and there is obvious advantage in setting up patrilocal residence.

The belief that the bride's parents and relatives should provide the house and house-site is strong among both the Southern and Northern Kalinga, but it is especially strong in Lubuagan. A family (and its relatives) which cannot provide a home for its daughters in Lubuagan is "shamed." Since "loss of face" is an extremely powerful negative sanction in Kalinga culture, every effort is made to observe traditional customs.

Among the Northern Kalinga, the matrilocal or uxorilocal residence pattern is less consistently followed. The greater intraregional mobility necessitated by the predominantly shifting form of agriculture, results in a more varied form of residence. Although couples commonly locate near the wife's parents' home (or even move into the same house) there are a number of instances of patrilocal residence and even more of neo-local residence in a hamlet different from that of either of the parents. Convenience to the swidden or rice fields usually determines the place of residence. Other things being equal, however, there is a preference for residing near the wife's parents' home.

Another difference between Northern and Southern Kalinga exists in the relatives who aid and contribute labor in the construction of a house for a newly married couple. In cases of matrilocal residence in Lubuagan, only the bride's relatives are responsible for providing labor and costs, but in Mabaca and the north Kalinga area generally, the responsibility is binding on both the bride's and groom's relatives. This difference is undoubtedly due to the fact that Mabaca, like other sparsely populated north Kalinga regions, considers itself a single kinship unit, and all its members believe themselves related.

One important point needs clarification. When informants speak of the "responsibility of relatives" in small group tasks such as house building, they actually mean the closest kin, hence siblings, parents, parental aunts and uncles, and perhaps first cousins and the spouses of some of these. It is unlikely that a whole kindred ever engages in group work.

Members of an extended household work together in common economic tasks. In the rice fields and swiddens both sexes help, though certain jobs are more specifically for men, others for women. Only men, for example, plow with carabao, while women characteristically attend to weeding. The transportation of loads from field to house is also usually done by the women, but men may use the balance-pole for carrying heavy loads. Around the house the women help one another in pounding and winnowing rice and attend to myriad other tasks. Except for house-building and house repair, men seem not to have as much to do around the house as women. Characteristically in a Kalinga home, one sees men and boys sitting or lounging around while women and girls are busy with household tasks. At home the Kalinga male has privileges and leisure not accorded the opposite sex. The Kalinga women are not subdued or abused and probably have a more equal position with men than the women of other Mountain Province peoples; nevertheless, on many occa-

One of the walls of this northern Kalinga dwelling is of split bamboo, and another of handhewn planks. The stone pot-supports on the cooking hearth are fashioned in the shape of cats.

sions women will be working, while men are merely around, watching and talking. This may be a phenomenon reflecting the past, when men of the household had to be free and ready to defend the home against an enemy attack.

While the extended family works together and the products of the field are shared, a single dwelling house is ordinarily the domain of the nuclear family, although occasionally a dependent relative may also reside there. In the north sometimes a married daughter or son and her or his children may live in it. Within, the couple construct special shelves along the walls to display the Chinese plates and jars which they have inherited from their parents. In a wooden closet or in a chest are other heirlooms.

agate beads strung in necklaces and chokers, and brass gongs, plus woven blankets and clothes for wife, husband and the children. These are the prized possessions of the family and determine its wealth. Hence this is one index prestige in the hamlet or region. The nuclear family also prepares meals and eats as a unit, but when visitors are entertained or on festive occasions other relatives will be accommodated within the house to partake of a meal. There is of course considerable daily visiting and members of the extended household freely enter one another's houses.

Young children sleep with their parents, while unmarried children above the age of six often sleep together in different houses of the extended family unit, one night in one house, the next in another, and so on. In Lubuagan unmarried youths often sleep in vacant houses called *obog*,[4] and girls in the homes of widows. Lubuagan informants also report that unmarried youths may visit girls staying in the homes of widows, or even visit girls in their homes at night, but only engaged couples are permitted to remain the night together and have sexual intercourse. Northern Kalinga patterns vary from those of Lubuagan. Here, a boy and a girl may arrange to have sexual intercourse, but this is always done secretly and not with parental approval. If a girl is forced into the act, the boy's relatives are assessed fines. If discovered, especially if the girl becomes pregnant, parents of the girl will whip her providing that she entered into the affair willingly. There is no punishment of the boy if the girl consented, except to try to force them to marry, an affair of the regional leaders (pangngats). (*See* also Barton 1949:244.) In the northern Kalinga area, unmarried youths and girls who are "properly raised" remain in the homes of the extended household at night and only an engaged couple may sleep together provided there has been a gift of beads following the performance of the ceremony called *Ingngilin*. (For further details on the subject of courting and marriage, *see* Life Cycle.)

It is difficult to locate the nucleus of authority in group tasks involving the extended household since direction and discipline, whether of children or adults, appear to be unstructured. Yet things get done and activity is not haphazard but orderly. Extended household decisions and work projects emanate from the older relatives, particularly the senior couple, but orders are so subtle that the extended family appears to act by precept rather than by a perceptible familial authority system.

The extended household is a kind of a segment of the larger kinship circle described below. While an older couple's daughters and their families live nearby, their married sons are dispersed in the residential areas of their respective wives' closest kin. Nevertheless, the families of sons and daughters, plus a host of other relatives, are members of the same kinship circle.

The Kinship Circle or Kindred

The important social unit of the Kalinga is a bilateral grouping of kin consisting, for any individual, of his siblings, first cousins, second cousins, third cousins, and the ascendants and descendants of these up through the great grandparents and down through the great grandchildren.[5] The spouses of all these are also included in the kinship group. Since relationships are always traced from a particular individual, who forms a kind of a hub in a circle of kin, the Kalinga kinship group is not a descent group. Eggan (1960: 30) refers to this grouping found among all of the mountain peoples of northern Luzon as a "personal kindred." It is important to note that as the Kalinga conceive of it, this kinship unit includes spouses, and it is in this sense that the term kinship circle or personal kindred is used in this study.

In addition to the Kalinga-type kinship circles, Eggan (1960: 29), reports bilateral descent groups for Sagada, i.e. the importance of "the descendants in both lines of certain prominent ancestors, founding fathers, and important living individuals."[6] In Sagada these descent groups are usually named after a male founder or ancestor and have certain corporate characteristics; for example, they own land, pine trees, and appoint a warden to regulate the gathering of wood. What appear to be descent groups have also been reported for the Ifugao by Eggan (*op. cit.*) and Lambrecht (1953, 1954).[7] With the exception of three "heads of families" responsible for areas of irrigated rice fields in Lubuagan, there is no evidence of bilateral descent groups among the Kalinga.[8] Lubuagan rice fields are said to be divided into an upper, middle, and lower field, and each of these has a "supervisor" who, in the past at least, was responsible for allocating water rights, announcing the times for planting and harvesting, and settling disputes over land in his area. Two men and one woman hold these positions at the present time, although their duties are reported to have lapsed in recent years. All three claim to have inherited these positions from their fathers who held them until their death.

No hint of descent groups was found among the Northern Kalinga except in connection with the recent peace-pact institution. Positions of leadership or prominence in a region in the northern Kalinga area are acquired through individual achievement, not because they belong to specific families. There are no positions which descend along family lines, and while certain families are considered to be more wealthy than others there is no ranking of common and prominent families. Nor are fields or property held in common by specific families. Inheritance patterns run along individual lines rather than along family lines.

The lack or unimportance of bilateral descent groups among the Northern Kalinga tends to refute Eggan's postulations (1960: 29-30) about the correlation of Mountain Province descent groups with shifting cultivation of root crops, smaller populations, and dispersed settlements.[9] Where there is some evidence for descent groups among the Kalinga, they are associated with rice fields and irrigation, and in Lubuagan where the population density is highest. In the north where populations are small and settlements dispersed, there is no evidence of descent groups. I did not have an opportunity to check the presence or absence of bilateral families in the Tinglayan Municipal District, but informants report greater attention devoted to agriculture in Bangad, with "head men" responsible for enforcing "no trespassing prohibitions" and other taboos in rice fields and granaries during planting and harvesting.[10]

I suggest rather the reverse, that attention to specific family lines came in with the wet rice complex: ownership and inheritance of rice fields, increasing population, and the need for greater controls and a permanent authority. (Compare Frake 1956:172; Goodenough 1956: 173-175). Wealth differentials, emphasized in the south, would be an additional factor favoring the singling out of certain families for special attention. In the north, authority is informal and changing, to the degree that the leader or leaders held the respect of the shifting swidden farmers. In the past, the situation may have been comparable to that of a band organization with band chiefs who acquired their positions informally and held them as long as they were responsible and respected leaders. To the extent that populations remained small and the boundaries of the region were specified and well defined, the kinship circle or kindred with its strong informal leaders functioned efficiently. Elsewhere, for example, among the Maori and in Tikopia, the bilateral descent group is associated with societies more complex than the Kalinga. In these societies factors of wealth and/or rank are closely associated and hence, descent from distinguished ancestors of wealth and rank is important. In Lubuagan the term *kadangyan* refers to a well-to-do and distinguished class but its members are not deeply rooted in the society and the pangngants, informal but influential leaders, come from all ranks. In the north there is not even an incipient development of the Kadangyan. A well-to-do individual or family is called *bagnang,* as indeed is also the case in Lubuagan and among the Kalinga generally. The important point is that in the south there is recognition of an emerging aristocratic class not yet firmly established, while in the north there is no such awareness. Among the Northern Kalinga, leaders were those who had distinguished headhunting records, and who in addition spoke with courage and conviction at public gatherings. With the cessation of headhunting, wealth has become an important criterion of leadership, but the ability to speak with eloquence at meetings is still an important trait of the regional leader among both the Northern and Southern Kalinga.

Members of kinship circles everywhere among the Kalinga are required to support one another in all disputes and conflicts. They are obligated to avenge any member who is killed, wounded, or wronged in any manner. They are responsible for seeing that the provisions of a peace pact are kept, and if any member has wronged a member of another kinship circle, all members of the personal kindred are required to contribute to the payment of indemnities. The relatives that compose the kinship circle are in evidence particularly on festive occasions, such as sickness rites or funerals. On such occasions, specific relatives have certain obligations regarding the contribution of wine or food, and they also receive shares of meat.

Barton (1949:32) found in Lubuagan that the kinship circle of any individual consisted of "his brothers and sisters, first cousins, second cousins and third cousins, and of the ascendants and descendants of all these categories with the exception of the descendants of the last one." Thus, above ego's generation the great grandparents and their siblings are included, but below, the descendants of the third cousins are excluded all together. In my investigations in Lubuagan, informants drew the limits even more narrowly around the outer boundaries of the grandparental siblings, second cousins and their grandchildren (*see* chart of the Kalinga kinship circle p. 69). This further change very probably reflects modern acculturative pressures already evident during the time of Barton's study when the descendants of the third cousins had been excluded from the kinship circle. Since the war there has been greater mobility, and members of a kinship circle are no longer in constant face-to-face interaction as in the past. Moreover, the large populations of southern Kalinga regions make it difficult to draw the limits of the kinship circle around more distantly related kin than second cousins. The kinship circle thus appears to have shrunk in size under the pressure of acculturation and population increase.

The acculturative factors which have apparently reduced the kinship circle or kindred of the Lubuagan Kalinga are also operative in the north, but the population increase has not been as phenomenal. None of the northern regions have the high population density of the Lubuagan region, and undoubtedly this factor is crucial in accounting for the reduction of the kinship circle in Lubuagan. The Northern Kalinga are still characterized by the larger kinship circle as initially described and indeed equate the territorial region with the kinship circle.

As we have noted, formerly the region was an autonomous political unit, insofar as the natives conceive of the region as comprising a kinship group. In actuality, of course, members of a region do not comprise a single kinship circle but because members usually marry within the region they tend to be closely related. With increasing marriages outside the group, it would be safe to predict that the region will diminish in importance as the modern municipal district begins to fulfill the needs of local government. The kinship circle, perhaps in diminished form as at Lubuagan, will undoubtedly persist in importance for settling disputes. Since so many social, economic, and religious functions are bound up in the kinship circle, the continuity of this organization is virtually assured. Indeed, despite strong acculturation pressures, this kin group has persisted in other areas of the Philippines.

In all Kalinga areas, marriage is strictly forbidden through first cousins. There is some objection to marrying second cousins, but these occasionally occur, while marriage with third cousins and beyond is freely sanctioned.[11]

Northern and Southern Kalinga informants report that formerly regional endogamy was strictly enforced. Marriages outside the region are beginning to occur, but the instances are not yet numerous. In southern Kalinga Barton (1949:37) found two Lubuagan men who married girls in Tanglag, the region most accessible to Lubuagan, and an informant told him about another case of a Lubuagan man who married a woman in Bangad and was living there. Barton (*op. cit.*) found only one case of a woman from another region who had married into Lubuagan and resided there with her husband. The woman was also from Tanglag. A genealogy of one man's "kinship circle" which I collected in Lubuagan, involved thirty-one married couples. Of these, five had married in from the outside. The cases involved four women and one man, all residing in Lubuagan, and they had all come from regions bordering the Lubuagan region. In Mabaca a similar genealogy of thirty-six married couples revealed only two marriages outside the region, a man married to a Balbalasan woman and another man married to a Tinguian woman from Abra. The couples were all residing in Mabaca. Marriages with Christian lowlanders are even fewer. A man from Mabongtot had formerly been married to a Tagalog woman in Manila and lived there. When she died he married a girl from Mabilong (a town of Lubuagan) and is now residing there. The present justice of the peace at Lubuagan, a Kalinga from Lubuagan, is married to an Ilocano woman. In Salegseg, an Ilocano teacher at the public elementary school has a Kalinga wife. Marriages between members of a parent region and its colonies are not reckoned as marriages outside the region even though such settlements may be at considerable distance from the parent region. Marriages between parent regions and daughter settlements are the rule even after the daughter colony has gained "political" independence.

The high mobility of the Kalinga in pursuit of education, wage work, and the like, will undoubtedly lead them into greater intermarriage

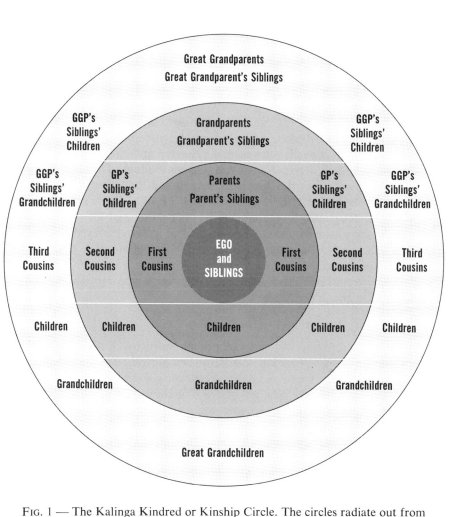

Fig. 1 — The Kalinga Kindred or Kinship Circle. The circles radiate out from Ego's nearest to farthest kin, thus from Ego and Siblings to the great grandparent generation, third cousins, and great grandchildren generation. Horizontal lines indicate the ascending and first, second and third cousins through the great grandparent generations and the great grandchildren generation are all part of Ego's kinship circle, as are all spouses. The terms shown on this chart are not translations of the actual terms used. For kinship terms, see accompanying charts.

with Kalinga from other regions and also with other Filipinos. Such marriages will result in the eventual breakup of the endogamous political regions and help to integrate the Kalinga into the general Philippine nation. Indeed, the Kalinga are extremely interested in modern Philippine politics and take an active part in local and provincial governmental affairs.

The Kinship System

The kinship system is patterned on the kinship circle and singles out those relatives who are embraced in the latter. It is organized bilaterally and generationally; the terms, behavior and obligations toward relatives extending outward from ego and his siblings. The terminology employed is similar to the American system and fits into the "Eskimo" type set up by Spier (1925) and Murdock (1949). Cross and parallel cousins are designated by the same terms, but those used for siblings are different and never extended to cousins. The terms employed for consanguineal relatives in reference and address and those used for affinal relatives are presented in conventional kinship charts (*See* Figs. 2, 3 and 4). These terms and other additional ones employed for relatives are contained in the appendix.

Significant Aspects of the Terminology

Some interesting differences between northern Kalinga and the Lubuagan region appear in the terms employed. These differences undoubtedly reflect social and cultural changes going on in the two areas. Thus, for example, the Kalinga of the Lubuagan region use the same referential term, *olitog,* for parents' male and female siblings, and the first and second cousins of parents (and spouses of all these relatives).[12] The Northern Kalinga use *olitog* for "uncles" but they have a separate term, *ikit,* for "aunts" and parents' female cousins through the second cousins (including wives of these relatives). The use of a single term for one's uncles and aunts is unusual in the Philippines and apparently does not exist among other Mountain Province peoples. Since the area in which this pattern occurs was the most isolated before the American period, this usage may be the earlier Kalinga pattern. Lubuagan informants claim that the Northern Kalinga have borrowed the term *ikit* from Ilocanos and that formerly all Kalinga employed a single referential term *olitog* for parents' siblings. Lubuagan informants report that the Northern Kalinga dialect has been profoundly influenced by the Ilocano. Indeed, a sample of Kalinga lexical items from the two areas indicates that Northern Kalinga vocabulary contains many more Ilocano words than Lubuagan. Furthermore, the Northern Kalinga are said by Kalinga

KALINGA KINSHIP TERMINOLOGY — TERMS OF REFERENCE

EGO = Male or Female

(N. Kalinga terms are given first, followed by Lubuagan terms in brackets, if different. Terms in parentheses are alternate terms.)

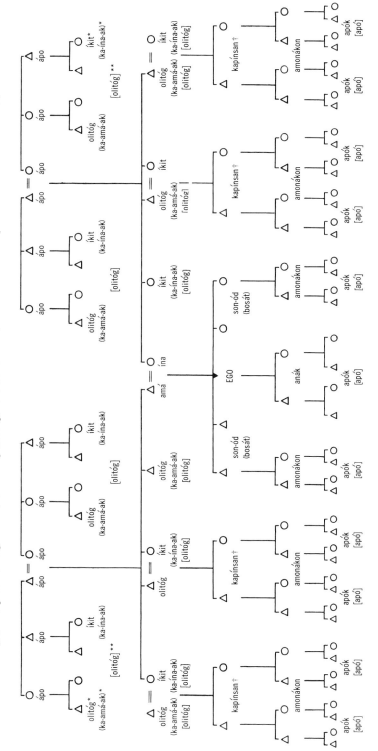

*Extended to parents' second cousins   **Extended to parents' first cousins

†third cousin: kapitlo/second cousin: kapidoa

of other areas to be more proficient in the use of this lingua franca. It may be significant too that among the Southern Kalinga, traditional forms of dress are much more in evidence, the Northern Kalinga having replaced their colorful native costume almost completely by Ilocano or lowland-type dress. Furthermore, in religious practices, beliefs, and other matters of culture, Northern Kalinga seem to grade almost imperceptibly into the Tinguian in Abra, and the latter have become almost completely Ilocanized in recent years. But the Southern Kalinga present a sharp break with the Tinguian, and the differences between the northern and southern Kalinga groups are also fairly pronounced. No obvious behavioral correlates have been made with these differences in terminology between the two areas.

Another important difference in terminological usage between the two areas is that the Northern Kalinga extend the terms of address for mother, *ina,* and father, *ama,* to parents' siblings, but the Kalinga of the Lubuagan region do not do this. Lubuagan Kalinga use personal names in address for these relatives, as indeed also for other relatives, while the Northern Kalinga employ kinship terms, e.g., Ego's first and second cousins. It seems possible to explain these changes by the rather phenomenal population increase in the Lubuagan region, an explanation which we have also suggested for the reduction of the Lubuagan kinship circle. Lubuagan Kalinga recognize that the use of personal names for relatives is a recent change. "We are too proud and are beginning to lose respect for our relatives," they remarked when I asked why they do not employ relationship terms as do their northern kin. Interaction in Lubuagan is depersonalized and even close relatives do not interact with the intimacy and closeness that characterize interpersonal relations in the north. Northern Kalinga frequently employ the term "Capitan" when speaking to important and influential men, but in Lubuagan even the mayor may be called by his first name. One is impressed with the humility and politeness exhibited by the Northern Kalinga as contrasted with the rather brash and outspoken behavior of the Lubuagan Kalinga. Lubuagan has an "urban" aspect with much of the same impersonalized and individualized traits that characterize urbanism elsewhere.

The nuclear or elementary family is not set apart as distinctly as at Sagada (Eggan 1960:38). While collective terms such as "father and child," "mother and child," exist, these are no more frequently employed than terms like "grandparent and child," nor are parent terms as widely extended. Teknonymy, which appears to be a device for setting apart the nuclear family in Sagada (Eggan *op. cit.*) by the use of such terms as "father of so-and-so," "mother of so-and-so," after the birth of a child, is not employed among the Kalinga. The greater importance of the

KALINGA KINSHIP TERMINOLOGY — TERMS OF ADDRESS

EGO = Male or Female

(N. Kalinga terms are given first, followed by Lubuagan terms in brackets, if different.)

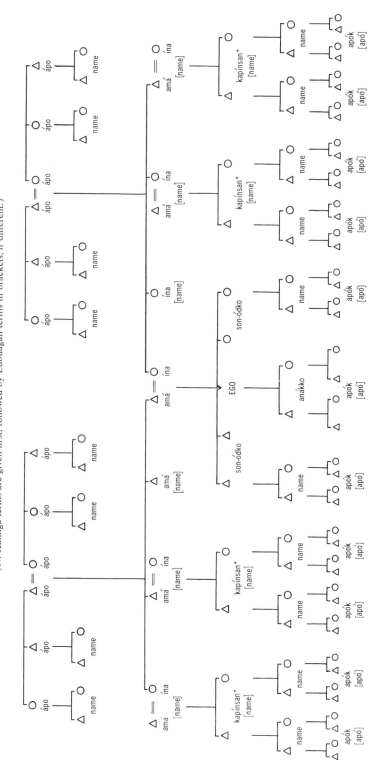

* First cousin term extended to second cousins, but not to third

KALINGA KINSHIP TERMINOLOGY — AFFINAL RELATIVES

EGO = Male or Females;   SPOUSE = Male or Female

(N. Kalinga terms are given first, followed by Lubuagan terms in brackets. Terms of address are enclosed in parentheses.)

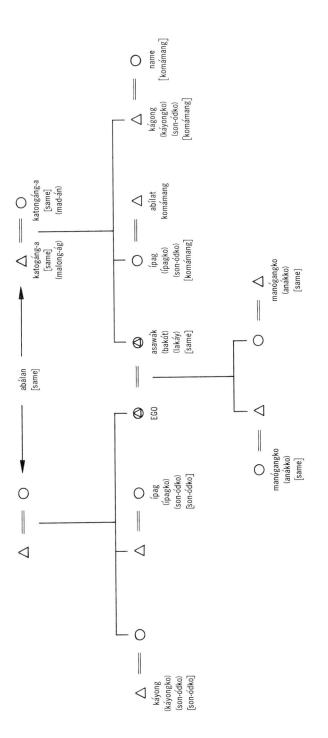

extended household also tends to de-emphasize the nuclear family. Thus among the Kalinga a wider circle of kin appears to receive greater attention in the terminology and in the behavior of relatives. This kin group is the personal kindred or kinship circle, whether the wider one of Northern Kalinga or the narrower one of the Lubuagan region.

Kinship Behavior

Obligations and responsibilities among kin are particularly emphasized on ceremonial occasions associated with the life cycle and in the operation of inheritance patterns. The life cycle and inheritance practices will be discussed in greater detail in special sections devoted to those topics; here we will record the generalized behavior among relatives that occurs during the round of daily life. We have noted that the Lubuagan Kalinga tend to address relatives by the use of personal names rather than by the use of kin terms. The Northern Kalinga use kin terms in address to a greater extent than the Southern Kalinga, but compared to Sagada (Eggan *op. cit.*) the Kalinga generally tend to use kin terms less extensively in address. As we have suggested, this phenomenon may reflect accculturative factors which have influenced the kinship circle in special ways. Intimate interpersonal relations among kin have been disrupted in Lubuagan by increased population; but the high mobility of the Kalinga everywhere has also modified the intimate face-to-face interaction among relations which we believe formerly characterized the regions.

Grandparent-grandchildren — Children develop a feeling of extreme fondness for their grandparents. This is because so much of the early period of a child's life is spent in the company of a grandfather or grandmother. With the predominantly matrilocal pattern of residence, the maternal grandparents are seen most often by the children but this is not an invariable rule. There is so much visiting of kin in the region that even if one's grandchildren are not near, there are frequent occasions when contact occurs. Then, as we have noted, not all married couples establish matrilocal residence; a few in each barrio or sitio live patrilocally, or in the case of Northern Kalinga, the couple may establish residence in a settlement where neither pair of parents resides.

Grandparents are the "baby sitters" of the Kalinga. While the parents are working in the fields, the young children are left in the care of a grandfather or grandmother or both. Children are delighted to be with them since grandparents are more indulgent than their parents. If a grandfather is still strong and active, he will transport his grandchild about the village in a blanket sling, thus permitting the child to see a variety of daily activities. Grandmothers restrict themselves more closely to the home with their charges, but both shower their grandchildren with affectionate attention.

A child is often given the name of a living or departed grandparent who has lived long. The Kalinga believe that conferring the name of a person on a child magically transfers the person's attributes to the name-sake — longevity, prominence, or any other desired quality. Related to this belief is the one that if a grandchild dies within a few months after the death of a grandparent, the spirit of the latter has taken the grandchild. The grandparent who has been especially affectionate to a grandchild is believed to be a kind of guardian spirit to the child after the former's death. Hence, a grandchild must be especially attentive to grandparents and fulfill all obligations entailed in the relationship.

Grandchildren have the responsibility to ensure that grandparents are well cared for in old age. While ordinarily the children do not inherit directly from the grandparents, they are, nevertheless, obligated to offer sacrifices at the time of a grandparent's illness or at his or her funeral. In Lubuagan during a *posipos* (curing rite) for a grandparent, the grandchildren join in singing. Also at Lubuagan, at the grandparent's funeral, grandchildren play conventionalized games and run races, prizes being awarded the winners. Thus as small children they are involved in ceremonies given for their grandparents and later, as adults grandchildren initiate or take a prominent part in their grandparents' illness rites and funeral ceremonies.

When a person is ill, the medium (*mangalisig,* Lubuagan; *mandadawak, mananito,* Northern Kalinga) often prescribes sacrifices to a dead grandparent after having "discovered" that the spirit of a departed grandparent has been offended or not properly propitiated. Most illnesses among the Kalinga are believed to be caused by dead ancestors, who make known their wants by sending illness or misfortune. If a medium names a grandparent as the cause of an illness, the patient and his relatives have a curing rite (*posipos,* Lubuagan; *dawak,* Northern Kalinga) and the animals butchered on the occasion are offered to the spirit of the deceased grandparents.

A mild form of joking exists between grandparent and grandchild. The former teases the grandchild about his or her lack of work aptitudes, failure to secure a sweetheart or wife, or flaws in the girl or boy he or she has been contracted to marry. In turn, the grandchild chides the grandparent about infirmities, and inability to do a full day's work. But this is all in fun and the relationship between grandparents and grandchildren is undoubtedly the most affectionate bond in Kalinga society.

Much of Kalinga culture, particularly with respect to ceremonial practices and beliefs, is learned from grandparents. A grandparent often selects a specific grandchild upon whom to lavish special emotional attention and affection. In such cases a strong bond of affection and dependence is forged, lasting until the death of one or the other. Such a bond existed between one of my informants from the region of Poswoy (northern Kalinga) and his maternal grandfather. The grandparent's death recently was a blow such that death of any other member of the family would not have been so keenly felt. My informant slept with his grandfather under the same blanket until late in his youth, and accompanied the former in travels in many parts of northern Kalinga. The grandfather encouraged him to continue his education, even though other members of the family wanted him to come home and take up farming. It is the advice and counsel of this grandfather that he now cherishes and hopes to follow in life.

Parent-child relationship — Between the ages of about two and six, children are usually left in the care of grandparents or older siblings. Mothers are busy with younger siblings or else performing essential household tasks and helping in the rice fields. Weaning takes place any time between the ages of one to five, depending on whether or not younger siblings have been born. If a child has no younger siblings, she or he may nurse until five years of age. Such a child sees a great deal of its mother and develops close ties with her, but when there are many children, only the youngest may get special attention. Field and household tasks demand so much of a mother's time that unless she is restricted to the house by a newborn infant, a mother turns over the care of children who are weaned and able to walk to older children or grandparents.

In Lubuagan, after about age six or seven, girls sleep together with age mates in the homes of widows, while boys go to an *obog,* a vacant house habitually used as a sleeping place. Thus, parents in Lubuagan become even more separated from their children after these ages. There is, of course, considerable interaction with children during the day and contact continues with those children, especially daughters, who bring their spouses to reside near the parental home. Nevertheless, parent-children relationships are not as intense and prolonged among the Kalinga as among other groups.

The Northern Kalinga do not segregate the children in the Lubuagan manner. Parents in the north maintain closer and more prolonged contact with their children. Thus children ordinarily remain with their families until the time they join or are joined by their contracted partner and a separate dwelling is erected. After this, interaction continues in extended household living or in the custom of frequent visiting.

Fathers in the evenings devote considerable time to children, playing with the young ones, carrying infants in blanket slings. Later the boys accompany their fathers to the fields, while girls remain at home to care for younger siblings, although some will also work in the fields. Boys

Spankings are rare among the permissively raised children of the Kalinga. Family relationships are not tightly knit after the age of six or seven, when little girls leave the homes of their parents to sleep with their age mates in the homes of widows. Boys go to an *obog* (vacant house) used as a sleeping place.

bring fuel, but their help and duties around the house are considerably less than the tasks required of and performed by their sisters.

Parents seldom resort to whipping, but scold or frighten children into obedience. Strangers often become bogey men, and children may be told that strangers will carry them away if they do not behave. Lubua-gan and north Kalinga informants reported spanking children in severe cases of disobedience, but this must be rare, and I personally did not observe it. Kalinga child-rearing practices may be generally characterized as indulgent and permissive. The Northern Kalinga will whip an adolescent girl who has sex relations with a man not contracted to her in marriage, or with a man already married or with one who has not promised to marry the girl. The prohibition of sex relations under these circumstances is because of the complications that such an affair is likely to cause in matters of support and inheritance for the child of such a union.

The boy or the man escapes punishment, unless he has forced the girl into the relationship; in the latter case, he must pay heavy fines. The Kalinga are motivated in these matters, not by moral or ethical principles, but by practical concerns. Support and inheritance are crucial matters, and when these are complicated or threatened, parents and relatives take action to see that sons and daughters are insured economic support and their inheritance protected. Marriages are arranged for this reason and while an engaged couple may break their contract, parents make every effort to hold together a couple whose contract is considered a sound economic arrangement. By safeguarding the inheritance due a son or daughter and by providing a good match, economically viewed, parents feel that they have fulfilled their primary obligation to their children. Moreover, they have also guaranteed their own future in this life and the next. Children are obligated to provide for the economic support of their parents when the latter become old or infirm, to offer the proper sacrifices when they are sick, and again at their funeral and to continue to make such sacrifices for their well-being in the hereafter.

The Kalinga are a practical people and the concern over their children is practical and realistic. Whereas parent-child relations are not completely devoid of affection, they contrast sharply with the warmth and love that a grandparent showers on a grandchild. The latter relationship is not ordinarily a bond of mutual obligations. The grandparent has already given his inheritance to his own sons and daughters who have the primary obligations for reciprocal payment, in the form of economic support and sacrifices.

Uncles and aunts: nephews and nieces — Aunts and uncles assume the status and responsibility of parents in the absence of the latter. If a child is orphaned, an aunt or uncle takes it into their household. Here the child becomes like a member of the family with rights of inheritance equal to those of the other children. The child also has equal obligation with his first cousins to support his foster parents in their old age and to offer sacrifices in their behalf. The behavior of an adopted niece or nephew is said not to differ in any respect from that of the other children. Indeed, it is believed that adopted children are often more attentive than real children to aged foster parents, and that they are more careful in offering sacrifices at times of illness and at the death of their foster parents.

The Northern Kalinga appear to have closer relations with their aunts and uncles than the Lubuagan people. We have noted the extension of parent terms in address to uncles and aunts among the former, but not at Lubuagan where the personal names of these relatives are used. There is also more sharing of cooperative activities, such as housebuilding, the construction of swiddens and the like. Undoubtedly this is due to the

A bamboo pipe provides a gravity stream of water at the village spring where clothes and floor mats are washed, pots are scoured, and village news exchanged.

smaller populations in the north where kinship relations are known and kept tab on more closely than in the south. Among both the Northern and Southern Kalinga, an adopted nephew or niece employs sibling terms for his or her aunt's or uncle's children with whom he resides, but sibling terms are not otherwise extended to cousins.

Often an influential uncle becomes a kind of father confessor and counselor to his sister's or brother's family. When this family is in difficulty they may consult the uncle who is always ready to offer sage advice and to perform many kinds of services for them. One of my companions and aides, a young man of about twenty-five who drew maps for me, counted houses in hamlets, and performed a number of other useful tasks, could not bring himself to tell me that he was needed at home and could no longer work for me. He walked from his own village to an isolated hamlet where an uncle lived and brought him over the next day so that the uncle could tell me that his nephew could no longer work for me! This incident also illustrates another interesting trait of the Kalinga. They cannot divulge unpleasant news directly but must bring a relative along, most often an uncle, to explain the circumstances.

The homes of uncles and aunts are constant visiting places for nephews and nieces. Most traveling within a region is to visit relatives and these are usually uncles and aunts. If a child is scolded or reprimanded in any way, he or she will take the first opportunity to visit an uncle or aunt, often traveling several miles to discuss the incident. Frequently he will return with the aunt or uncle to talk over the matter with his parents, the uncle or aunt attempting to smooth over the difficulty.

Siblings and cousins — Ego and his siblings, Ego's first cousins, the latter's parents and Ego's own parents form a circle of kin where obligations and privileges are most clearly defined. This is the group of relatives among whom intermarriage is strictly prohibited, even with former spouses of the group who have been widowed or divorced. These relatives support one another in all disputes and troubles and also rejoice together in any good fortune that befalls one of their members or the group as a whole. Respectful behavior marks the relationship among all these relatives.

Beyond first cousins, laterally, obligations and privileges extend to second cousins in Lubuagan and among the Northern Kalinga to third cousins. In the north where kinship group and region are believed to be co-extensive, obligations and privileges of the kinship circle are extended to all members of the regional population. If a regional member is killed, wounded, or injured in any manner by someone from the outside, all those living in the region are obligated to avenge since they are all considered relatives and very likely can trace relationships to at least the third-cousin degree. If an offense is committed among members of the region, the matter is taken up by the influential leaders of the region who discuss the matter and decide on fines and payments to be made. Since all consider themselves relatives, vengeance is seldom resorted to in intra-regional disputes. While injuries are often inflicted by hot-headed individuals in a quarrel within a region, influential leaders are ready to separate such individuals. Heated arguments are usually stopped before they go very far by emphasizing that "everyone is related and [all] must support one another."

In the densely populated Lubuagan region, kinship allegiances and responsibilities have become complicated and confused beyond the first-cousin degree of relationship. While kinfolk within the second-cousin degree of relationship (the lateral boundaries of the kinship circle) are all required to support one another, increased populations have disrupted face-to-face relations and one is not always sure which relatives he is supposed to defend or avenge. This is particularly so since second cousins may marry; therefore, in disputes involving individuals related to both parties it is not always possible to know whether one should take vengeance, pay indemnities, take precautions not to be avenged upon, or collect indemnities. The results are considerable feuding and fighting and even occasional killings within the region (cf. Barton

1949:69–83). The important difference between Lubuagan and the northern Kalinga regions is that in the former region the vengeance pattern is frequently invoked, whereas in the north, vengeance tends to operate only interregionally, and intra-village disputes are informally resolved by amicable settlement.

The Lubuagan situation appears to characterize all densely populated regions of the south where the kinship circle has become narrower and intraregional conflicts are of common occurrence. In these regions there is an urgent need for an effective organization beyond the kinship group to cope with these problems. The pangngats, influential leaders of a region, might have eventually become such an organization, but they are not a united body and generally act as individuals; moreover, at present their power and influence have diminished considerably. It seems safe to predict that, in the future, modern municipal officials will take a greater role in problems which the traditional kinship organizations are incapable of resolving. This problem is discussed in greater detail toward the end of this chapter.

Affinal relations — All spouses married to consanguineal relatives of the kinship circle are also members of the group and theoretically, at least, have the same responsibilities and privileges. Again it is important to note that as in the case of relatives more distant than first cousins, spouses have divided loyalties and obligations to their own consanguineal kin; thus, their cooperation is complicated in the Lubuagan region and in the southern Kalinga regions where kinship group and region are not considered to be co-extensive. The endogamous regions of the north work as a unit and spouses are part of this relationship.

The sibling term is extended vocatively to men and women married to Ego's siblings. They are treated in a respectful manner, but there are no avoidance patterns. As elsewhere in the Mountain Province (Eggan 1960:38), children are essential for a stable and enduring marriage. If no children result from a union, separation or divorce is customary and the gifts exchanged are returned or some settlement agreeable to both families is made. Each may then contract another marriage with the hope that the new relationship will produce children.

Parents-in-law are treated with respect and obedience much in the same manner as real parents, but they are not addressed by parent terms. A marriage unites the parents of the couple in a special relationship and henceforth they become *abalan,* "co-parents-in-law," to one another. While the son-in-law or daughter-in-law treats his or her parent-in-law with respect and obedience, there are no avoidance or restrictive patterns between them.

Because of the uxorilocal character of Kalinga extended households, it is the men who most often change residence to live in the proximity of their in-laws. Thus, the man ordinarily makes the greatest adjustments after marriage with respect to relationships with in-laws. The inability to get along with in-laws may sometimes lead to separation and divorce, but this is rare. The overwhelming cause for divorce is attributed to the lack of children. In the southern Kalinga area, kinship feuds within the region were also given as a cause for divorce, but there are many cases where a man and woman remained married despite family disputes.

The kinship system of the Kalinga is involved almost exclusively with consanguineal and affinal relatives. Except in connection with the peace-pact institution, which is a recent development, there is no evidence of an indigenous fictive or ritual kinship organization. The trading partnership, *aboyog,* bound two individuals from different regions into a pact of mutual obligation of hospitality and physical protection for one another and their companions, but such relationships were usually short-lived. Moreover, neither the two individuals nor their families were bound into a "blood brother" relationship as exists elsewhere in the Philippines and in southeast Asia. There was also no extension of kinship terms to one another or their families and no behavior that would suggest even remotely a feeling of kinship between the relatives of the two individuals bound in an *aboyog* relationship. The development of the Kalinga peace-pact institution has essentially replaced the trading partnership, and trade, visiting, and other interregional contacts now go on under the protection and privileges extended by the peace pact.[13] Between peace-pact holders of two different regions and their families, some aspects of the kinship system have been extended. There is no ritual to make pact-holders "brothers" but they are considered as such, and marriage prohibitions are binding on their relatives just as if they were all members of the same kinship circle. Obligations that are traditional to members of a kinship circle, such as attendance and assistance at marriages, funerals, and the like, are also extended. Distances between regions and difficulties of travel, however, make it impossible for pact-holders and members of their kinship groups to fulfill even minimally such obligations. There is also no extension of kinship terms, even among the two pact-holders themselves. A peace pact is intended to open up intermarriage privileges between members of the two regions (except for the pact-holders and their families), but traditional vengeance and inheritance patterns conflict with such practices and "mixed marriages" are placed in a difficult position.

The system known elsewhere as *compadrazgo* (Mintz and Wolf

1950), introduced among lowland Christian Filipinos by the Spanish, has had little effect on the Kalinga. Occasionally a Kalinga will exchange *compadre* and *comadre* terms with Ilocano baptismal or marriage sponsors (his own or those of his children), but the obligations inherent in the system are either unknown or, if known, ignored.

The Life Cycle

Kinship relations are highlighted at certain periods in the life span of an individual, and these are occasions for social and ceremonial festivities. Other social and ceremonial activity is associated with the subsistence economy: hunting, clearing of swiddens, construction of rice fields and the planting and harvest of rice. The social and ritual activity related to Kalinga subsistence economy will be discussed in the section on economics. There are no fixed dates for social or ceremonial events, unless one so considered the introduced Saint's Day celebration conducted by the Roman Catholic Church on the patron saint's day of the church at Lubuagan and Salegseg. But these events have not become an integral part of Kalinga social and ceremonial life. There are also no "rest days" among Kalinga like there are at Bontoc, Ifugao, and Sagada.[14] Kalinga ceremonies differ from ceremonies of other Mountain Province peoples in that, among the Kalinga, all occasions on which animals are sacrificed are prestige feasts. In Lubuagan funeral celebrations, particularly those of grandparents, require the largest number of sacrificial victims, but with the well-to-do, even the death of a child may be celebrated in an elaborate fashion. Perhaps because all ceremonial occasions are prestige affairs, the carabao is a proper sacrificial animal in virtually all Kalinga ceremonies. The large size and cost of a carabao bestows prestige on the family which offers it as a sacrificial victim. Among the Ifugao, Bontoc, and Sagada the carabao is not considered a proper sacrificial animal except in marriage ceremonies, undoubtedly because of its recent introduction in the Mountain Province.

Four stages in the life cycle of an individual are given social and ceremonial significance among the Kalinga: birth, marriage, sickness, and death. Appendix II presents in summary form pertinent data on the ritualistic observances made on these occasions for Lubuagan and the Northern Kalinga, specifically the Poswoy and Mabaca regions. There is considerable variation in the manner in which these ceremonies are conducted in the different regions, and some life-cycle events recognized in one region may not be presented in another. There is, however, a similar pattern of life-cycle observances among all Kalinga despite regional variations.

Between the hamlets of Liglig and Gawa-an, a footbridge of plaited bamboo spans the Saltan River from one rocky bank to the other.

Pregnancy and Birth

Children are greatly desired among the Kalinga, and although large numbers are born, many do not survive into adulthood. Sample genealogical records for the regions of Lubuagan and Mabaca indicate averages of seven children per family over the normal childbearing period of a woman, while the size of households are 5.5 for the Mabaca region of northern Kalinga and 4.8 for the Lubuagan region of southern Kalinga. There seems to be a high rate of barrenness among women, and perhaps the fertility rate of men is also low. At any rate, there are a number of marriages where no children are born. Normally in such cases the couple will separate in order to try their luck with other partners. If there are no children from an individual's second marriage, he or she will separate again. The number of divorces is high among the Kalinga; as many as 50 per cent of the men presently married at Poswoy have been divorced at least once. Such divorces are almost always because the woman did not conceive. A woman refuses to accept as a fact that she is barren and keeps trying to have children with different partners until the onset of menopause. In many cases a wife will permit a husband to have a mistress (*dagdagas*) with the agreement among all three that if there are any children from this arrangement one of them will be raised as the married couple's own. In other cases, a devoted couple who do not wish to separate may adopt the child of a relative so that there is an heir to property and someone to offer sacrifices for the couple in time of illness and after death.

The inability of a woman to have a child is attributed to three possible factors among the Northern Kalinga: 1) to a disregard of bad omens at the time of marriage; 2) the activity of the *ngilin*,[15] a malevolent water spirit who is believed to have the appearance of a human pigmy; and 3) to an organic or physical defect in the reproductive organs of the woman. In the first and second instances, the couple "pretend to separate" in order to make the ngilin believe that the couple have given up trying to have a child. It is believed that by this action the ngilin will turn its attention elsewhere and while it is distracted the couple can resume sexual relations, assured that without the machinations of the ngilin the wife will conceive. The ngilin consumes the spirits of human newborn embryos or newborn children. Other spirits, particularly the ancestral spirits of grandparents, are also believed to take unborn or newborn children with them into the spirit world.

An organic or physical defect in a woman which prevents her from conceiving is diagnosed by a woman doctor by examination. Such a native doctor, of which there are a few in every region, will treat the wife and prescribe certain acts for both the wife and the husband to perform. In Poswoy there are three women whose bathing and massaging of the woman and administering of herbal drinks to both husband and wife are believed to bring about fertility in the woman. In the case of a tilted womb, native women doctors are able to straighten the organ. This is done immediately after menses when the womb is soft and the opening into the uterus is enlarged.

Informants from Poswoy and Asiga regions (northern Kalinga) denied that there were sacrifices performed by native doctors to induce fertility. In Lubuagan, however, a medium is called to perform a ceremony (*makobin*) over a barren woman. A medium butchers a pig and sings the chants that are appropriate for the ceremony. She instructs the woman to visit her husband's parents and tells the husband to distribute gifts among his wife's relatives. Apparently the general good feeling thus generated between the two sets of relatives, wife's and husband's, is believed to bring about fertility.

Pregnancy among the Kalinga is marked by intricate ritual practices and observances of numerous restrictions by both husband and wife. These customs are observed in order to maintain the health of the mother, to facilitate easy birth, and to safeguard the health of the unborn child. While there are differences in detail among the Kalinga from region to region in customs associated with pregnancy, there is in general an over all similarity. The practices and beliefs described here are specifically those of the Poswoy region of the Northern Kalinga, but differences with other northern Kalinga regions and of these with the Lubuagan region are noted where they occur.

The Kalinga woman is considered to be temperamental and jealous of her husband during pregnancy. She becomes angry if her husband comes home late from the fields and is morose and sullen if her husband spends too much time with friends. She is likely to flare up with anger at her husband on the least provocation and may tear his clothes, or release her anger by spanking her children. A pregnant woman also develops a peculiar desire for special foods, such as shrimp, and fruits that are difficult to obtain. A particularly typical craving of pregnant Kalinga women is for sour fruits and vegetables.[16] The husband is said to be patient and understanding during this time and will attempt to humor her and fulfill as many of her desires as possible.

Naturally, as in almost every society, some women are nauseated during pregnancy and cannot retain their food. It is believed in Poswoy that this condition is caused by the husband eating foods such as beef, cow's milk, eel, frogs, taro (*colocasia*), and dog meat, all of which are prohibited to a couple during the wife's pregnancy. If the woman has serious trouble in retaining food and grows thin, a medium is called to perform a ceremony called *yabyab* (*see* below).

During the wife's pregnancy, both husband and wife must avoid places where ngilin the water spirit, might be encountered. The ngilin resides in streams, particularly in pools and waterfalls. It is believed that the ngilin is attracted by the odor of a pregnant woman and even a husband or her children may carry this odor. If the ngilin smells the odor, he learns of the pregnant woman and will devour her unborn child. To prevent the ngilin from knowing that there is a pregnant woman in his home, a conscientious Poswoy Kalinga will carry one of the following objects on his person: 1) a piece of the bark of *sugaga,* a small tree which looks like an outstretched hand signaling a halt; 2) a dog's tooth, because the ngilin is afraid of dogs; 3) a crocodile tooth, because the ngilin will think you are related to the crocodile who also inhabits rivers (the two are mortal enemies); and 4) a ferret fox's tooth, because the smell of the fox is repulsive to the ngilin.

Other observances during the period of pregnancy are the following: a pregnant woman must not eat eggs or the baby may be born blind; she must not use a cup made out of taro leaves for drinking because this would cause her child to be easily dominated by others; older children must not sit by doors or windows when a baby is expected, lest the baby be born in a breach position; the father avoids playing the flute during labor because the child may become an incessant crybaby.

After birth the child is still in danger of being harmed by the ngilin. These fears of the ngilin are lost only after the removal of restrictions on visiting and food taboos following a ceremony to remove such restrictions.

Kalinga everywhere genuinely want children and, as mentioned previously, the high separation and divorce rate is found among those couples in which the wife is unable to conceive in the first few years of marriage. While there is a desire for children, and a home without children is not considered the natural state of affairs among the Kalinga, Kalinga women also feel that too many children effect hardships on the mother. In the north, at least, some women who have too many children consult an abortionist. There are specially knowledgeable women who perform abortions by administering a drink prepared from an herb called *gallopot,* and with the aid of massage. In the region of Poswoy (northern Kalinga), a woman who has had eleven children, ten of them living, considered abortion for future pregnancies, but her relatives advised against it. Restricting the size of the family becomes a problem for the bilateral kin group because of inheritance customs. All children are entitled to a share in the property of parents and that of the grandparents as well, if the latter's property has not been divided. The parents of a large family may claim a greater share of their own parents' property; hence, a large family poses problems not only for the nuclear family involved but for parental siblings and their children as well. Abortion is then not only a concern of a wife and her husband but of all the bilateral kin whose share of inheritance might be smaller if more children were to share in the division of property. In this particular Poswoy case, the bilateral kin advised against abortion thereby leaving open the possibility of more children and hence more claimants to inherited property.

The Lubuagan Kalinga have a special ceremony, *manilom,* to celebrate pregnancy of a woman, offset evil consequences, and placate the spirits. When a girl realizes that she is pregnant she informs her husband and her parents and arrangements are made to have the manilom. Pigs are butchered and the medium comes to sing and bless the event. The celebration is a two-day affair with a gathering of relatives from both the husband's and wife's side. At this time the husband will recite his accomplishments (*i-iyab*), and formerly he also recounted his killing exploits (*palpaliwat*).

The Northern Kalinga do not have anything comparable to the Lubuagan manilom. Poswoy has a special sickness rite, the yabyab, for pregnant women but this is a curing ceremony rather than a celebration rite. Of course, the manilom is not simply a celebration rite either, since its performance is also or perhaps primarily to ward off any possible ill effects on the woman and the expected child and hence to insure a safe and satisfactory delivery.

The Poswoy yabyab ceremony is performed only for a special type of illness to which pregnant women are believed to be subject. This malady causes the woman to lose weight and to become gaunt and weak. A medium is engaged who sacrifices a small pig. The heart of the pig is rubbed on the breasts and back of the woman. A feast is prepared to which all the relatives of the couple in the immediate vicinity of the sick woman's house are invited. For other types of illness suffered by a pregnant woman or for a difficult labor, the medium performs the regular Kalinga curing rite called *dawak* (northern Kalinga) or posipos (Lubuagan). The chants sung by the medium for yabyab differ from those of the dawak or posipos, although there appears to be considerable variation in the curing chants from region to region (*see* section on religion).

A curing rite for the married couple also exists in Poswoy. This rite, *sabblay*, is specifically for husband and wife in Poswoy. If both husband and wife become ill, a medium is engaged to perform the ceremony. The rite involves the sacrifice of a pig and the recitation of chants appropriate to the ceremony. For an illness of husband or wife alone, the appropriate Poswoy curing ceremony is the dawak.

Delivery takes place within the house.[17] When labor pains begin, the expectant mother tells her husband who calls her mother and other relatives of the extended household. A rope is suspended from the rafter and the woman sits on the knees of her husband or another relative. She draws on the rope while the relatives take turns in kneading and pressing on her abdomen. As the baby emerges, the woman's mother receives it. She cuts the cord with a bamboo knife and washes the baby in water which has been boiled. She then wraps the baby in the soft brown bark of the *alimit* tree. After one week the grandmother will wash the baby again, mixing the bath water with an herb prepared from the *solsolkop* tree. This tree has hard joints and it is believed that the baby's arm and leg joints will likewise become strong.

The birth of a baby among both the Northern and Southern Kalinga is attended by restrictions in the activities of the household and by the observances of food taboos. The general name for this period of restrictions is the same name given to the malevolent spirit which might bring harm to an unborn or newly born child. As soon as the baby is born an adult man or woman of the household places four knotted runo shoots (*poldos*) at every corner of the house on the outside. The runo shoots indicate that the family within is under restriction; and visitors, including relatives who do not sleep in the house, are prohibited from entering it. Food restrictions for the family at this time include the following: beef, cow's milk, eel, frogs, gabi, and dog meat. Most important of all, the father must not go outside the bounds of his village during the period of restrictions.

About one month after the birth of the baby, a medium is called who asks an old woman to sweep the house with the native raincoat made of palm fronds, *ana-aw*. Then the old woman or the medium herself removes the knotted runo shoots signifying the end of the ngilin. The medium pronounces the mother and child safe and instructs the household to resume its normal functioning with all restrictions removed.

After the ngilin, the mother resumes her usual heavy duties around the house, but with the added task of nursing her baby. If the milk is inadequate, she finds a mother with an extra supply of milk to supplement her feeding. Finding a wet nurse presents difficulties since the Kalinga mother believes that a woman with a baby of the same age as her own should be located. She proceeds from the nearest to more distant relatives in locating a woman to nurse her baby and she usually finds one in the large numbers that compose her kinship circle. At present some Kalinga mothers also use canned milk preparations to supplement feeding, but canned milk presents problems. It is difficult to keep milk from souring and Kalinga mothers have difficulty in observing the precautions needed to safeguard the use of canned milk. As a result, there is considerable illness among babies whose mothers have an inadequate supply of milk.

The Kontad Ceremonies — infancy and early years

In all Kalinga areas the first year and a half of a child's life is filled with a series of rather complex ceremonial rituals called *kontad* (northern Kalinga) or *kontid* (southern Kalinga). The word "kontad" in the north Kalinga dialects means "request" or "supplication." The child in its first year is considered to be most vulnerable to the machinations of malevolent spirits. The Kalinga believe that the malevolent spirits must be placated and hence are meticulous in observation of rituals. The series of ceremonies is performed by mediums who know the appropriate rituals, prayers, and chants. The Kalinga refer to these mediums by a special term, *mangkokontad,* rather than the general term for mediums, *mangalisig* (southern Kalinga) or *mandadawak* (northern Kalinga).[18]

Kontad rituals involve characteristic Kalinga ceremonial features and practices such as the sacrifice of chickens or pigs, the singing of

Since young children are believed most susceptible to the mischief of evil spirits, the first eighteen months of life are marked by a complex set of rituals called the *kontad,* performed by a medium and aimed at turning aside the malevolence of the spirit world.

chants, examination of the pig's liver for omens, and in some of the stages of the kontad, the erection of a spirit house or platform. The baby is given a name during the period of the kontad. In Poswoy the medium gives a child a name from one of its ancestors. The name might be changed later if the child becomes ill. This is done to deceive the malevolent spirits who are believed to be making the child sick. The spirits will stop the machinations, believing that their magic has worked since they do not recognize the child under the new name.

A deceased grandparent or other near relative is also believed to make a child ill in order that the child may join him in the afterworld. The kontad ceremonies are performed to placate both malevolent and ancestral spirits. The belief that ancestors are responsible for illness or misfortune is stronger in the south; the Northern Kalinga emphasize the activity of malevolent spirits as causative agents. In Poswoy, prayers by the medium are addressed to *mandodwa* — a designation said to include all benevolent spirits.

A simple ceremony for teething called *káwol* is performed in Poswoy when the child is about four months old. A woman inserts a *sang-al* bead (the most valuable of the precious beads) into the mouth of the child and as she takes it out she says: "Come front teeth, this is the bead you have been waiting for." In Lubuagan, at about the same age, the father's parents give the child a special gift, usually a bead necklace. A pig is then butchered and close relatives of the child's father and mother are invited to partake of the festivities.

The solidarity of the kinship circle bond is periodically reinforced during the first and second year of a child's life. In Lubuagan when a child first mentions the name of a relative, a formal visit called *omo pasibit* is made to the particular relative's home. Similar formal visits to members of the bilateral kin group at Poswoy are called *omapó*. The first time that the baby is taken to visit the father's parents is the occasion for a special celebration called *balon di babat* (Poswoy) or *Mamilók* (Lubuagan). At this time, a large pig is butchered and the kinship circles of both the mother and father join for a grand celebration. The forefront of the pig, *long-os,* is taken to the wife's relatives and the carriers are given a peso or two each. The hind quarter is cut into strips and the shares, *ilang,* distributed among the father's kindred. In addition to the large pig, additional pigs, chickens, and carabaos are also butchered on this occasion depending on the wealth of the father's relatives. Large quantities of sugarcane wine are also passed around and consumed. The celebration is a prestige feast and the father's relatives make every effort to make the occasion an impressive one. In the sparsely settled regions of the north, as many as one-third of the regional population might attend the affair, and all will receive a share of the meat. In Lubuagan and other densely populated regions of the south, far more people come than can be given shares of meat. Since some of those who do not receive a share of meat also reckon themselves related to the father, bitter arguments occasionally occur between the near and distant kin over who is entitled and not entitled to meat shares. Sometimes these arguments flare up into spear and headaxe fights and a killing may occur. Northern Kalinga festive occasions are much more peaceful, although the men get drunk and there is formalized boasting about one's accomplishments, *manyamyam, i-iyab;* or war exploits, *pokao, palpaliwat.* Festivities in the *balon di babat* start in mid-afternoon and go on far into the night with gong music and danc- ing of the *tadok* (*see* section on dance and music). As the couple leave for their home the father's family presents the child with a precious gift, the *balong.* This is usually a necklace of beads to be cherished by the child for the rest of its life. It will form a part of its heirloom collection along with valuable Chinese jars, plates, and gongs.

Constant reiteration of the kinship bond in festivities and in daily relations among members of a region is a striking feature of Kalinga society. There is continual mobility within the region, and relatives visit one another and may remain overnight. This pattern of interaction, (almost exclusively of the regional population) even though the settle- ments are widely dispersed, is especially characteristic of the Northern Kalinga.

In the south, intimate and frequent contacts among relatives, which we believe were also a pattern there in the past, have diminished with increased populations. Indeed, change is beginning to become evi- dent now in the north as well. Modern conditions with the development of bus travel, trade, and wage work are beginning to disrupt the close intraregional interaction of relatives. Present conditions are bringing the Kalinga into intimate relationships with other mountain peoples and with lowlanders. In the process, old antagonisms are cast aside and non-kin- ship bonds are formed with every indication that such contacts will be more frequent and enduring in the future. The peace pacts broke up rigid intraregional interaction, but at first this involved only Kalinga of differ- ent regions with one another. Present conditions, however, are establish- ing far wider relationships. The trend will undoubtedly result in the eventual Filipinization of the mountain peoples. This may be far in the future, but it will be relatively rapid for the Kalinga.

Weaning and toilet training are carried out in a relaxed atmosphere with no apparent fixed or rigid rules. There are no regular periods of feeding the infant; it is given the breast whenever it so desires. There is also no set time for weaning; most children continue to nurse until quite old, up to the age of four or five, if there are no siblings. If other children come, then the mother may discourage nursing by rubbing her breasts with powdered *sili* (chili peppers). This is said to be effective with most children; with others, "shaming" is believed to work. Thus, the mother works on the pride of the child by telling him that he is too old to nurse, or by comparing the child adversely to younger children in the village who have been weaned. Early, the infant is given solid food such as rice, bananas, sweet potatoes, and is allowed to suck sugarcane. The process of weaning is, therefore, accomplished with minimal effort and Kalinga mothers do not consider it a serious problem.

Toilet training is also treated in a similarly relaxed fashion. Bark cloth, made especially soft by careful pounding, was formerly used as diapers and today cotton cloth is sometimes employed. Most often, however, infants and toddlers are completely without clothes. Indeed, clothing does not appear on the child until it is seven or eight years old and then it is usually a simple shirt or dress. Little attention is paid to the toddler who relieves himself on the floor of the house. If an older member of the household catches the child in time, it is quickly picked up and held over a portion of the floor where the bamboo mat floor can be lifted. Outside, the small child may relieve itself or defecate anywhere. Pigs and dogs who roam freely about the village quickly clear up the refuse. Indeed, pigs follow naked children around alert to clean up after a child who has a bowel movement.

For older children, parents advise them to go to the edge of the village. Outside privies are a recent introduction and most villages still do not have these facilities. Bed-wetting problems are handled in much the same way as weaning, by "shaming." In general, toilet training is accomplished without prescribed rules, simply by permitting the child to follow his own inclinations until such a time as he can understand the behavior of older children and adults in his village. The child adjusts his toilet practices to the group in order to prevent censure and ridicule.

In addition to the kontad series of ceremonies performed for health and well-being of the child, a ceremony called *gabbok* is performed in different regions of northern and southern Kalinga. In Lubuagan, the ceremony is considered a thanksgiving celebration and performed three or four months after the birth of the child. A medium chants the appropriate songs associated with the ceremony. Chickens and pigs are sacrificed and relatives and friends come to join the parents in celebration.

In Poswoy, gabbok is a curing rite which takes place only if the child becomes ill after the series of kontad ceremonies have been completed. A mature pig is sacrificed by the medium, and special chants different from those of the kontad or the general curing rite, dawak, are sung.

Dawak is the general curing ceremony for northern Kalinga, while its counterpart in southern Kalinga is called posipos. Upon completion of the kontad series and the intermediate gabbok rites, any subsequent illness or misfortune suffered by the child entails the performance of this general ceremony. A description of the dawak ceremony and the story chanted by the medium during its performance are included in the chapter on religion.

Later Childhood

Children are brought up in a seemingly unstructured and permissive atmosphere. Up to the age of six or seven few restrictions are placed on them. With boys this permissive pattern may be carried on considerably longer. The activities of boys and girls during the first three to four years are undifferentiated. As infants, they are carried about in blanket slings by older sisters or aged grandparents. Indeed, until an infant is able to crawl it is rarely put down. The belief is strong that an unattended baby's spirit will be carried off by malevolent or ancestral spirits. Hence, an older sibling or adult is always around an infant. At night the baby sleeps next to the mother, usually between the parents. From ages three to six, children may occasionally accompany their parents to the fields, but most commonly remain in the village. Undoubtedly this is a practice from former times when the enemy was likely to attack those away from settled areas. Men and women in the prime of life could defend themselves or run back to the safety of the village, but old people and children would not be so nimble; hence they remained in the greater security of the hamlet or village.

There is no marked preference for boys or girls in the society. Since the residence pattern is predominantly matrilocal, and since women do most of the work around the house and fields, one might expect that girls would be favored; but past conditions when enemy attacks were common still dominate Kalinga thinking. Men did all the fighting and distinguished war records determined the influence and prestige of families. It was therefore important to have sons and a family without sons was considered very unfortunate. The custom of placing few restrictions on the activity of males in the family is a reflection of conditions in earlier days when the males of the family defended homes and youths brought back heads from the enemy. Girls at an early age assume heavy household tasks and responsibilities. They care for younger siblings, pound and winnow rice, scrub the bamboo floor mats, tote water and help in the fields. Young boys are responsible only for bringing fuel; the rest of the time they loll around whiling away time in idle gossip. For those youths who have been promised in marriage, activities are more circumscribed. They take up residence in their future wife's household and perform various services for the family. But even these youths have it far easier than girls of comparable ages.

Discipline as such is not disapproved of by Kalinga. They believe, however, that discipline should be dispensed by individuals with the authority and qualifications to do so. Parents are not considered to have these prerogatives over their own children. They believe as parents their functions are mainly to provide love and affection. While they may suggest or "shame" their children into proper behavior, serious disciplinary problems are taken to an uncle or an influential man of authority. At present, school teachers and outsiders who employ Kalinga are also granted the right to exercise discipline. Thus, school teachers and non-Kalinga in authoritative positions are often asked by parents to be firm and strict with their children and to spank them "if they need it."

Serious parents deplore the idle behavior of their young sons at present, but they seem at a loss for solutions. The freedom which boys have is, of course, a carry-over from earlier days, as has been explained. Boys early developed a pride in warfare activities. They practiced under the supervision of older males and soon became proficient in the use of the spear, shield and headaxe. But warfare is an activity of past generations; idleness today can and does lead to trouble. Young boys having no concrete and purposeful tasks often break into houses to steal or vandalize; with increasing frequency young boys become involved in arguments and disputes with relatives. Kalinga parents are ineffectual in providing guidance and in controlling the deviant behavior of their children. Indeed, they admit readily that they do not know how to resolve the conflict between being an affectionate parent and a stern disciplinarian. Such conflict we have seen leads them to assign tasks of discipline to others.

Corporal punishment is usually avoided by the Kalinga since this may lead to reprisals or demands for the payment of fines by angry relatives. Foreigners are exempt if they occupy positions of authority. If a Kalinga lays a hand on a child, the parents out of a sense of pride and the urge to preserve traditional customs must "revenge" or demand the payment of indemnities. No action is taken against a non-Kalinga, who in a recognized position of authority employs corporal punishment. Indeed, parents might even express gratitude to such a person for giving their child "proper training."

Kalinga vacillate over the matter of having local natives as school teachers. On the one hand they feel proud that local talent and intelligence are recognized by school authorities; on the other, they believe that their children do not receive the proper disciplinary training. Many feel that it is best to have outsiders as teachers since such teachers are free to exercise strict disciplinary measures in the classroom, even corporal punishment if need be, without the fear of retaliation to which a local Kalinga teacher would be subject.

While no clear cut preferences for male or female children are made, Kalinga have strong negative feelings about twins. In the past, one of the pair, the one judged the most frail, was usually exposed to perish while the stronger one was permitted to survive. Sometimes the spirits were deceived by pretending to abandon one of the twins but recovering it later, or by changing the name of one of them after a time. Another method was to give one of the twins to a relative to raise. The reason for the taboo on twins is unknown, but it is undoubtedly related to the difficulty of nursing two infants at once under the former difficult subsistence economy of swidden farming.

In Lubuagan it was customary in the past for boys to be circumcised at about the age of seven. A number of old men without any special position in the society had the knowledge to perform the operation. Which one of these men was selected to circumcise a particular boy was up to his parents. The "surgeon" received a small payment either in produce, materials or money. The man who performed the operation abstained from eating taro until after the operation healed; otherwise there was no prescribed ritual associated with circumcision. The operation is rarely performed now in Lubuagan although it was reported that circumcision was once characteristic of all the Kalinga south of the Pacil River. Informants all denied that circumcision was ever performed in the northern Kalinga areas although informants from the north knew that southern Kalinga boys underwent the operation.

From ages four through ten, boys and girls play a variety of games. Perhaps the most common is a simple hide-and-seek played in the evening by both girls and boys. For boys, spinning tops is perhaps most popular; boys aged seven to fifteen play the game. Top games are not played by girls. There are also many unorganized games. Every village has a stream and pool nearby where women get water and where clothes are washed. Here, children from three to ten years old bathe, swim, and play games while women relatives wash clothes, scour pots and pans, and perform other household tasks.

The Kalinga delight in performing tasks which bring attention upon themselves as individuals. We will discuss later the exhibitionist qualities of adults, but children learn early to strive for activities which will make themselves visible. Plays and skits are popular and parents plan recitations for children to perform at public gatherings. The themes of these performances often come from their own school experiences. A poem or a piece of prose learned by a parent when a child perhaps under an American school teacher is taught to a young son or daughter. The child recites the poem at a peace-pact gathering or at a regional festive gathering with dramatic vocal emphases and exaggerated hand gestures. There is always considerable applause which reinforces the strong drive for individual achievement and distinction.

Beginning about the age of six or seven, boys and girls tend to separate themselves. The relationship between brothers and sisters becomes one of respect, almost of avoidance. While distantly related boys and girls may tease and throw stones at one another, a brother and sister will not align themselves on opposing sides in such groups. The respect patterns continue into adulthood.

In Lubuagan and in the southern Kalinga area generally, girls in their teens usually sleep together in the homes of widows while boys sleep in vacant houses. This is not an invariant pattern, however, since some girls and boys prefer to remain in their own homes at night. The predominant sleeping arrangement of Southern Kalinga teenagers is known among Northern Kalinga who strongly disapprove of such a custom. In the north, boys and girls remain in their own homes at night, unless they are visiting a distant hamlet and decide to remain the night.

Marriage

Arranged marriages were reported to be more prevalent in the past, although free choice of marriage partners apparently always existed as an option. A genealogical survey of marriages and other data for the Poswoy region indicated about half of the marriages had been contracted; the marriage partners of another one-fourth of the marriages had been contracted to marry others but had broken them for one reason or another; while another one-fourth had married through free choice. Samples were not taken from other areas although both northern and southern Kalinga informants indicated that these ratios seemed reasonably representative for the two cultural areas of Kalinga.

It was also reported that formerly individuals rarely broke marriage contracts, whereas at present there is an increasing tendency to break them. This statement is undoubtedly true. American attitudes toward marriages have diffused widely throughout the Mountain Province. Missions, boarding schools, recent opportunities for wage work and trade are all factors which have weakened the custom of arranged marriages.

Occasionally parents use pressure to force the consummation of marriage engagements they have made for their children. A school teacher now happily married to a man of her choice reported this incident:

> My contracted partner was the son of a prominent man, whom I scarcely knew although the first exchange of gifts beginning the marriage contract had been made while we were both babies. I had nothing concretely against my marriage partner, but we had developed in completely different ways and I could not think of a compatible life with him. He had had about two years of school, and then had gone to work on his family's fields. Through the years he and his parents had enlarged their land holdings and they owned perhaps more rice fields than anyone in our hamlet.
> My own life had gone on quite differently. I went through the high school program offered at Saint Teresita's mission in Salegseg and then had gone on to the Catholic junior college in Lubuagan. There I had met

my present husband and a horizon of new experiences had opened up before me. I wanted to return to the north Kalinga area to teach, but I wanted no part of the old life where I would labor in the fields and pound rice from early mornings until late in the evening and perform all of the other work that quickly make Kalinga girls into old women.

While I was yet in high school I told my parents that I had no intention of going through with my contract but they said I would see things differently later on and went on with the different stages of the engagement. When the gifts of the *ingngilin* [consummation of the marriage contract] were made my father and mother told me I now must join my husband-to-be and spend the night with him. I refused. They persisted in their demand that I live up to the contractual arrangement. Finally they seized me and locked me in a rice granary. That night my marriage partner came to the granary. He had been given the key and he opened the door and said that he was prepared to force me into sex relations with him which would make the marriage contract binding. I tried to persuade him that this marriage was not right for us, but he said that all of the necessary steps leading to the consummation of the marriage contract had been fulfilled and his family had no intention of backing down on the arrangements. If my family decided to sever the engagement they would have to pay back the equivalent costs of the gifts they had received and I knew they could not afford to do so. The only thing that I could do is run away and never return then the entire blame would be mine and not my parents. Relations with this man were abhorrent to me and I knew that if I consented I should very likely not have a chance to marry. I decided to play along for a while and try somehow to escape.

I told him that I would go through with the agreement and he immediately relaxed and laid the key of the granary lock on the floor. As he took off his clothes I pretended to do likewise, but then I picked up the keys, went out and quickly closed the granary door and snapped on the lock. I began to walk toward the village, but I realized that no one there would approve of what I had done, so I started off for Lubuagan; I knew I would find refuge with the Catholic Sisters at the mission. Many hours later I reached Lubuagan exhausted and hungry, but I knew the sisters would not take me back to my family. I did not return home until many months later and then with my present husband. My family was reconciled, for my younger sister had been substituted in my place. She was still very young and the time for consummating the marriage was still several years in the future for her. Everyone was pleased, the two families were still on good terms.

The case of the school teacher is not an isolated one. I have a number of other examples of the use of both force and resistance on the part of either the girl or the boy. Northern Kalinga parents of a girl try to comply with contractual arrangements once begun, more than do those of Lubuagan. This is probably because the boy's parents in the north contribute more gifts (what actually amounts to a bride price, *bansak*), than in Lubuagan where the gifts exchanged between the two families are about equal.

While Kalinga parents use force occasionally they are not as severe in enforcing marriages as parents elsewhere in the Mountain Province. Among the Ibaloy of Benguet Province, for example, the go-between who makes the arrangements for marriage uses rather drastic measures to consummate a marriage where the girl opposes the marriage. He strips the clothes off the girl and then binds her in a room and sends in her betrothed to have sex relations with her. If both object to the marriage, they are stripped of their clothes, bound together in a carabao hide and placed together in a locked room (cf. Leaño 1958:79–80).

Once it is common knowledge among the Kalinga that a girl has gone through the ingngilin, the marriage is considered consummated, although the final distribution of gifts and the wedding feast will not take place for another five months. No man would court a girl who has passed through this stage of the marriage contract. This is because such a man would be required to pay back all of the gifts exchanged between the two families through the years and he would be fined for making overtures to a girl whose marriage was already considered consummated. Hence, men will have nothing to do with a girl who has gone through the ingngilin stage of the marriage contract. It is important to emphasize that the avoidance of a girl who has passed through this stage of the marriage contract is not for moral reasons, but because of the practical and economic difficulties involved in the situation. If a man tried to marry such a girl it would be tantamount to making advances to a married woman, and he would be inciting the wrath of two extended families, the girl's and the contracted partner's. The ordinary Kalinga man, though he may be interested in a contracted girl, would have nothing to do with one who has gone through this crucial stage of the marriage contract.

Contract Marriages — The details of contract marriages vary considerably from region to region, but they do have a similar, over-all pattern. The one described here is specifically for the region of Poswoy. Children are engaged soon after they are born. Ideally, the boy should be a year or so older than the girl. Both the girl's and the boy's family make sure beforehand by various subtle overtures that the planned engagement meets the approval of both parties. The boy's parents make the initial overt advances in arranging the marriage contract. They select a man or two men related to both parties to act as "go-betweens," *manggogod* or *mambaga*. The mediators observe all omens (*see* section on omens — chapter on religion) and proceed to the girl's house only if all signs are favorable. Once at the house, again traditional omens are observed and a pig is killed and its bile sac examined for the proper favorable sign. If everything goes well, the mediators present the parents of the girl with valuable beads, *masilap* and *abali*. A feast is celebrated in the presence of

Lounging is infrequent for the busy Kalinga woman whose work begins before dawn and lasts well into the night. Typically, a moment of respite may be spent in squatting and smoking a cigar.

the girl's relatives and the mediators are treated as honored guests. Upon leaving they are presented with gifts for themselves and the forefront of the pig (*long-os*) as a present to the boy's parents.

The acceptance of the beads and the feast, called *banat,* is the first step in the contractual arrangement. After the banat, the parents of the boy and the girl are invited to all feasts given by either set of parents and are given meat shares.

When the boy is between twelve and fourteen, he is taken to the girl's house by his relatives, who again observe all the omens and taboos ordinarily prescribed for the beginning of a crucial journey. In the girl's home, the boy performs services such as hauling fuel, working in the fields, and such other duties as may be required of him. Occasionally he may go home, remain for a few days, and then return to the house of his betrothed. This custom, a form of bride service, is called *magngotogaw*.

At about the age of seventeen or eighteen the boy is again formally escorted to the girl's house. This is the final journey to the girl's home and will culminate in marriage. The relatives who escort the boy may be aunts or first cousins, but never the parents of the boy. If parents accompany the boy, it is feared that the spirits will believe that the parents are tired of their son and want to get rid of him and hence bring illness or misfortune to the members of the escorting party. This formal escort preceding the series of events that terminates in marriage is called *tolód*. All of the omens are carefully observed and if these are unfavorable the journey may be postponed for a day or more until they are favorable. If the marriage is to be between partners from different regional units, a group of men playing the *pantángkog* (bamboo sticks struck against each other) precedes the escorting party. The tolod is also performed for marriages resulting from individual choice when the groom joins his bride immediately preceding marriage.

The arrival of the escorting party is an occasion for feasting. The boy's relatives are feted and return with gifts for themselves and the boy's parents. When they leave they carry back with them the forefront of the pig butchered for the occasion. Shares of meat from the pig will be distributed to all of the relatives of the boy. This occasion is called *kagítkit* in Poswoy.

About two weeks later, valuable gifts are given by the boy's family to the girl. These gifts usually consist of sixty precious Chinese beads and about twenty Chinese plates. After this gift-giving, the boy and girl may sleep together as husband and wife. This stage of the marriage ceremony is called ingngilin.

The official fulfillment of the marriage contract occurs about five months after the ingngilin. This is the wedding feast celebrated in all regions of Kalinga, although the designation of the feast varies considerably. In Lubuagan it is called *togtogaw;* in Salegseg, *among;* and in Poswoy, *pasingan.* At this time, relatives through third cousins from both sides of the couple's families are invited to the feast and receive meat shares of carabaos killed for the occasion. A basket of gifts called *gala* is given by the boy's relatives and another by the girl's relatives to the couple. The relatives are extremely competitive in this gift-giving, each set attempting to outdo the other by contributing the most precious and valuable gifts. At this time, too, the *banbansak* is decided. This represents the gifts given by the boy's relatives to the girl's relatives. The most valuable gifts such as *gosi* (Chinese jars), carabaos and rice fields go to the eldest brother, parents and grandparents of the girl, while the girl's more distant relatives, such as first and second cousins, receive plates and money. The amounts given to the girl's relatives, of course, depend on the wealth of the boy's relatives.

Wedding feasts are highly competitive affairs, each kinship group attempting to display its bountiful economic resources. Among the Northern Kalinga where the bulk of the gifts are contributed by the boy's relatives, the wedding feast highlights particularly the wealth and prestige of the boy's kindred.

At the time of the wedding feast, the parents of the couple also give their daughter or son a part of her or his share of the family inheritance. This consists of rice fields, carabaos, Chinese jars, plates, beads, and the like with which the couple may set up their own household. The inherited property collectively is called *tawid.* Since the ingngilin, the couple have been living with the girl's parents, but after the wedding feast, a separate residence is constructed for them. Residence in northern Kalinga is statistically only slightly matrilocal. If the girl's family has sufficient land for a house site, the couple's house is ordinarily built on such a site, otherwise the couple may build their house near the boy's family or on a site in a village where neither of the parents live. Primary consideration in determining a house site for the couple is nearness to the land to be farmed, either hill farms or irrigated rice fields. In building the house, both the relatives of the boy and the girl contribute their services.

The wedding feast lasts for a day and night. *Basi* (sugarcane wine) is consumed in large quantities while two or more *ganza* (gong) orchestras take turns in providing music for the *pala-ok* and *tadok* dances. Prominent men boast of their war records (*pokaw, palpaliwat*) or of their economic resourcefulness (*manyamyam, i-iyab*).

Variations in the pattern of the Kalinga contractual marriage custom as described for Poswoy are evident in the different regions. Crucial features which appear to be present in all areas, however, are the following: 1) selection of a go-between or go-betweens by the boy's parents; 2) formal visit of these mediators to the girl's parents, the presentation of a gift and their return with gifts for themselves and the boy's parents; 3) formal escort of the boy to the girl's home shortly before the marriage feast; and 4) a marriage feast with the exchange of gifts between the girl's and boy's relatives. The banbansak which designates the custom of presenting expensive gifts to a wide range of the girl's relatives does not occur in Lubuagan at the time of the wedding feast, but takes place later, after the couple have had a child. This custom is called *atod* in Lubuagan according to Barton (1949:46). The gifts given to the girl's relatives by the boy's kindred in Lubuagan do not compare in value with those of the banbansak in northern Kalinga. Gift-giving to the girl's relatives among the Northern Kalinga takes place in an atmosphere of exaggerated generosity and runs to several thousand pesos value in the case of the wealthy. Wedding feasts among the Northern Kalinga are therefore occasions on which the prestige of both kindreds is demonstrated, but particularly the boy's. Marriage of a couple where the partners come from different regions was formerly arranged by the influential leaders of the two regions. This type of marriage is called *gawayan*.

Uncontracted Marriages — While a considerable number of Kalinga marriages result from the betrothal of infants, individual choice of marriage partners also exists. As we have noted, in about one-fourth of Poswoy marriages there had been no betrothal of either partner, and in about another one-fourth neither partner had been contracted; hence, about one-half of Poswoy marriages were contracted by individual choice. Since a definite courting pattern exists among the Kalinga, we may assume that the individual choice of marriage partners is also an old practice.

Arrangements for a boy and a girl to see one another are made by themselves; it is not customary to employ a go-between in arranging a meeting. If a boy is interested in a girl, he finds an opportunity to intercept the girl on her way to fetch water, or to catch her attention at a public gathering. The initial contact is extremely subtle, for Kalinga etiquette forbids girls and boys to talk to one another in the open. A boy constantly seeks occasions on which he can catch the eye of the girl in whom he is interested. A vague sign unnoticed by others, such as a subtle wink, a raised eyebrow, or the sudden lowering of the eyes with a faint smile might be indicative that the boy has found favor in the girl. Emboldened by such a sign of approval, the boy will present himself at the girl's home in the evening. The boy prepares special courting songs, *olalim* or *bala-goyos,* and practices on the lip flute, *paldong,* and nose flute, *tong-ali,* and then serenades and woos his girl friend.

If the arrangement is satisfying to both the girl and the boy, the girl may arrange to see the boy under more private circumstances when her parents are away. Among the Southern Kalinga where girls customarily sleep in the houses of a widow (obog), he may visit her there at night. In time, the couple decides to marry, their parents are informed and a date is set for the marriage feast. The girl's parents give the first feast and are hosts to the groom's parents and his kindred. This feast is later followed in some regions by a similar one given by the groom's parents, the latter acting as hosts. After this ceremony the couple are considered married and reside temporarily with the girl's parents. Soon, however, as was discussed previously, a house is built for them, commonly near the girl's parents' home. Ideally, a girl's parents should provide the house or house site, but occasionally if the boy's parents are economically better off, the couple may go to live in a house provided for them by the boy's parents. Among the Northern Kalinga where swiddens and rice fields are dispersed, residence may actually be neolocal; that is, in a village where neither of the parents reside, but near fields which the couple have been given to cultivate.

Dating patterns of the western world are absent among the Kalinga, and indeed except in urban areas were not observed in northern Luzon. Young men and women do not date in public; it is only at night and inside a residence that couples may see one another. Flirtation patterns are also conspicuously absent; arrangements to meet at night are conducted so subtly that unless one is familiar with the cues and signs employed by the girl and the boy, it is virtually impossible to note the manner in which young people of the opposite sex attract one another.

Mistresses

Taking up with a mistress, *dagdagas,* is condoned, but permission of parents is usually necessary. A man gives beads or other objects of value to a woman who has consented to be his mistress. Children of mistresses are entitled to some of a man's inheritance, although they do not receive as much as a man's children from his legitimate wife. In the event that a man has no children from his "legal" wife, then his children from his mistress will inherit as if they were his own. A son may have a dagdagas when still a bachelor but the permission of his parents is essential in such a case. Under any circumstance it is good to have the permission of parents, for the eventual disposal of inheritance property may then be anticipated and taken into account by the latter in the event that there are children from such a union. It is important to emphasize that no child, whether of a legal union or a mistress, is denied support or inheritance rights. The leaders of a region, pangngats, see to it that every child is properly cared and provided for. Mistresses come from poor families, *kapos,* while men who take mistresses are of the prominent and wealthy class, *baknang.* A wife does not object if her husband takes a mistress when she is old or if she is barren. Indeed, a barren woman might ask a man to take a mistress so that one or more of the children by her husband and his mistress may be raised as their own and hence inherit their property. Mistresses are often women of other villages than one's own. Peace-pact holders and traders often take mistresses in the villages of the regions with which they have pacts and conduct trade. Much more rarely, a prominent and wealthy man might take a mistress in his own town, a practice almost completely restricted to the more densely populated communities of the south. In the latter case, the relationship is apparently fully condoned by the wife, as the mistress then becomes a kind of second wife under the domination of the legal wife. The mistress is housed nearby with her children (if any) and helps the wife with her household duties. Should the first wife die during the time the husband has this type of dagdagas relationship, then the mistress attains full and accepted status as a wife.

It could not be determined exactly how many men kept mistresses in any of the regions, although the practice seems to be typical of men of the baknang class whose wives had passed the child-bearing period. In this class the dagdagas system appears to have complete acceptance and adds to the prestige of prominent, wealthy men.

Prostitutes are said not to exist anywhere among the Kalinga. Detailed census data and occupational information on individuals obtained for the regions of Poswoy and Mabaca revealed no prostitutes. While comparable data was not compiled for any of the regions in southern

Kalinga, Lubuagan informants were emphatic that there were no prostitutes in their regions.

There is no clear distinction between adopted children and servants. Well-to-do families have one or more of them, although they are most common in the densely populated communities of the south. An adopted child is called *in-anak* and a servant *poyong,* but the treatment accorded to either seems not to differ markedly. Indeed, adopted children and servants become in most respects like other children of the household. They receive a portion of their foster parents' inheritance, although not as much as actual children. They are well treated and Kalinga custom law extends protective controls over them in the same manner as over other individuals. Adopted children are usually orphaned relatives, while servants come from poorer families. If a servant comes from another region, the peace-pact regulations of both regions protect the individual. The physical safety of the servant is thus even more secure than that of other individuals. Servants receive no compensation for their services, but are usually in better circumstances than they would be in their natal homes since only better-to-do families can afford to keep them. An adopted child may be contracted in marriage like an actual child, but a poyong must seek a wife on his own initiative, or if a girl, becomes a wife by individual choice. A girl servant often becomes a mistress. As a mistress or a wife she loses her special status as a servant, and her husband or lover must provide for her or compensate her in the same manner as any other woman. Adopted children and servants, like other members of a region, have the right to appeal to regional pangngats for inheritance property and adjudication of wrongs suffered either from their masters or from others. All individuals, whatever their socio-economic or personal status, appear to be treated fairly and equally among the Kalinga everywhere (cf. Barton 1949:64–65).

Divorce

Divorces, as pointed out earlier, have a high correlation with childless marriages. If a couple does not have a child in a year or two, they almost certainly will separate to try their luck with other partners. Some childless couples remain married by adopting a child, either a son or a daughter of a relative, or more rarely, a child born of the union of the husband and his mistress. The Northern Kalinga, who are perhaps more sensitive to the Roman Catholic priest's admonitions, rarely present themselves to be married by him until a wife is well along in pregnancy, or may even wait until after a child is born. This is because the Catholic priest emphasizes the permanence of marriages which he performs and Kalingas realize that only when a child has arrived, or is safely on the way, can a marriage be considered a permanent venture. A child is essential for the stability of every marriage and the banbansak (north Kalinga) or atod (south Kalinga) which designates the custom of gift-giving by the groom's to the bride's relatives does not take place until the couple have lived as husband and wife for about five months and the wife is pregnant. Among the Northern Kalinga the marriage feast and a partial distribution of the tawid (inheritance) does not take place until five or more months have elapsed from the ingngilin.

In Poswoy, the majority of those individuals who had been divorced one or more times (approximately fifty per cent of the population), had divorced because they had had no children in their previous unions. We have already observed that divorces for reasons other than the lack of children are rare. It was reported, however, that a man might divorce a wife if she were not pleasant and hospitable to his guests. Kalinga culture places high value on hospitality and girls are taught from early childhood to be gracious hosts to visitors. There are few wives, therefore, who are not mindful of this highly valued precept. A wife who is sullen and unpleasant to her husband's guests, whether relatives or friends, suffers censure not only from her husband but from the whole society. Industry and hard work are other traits that are given high value in Kalinga culture and the rare wife who is lacking these qualities is unlikely to remain married for long. Other factors, such as adultery or the dagdagas system appear to be negligible in divorces. Perhaps because of the custom of infant betrothal, early marriage and the mistress system, promiscuity in women or the incidence of adultery by either men or women is not a serious problem. The rather severe penalties imposed by custom law on those who transgress the accepted sexual privileges provided by marriage and the dagdagas relationship may also be a deterrent to adulterous and promiscuous behavior. A man has the right to punish his wife severely and even to kill her should she be caught in the act of adultery. The case of a man who commits adultery or seduces an unmarried girl is taken before the regional leaders who impose heavy fines and if a child is born of the relationship, the man is required to support the child and set aside a portion of his inheritance property for the child.

Adult Life and Occupational Activities

After marriage, men and women enter actively into adult life. The normal and continuous work of men involves the clearing of swiddens and the plowing of rice fields. While men work hard at these tasks, their work is ordinarily confined to daylight hours. This is in striking contrast to the duties of women whose work begins in the dark of early morning and continues far into the night. In the village, unless a house is under construction, men loll around or are assembled together in loud and boisterous conversation. During the dry season, after the rice harvest in January and before the clearing of swiddens in March, men travel about extensively. This is the time of peace-pact celebrations when men have the opportunity to trade and buy and if skillful, to advance the economic well-being of their households and thus bring prestige to their kinship groups.

There is little change at present in the pattern of activities for a man from a young married adult to old age. Prestige and status are advanced primarily by increasing land holdings, the acquisition of pigs and carabaos, and the accumulation of heirlooms in the form of Chinese plates, jars, and gongs: to this must be added the acquisition of large lowland type houses with galvanized roofs. Those who acquire these possessions are men of the bagnang class to which every married man aspires. While a man becomes a member of this privileged class by business acumen, some have entered the class by accidental circumstances. A number of Kalinga men were recognized as furthering the war effort through their participation as guerrilla fighters during the Japanese occupation. These individuals receive United States Government checks and are also entitled to buy American goods in the U.S. Government commissary at Camp John Hay in Baguio. The goods they buy are promptly sold at increased prices in black market establishments in Baguio. While the amounts such individuals realize from government checks and sale of commissary products are minimal in terms of United States economy, they represent small fortunes among the Kalinga.

Modern conditions have brought about important changes in positions that determine status and distinction among men. It is no longer possible at present to become renowned as a courageous warrior, mangngol. Education is now considered to be an essential step to most positions to which one would aspire. While a few illiterate old men still retain important status positions as regional leaders, younger pangngats or lakays are those who can read, write, and speak English. Schooling in other positions is even more important. In Balbalan District, which embraces most of northern Kalinga, individuals who hold positions from barrio lieutenants to the municipal mayor must be literate in English. For school teachers, positions which appeal to young Kalingas, a teacher's certificate is required and cannot be attained in less than two or three years of schooling beyond high school.

Except in rare instances, men have not been mediums among the Kalinga. The position of a medium has been essentially restricted to women who have assumed these positions if they were psychologically disposed. There were no purely ceremonial or religious offices for men.

A man could become a courageous warrior or a regional leader by personal achievement; these consitituted the only socio-political positions open to men in the past.

Beginning in the mid-eighteenth century, some men became part-time traders, but no one became exclusively a trader. Other occupational tasks performed by men were also part-time, such as blacksmithing and basket weaving. The weaving of cotton cloth and the making of pottery were the occupation of women who carried on these tasks on a part-time basis. Thus, there were no full-time specialists among either men or women.

The Kalinga of the past was mainly a subsistence farmer — in early times growing rice in swiddens and in more recent years shifting to irrigated rice. At present an increasing number of individuals are becoming wage workers, either as municipal employees or as laborers in Baguio or other cities of Luzon. The bulk of the Kalinga populations, however, continues in subsistence farming.

Women not only assist their men with farm work, but do all of the work around the house: nursing and the care of children, pounding and winnowing rice, preparing meals, scouring floor mats, and carrying water. During feasts and the visits of friends and relatives, they accelerate the normal activities of housework and must in addition appear as smiling and gracious hostesses. The lot of a wife of a prominent man is considerably harder, although such women do occasionally have extra help. In the homes of the baknang, there is almost a continuous series of visitors who must be fed and entertained. These occasions are called *palanos*. These feasts help to promote and maintain the position of influential leaders and to elevate the status of their kinship groups. While the men of the extended household circulate about the guests, women are busy cooking and serving food and dispensing basi. After the palanos, men of the kindred segment in the village may lounge about outside receiving the congratulations of neighbors for having given an elaborate feast and providing gracious hospitality to the visitors. But the work of the women goes on; they wash and scour to prepare the house again to receive guests — always ready to serve and provide generous welcome to the friends of their menfolk. The women of course take great pride and enjoy the prestige these occasions reflect on the kinship group.

The only semi-professional position for women among the Kalinga up until the present has been that of the curer or medium. A woman becomes a medium, not by individual choice or inclination, but, as has been said, by being psychologically disposed to it. The Kalinga believe that mediums are selected by the spirits. A woman thus "called" exhibits peculiar food and behavior habits recognized by the Kalinga as summons to assume the role of a medium (*see* section on religion). In the regions

The bamboo mat floor is a common feature of Kalinga homes, and is taken frequently by the housewife to the nearby stream for washing. The cooking hearth is also shown.

visited, mediums are all women past the age of thirty. In Poswoy, a region of approximately five hundred inhabitants, informants reported that there were about a dozen mediums.

In addition to mediums, a few women (three were reported for Poswoy), become specialists in the treatment of women who have trouble in bearing children or who wish to abort after conception. These women are not midwives; the Kalinga apparently do not have midwives. Women of an extended household, usually the mother, assist at childbirth. Should there be difficulty at birth, one of these childbirth specialists is called. The primary function of these women is then to help a barren woman conceive, to assist in difficult births, and to perform abortions. Such work is always conducted on a part-time basis; most of the time these women carry on the normal duties of housewives.

Mediums come nearer being full-time specialists. They are called for illnesses and funerals where they direct the sacrifice of chickens and animals and perform curing rituals (*see* section on religion). The services of mediums are in constant demand and they are extremely busy; nevertheless, they are not exempt from the usual work of women, and when not engaged in ritual activities, they are involved in normal tasks of women.

In recent years women have been able to get into other non-traditional positions. These are positions such as school teachers and municipal clerks for which schooling beyond the high school is required. Schooling receives high value in Kalinga culture and the desire to achieve an education will undoubtedly lead more and more men and women into professions new to traditional Kalinga society and culture. But for a society still engaged predominantly in subsistence farming and stressing periodic prestige feasts and generous hospitality to frequent visitors, the lot of most women will continue to be characterized by hard work both in the fields and at home.

Men and women during the courses of their lives will very likely become involved at least once in some kind of litigation proceedings within their own region. Kalinga custom law consists of a remarkably large body of jural procedures known to most adults but about which the pangngats or regional "arbiters" are especially knowledgeable. (*See* Barton 1949 for an excellent study of Kalinga custom law.) Since there are so many infractions which require litigation, it is virtually impossible for a Kalinga, or some member of his kinship group, to escape involvement in the Kalinga jural system. The Kalinga are sensitive people and the actions of others which cause physical harm or wound the pride of an individual or group must be compensated either by inflicting counter harm or by the payment of indemnities. The principle of group responsibility and the substitutability of one individual for another in his kinship group is foremost in the litigation process. Thus, in most offenses any individual, not necessarily the one responsible for an infraction, may be punished and if indemnities are to be paid, his entire kinship circle must contribute. Similarly, indemnities collected are not only for the victim or his immediate kin but for all members of his kinship group.

Another characteristic of Kalinga custom law is that distinction is rarely made between an injury inflicted through intent or one through accident. Both acts are likely to be punished in the same manner unless it can be proved beyond any doubt whatsoever that the action was accidental. The individual who has inflicted such an injury accidentally, however, is usually so uneasy about possible retaliation that he and his relatives are likely to make a payment even though there may be no demand.

In settling disputes and assessing fines and indemnities, the arbiters make pronouncements which are usually accepted as the proper interpretation of custom law. Such interpretations, however, are always made by regional leaders only after a careful survey of public opinion on the matter. Thus their judgments are rarely in conflict with group feeling.

Illness and Death

When illness or injury occurs the services of the medium and curer (*mangalisig,* southern Kalinga; or *mandadawak* or *mang-anito,* northern Kalinga) are engaged. Animals are sacrificed to appease ancestral and malevolent spirits, the numbers sacrificed varying with the age and importance of the patient. Sickness rites for prominent individuals in the grandparent generation are most elaborate. When a grandparent of the wealthy class is seriously ill, the rites reach the proportions of a celebration. Relatives of the patient down through the third cousins attend and receive shares of meat distributed by a pangngat. In Lubuagan, women sing *mambikbik* and *dangdang-ay.*

If all the efforts of the medium and curer fail and the patient dies, a relative goes outside and shouts the news (*mamípkak*). The information is relayed quickly throughout the region to members of the victim's kinship circle.

In Lubuagan, at the death of an adult, all relatives down through second cousins contribute wine for the wake (*kodomál*). Pigs and carabaos are sacrificed for adults, but for a child only a pig may be butchered.

Funeral Rites — Funerals *(bagongngon)* are more elaborate in the Lubuagan region than in the north. A bamboo chair *(sangngádil)* wide enough to accommodate the corpse and the widow or widower is made. The corpse of an adult was formerly watched for ten days or more; at present the period has been reduced to about three days. During this time the widow or widower (or in the absence of these, the closest relative) sits much of the time beside the corpse and drives off the flies with a fly switch *(wasiwás).* Wailing and sobbing, the spouse asks the deceased to pity him and their children and not to send illness. Other close relatives also go through conventional patterns of wailing and sobbing, but do not sit beside the corpse.

Among well-to-do Lubuagans the first night of the wake of a grandparent is a festive occasion. Gongs are played for dancers *(matatadok),* women pound rice *(kitkitong),* and pangngats recite their accomplishments *(i-iyab).* The children and grandchildren run races and play games while adults sing songs and chant *olalin* (*see* appendix for songs).

Northern Kalinga funerals are more subdued, but they, too, are festive rather than somber and sad affairs.

Among all Kalinga the wake is conducted and the sacrifices are offered in order to honor the spirit of the deceased who is asked to accept the sacrifices and not to bring misfortune and illness to the living.

The death chair is used primarily for adults, but a child of a wealthy family may also be placed in a chair and mourned. Ordinarily, however, young children are buried quickly, and the wake and funeral are shortened to a day. Among the Northern Kalinga the surviving spouse or close relative sits in a corner, shielded by a blanket from the rest of the room, instead of next to the death chair as in Lubuagan. There is no singing at funerals among the Northern Kalinga, but games are played and women pound rice ritually *(manggattong)* as at Lubuagan. A popular game at funerals among the Northern Kalinga is *bitlag,* a thigh-slapping contest.

Children are buried near the house or under granaries. Formerly in northern Kalinga areas there was secondary burial of the bones of adults in jars. Adults are now most commonly buried in graves about six feet deep and three feet wide, lined on the bottom and sides with small rocks and smoothed over with lime plaster. Large slabs of flat rock are placed on top of the corpse and the rest of the pit filled with dirt. A thatch-roofed arbor supported by four bamboo poles is then erected over the grave. At present some Kalinga bury their dead in concrete tombs; this is especially characteristic of the well-to-do in the Lubuagan region. Such tombs contain the remains of several individuals; they are rather large and properly should be called family tombs.

In Poswoy, *gongwoy* (betel nut preparation), charcoal and lemon leaves are placed on top of the grave or tomb. Giant ghouls, *alan* or *kotmó,* who seek to feed on corpses are believed to be repelled by these objects. A food offering in the form of rice bread is also hung from the thatch-roofed ceiling above the grave or tomb in Poswoy. Also in Poswoy, nine days after burial all the personal belongings of the deceased, such as spear, headaxe, raincoat, digging stick, or bolo, are placed on the grave. A man's belongings are put in a carrying pack *(pasiking)*; a woman's possessions in a basket.

Mourning and food taboos are strictly observed in all areas of Kalinga by the closely related kin of the deceased. For about a month in Poswoy, a surviving spouse (*pang-is,* man; *bilog,* woman) cannot eat meat, fresh-water fish, or root foods; the diet must be restricted to fruits and vegetable greens. During this time, it is also forbidden to pick fruit and to cook one's own food. The sacrifice of a chicken about a month after the death of one's spouse removes the food taboos and the restriction on cooking and picking fruit, but mourning continues for another year. A spouse cannot marry for a year and, together with other members of the household, is required to observe the following restrictions: dancing and singing are prohibited, a strip of black or brown cloth must be wrapped around the forehead, arm, or chest; both sexes must let their hair grow freely and not oil it.

Approximately a year after the death of a parent or grandparent, a ceremony or celebration called *koli-as* is given. This ends the mourning period and removes all the restrictions from household members. Koli-as is a big feast where one or more large animals are butchered and served to relatives, neighbors, and friends. The number of animals butchered and the size of the feast vary with the wealth of the household and closely related kin. There is dancing of the *tadok* and singing of *ogayám, dangngó, adí,* and *salidomáy.* The first to dance is the father of the deceased, followed by the widow or widower and then the other members of the household. There is also the recital of war exploits by those who have killed, and the recounting of outstanding achievements and accomplishments by wealthy and prominent individuals. The koli-as is approximately a twenty-four hour affair, beginning in the morning of one day and ending in the morning of the second day.

In all Kalinga areas the mourning period for a child under the age of one is only about a month. Mourning is extended somewhat for older children, and for adults it is ordinarily no less than a year. For all deaths there is a feast to remove behavioral and food restrictions, although the age and importance of the individual determine when mourning will be terminated. The older the deceased and the greater his prominence, the longer will be the mourning period and the more elaborate will be the koli-as.

Formerly a man whose son or parent died went to another region to hunt for a head. It was, and is, the belief of the Kalinga that one life atones for another and that the life of an enemy pleases the spirits and will keep the spirits from sending misfortune to the living. In earlier times if a man brought back a head he was welcomed with an elaborate celebration in which he danced. A successful headhunting expedition was believed to remove all sorrow over the loss, and it therefore ended mourning.

The koli-as or end of the mourning period is also believed to remove sorrow over losing a near and beloved one. Crying and continuing despondency after the koli-as are considered very bad and likely to produce another death. A man or woman whose sorrow cannot be consoled is asked to exhume the bones of the deceased and wash and rebury them, or else to take a journey on which a large river is crossed. Such acts are believed to be effective in restoring a sorrowful and despondent individual to normal life.

The preceding discussion of the life cycle highlights birth, marriage, sickness, and death as especially important occasions in the life of an

The Kalinga family tomb is close to the home of the living as this one regarded with doubtful curiosity by a Lubuagan child. Ancestral spirits are represented as not always of the friendliest sort.

individual. We have seen that headhunting activities were also emphasized in former times, especially for young adults. Ritual headhunting, however, is now a thing of the past. In part, peace-pact celebrations have substituted for the activities previously associated with headhunting, but the peace-pact meetings also serve other functions. They are new occasions for social interaction and with people formerly considered the enemy.

Kalinga celebrations, whether associated with the life cycle or with peace pacts, are primarily social and prestige feasts. At present sacrificial butchering and food-offering to the spirits appear to be secondary in importance, and much less emphasized than in previous times. Even sickness and death rites are essentially prestige and social events.

The Kalinga appear to be concerned about spirits and even fearful of them, but they do not adhere rigidly to prescribed forms of ceremonial ritual. They undoubtedly contrast in this respect with the Bontoc (Jenks 1905) and the Ifugao (Barton 1946, Lambrecht 1932–1955). In all of the ceremonies there is evidence of a greater concern in the past for the proper performance of ritualistic activities. At present, however, the Kalinga are haphazard in the execution of these rites, often omitting features which appear to be important. A number of ceremonies apparently important in the past, especially those connected with agriculture, have lapsed completely. Matters crucial to other pagan peoples of the Mountain Province such as knowledge of good and bad omens, observance of restrictions and taboos before beginning an important task or a journey, are only imperfectly known and usually omitted. Furthermore, if precautions are taken or observances made, these are in a careless manner and an atmosphere of amusement. Mediums are engaged for the important events in an individual's life cycle, but the attitudes toward them are characterized by amused tolerance. Educated Kalinga frequently deny that mediums still exist or refer to them deprecatingly as "quack doctors" whose services are used by only the most ignorant and backward persons. In the light of these attitudes, it is not surprising that the ceremonies of the Kalinga, especially, in the north, have come to emphasize the more secular aspect of such activities, namely, the social and prestige features.

Status and Class Structure

The determinants of status and leadership have undergone important changes among the Kalinga. Long ago, perhaps sixty or seventy years ago, men with distinguished headhunting records enjoyed the highest status. Such individuals frequently boasted about their war record in regional gatherings and tried to belittle their headhunting compatriots. A man with a good headhunting record, who could speak fearlessly in regional gatherings and use good judgment in settling disputes, might achieve a regional pinnacle of influence. Indeed, the possibility of becoming a renowned leader was the avowed reason for the boasting sessions, *palpaliwat* or *pokao,* which are still a feature of most regional festivals.[19] Old men report, however, that these sessions no longer have the importance they formerly had, and my own observations confirm these statements. The brave warriors who became influential leaders because of undisputed war records, clever oratory, and wise adjudication of offenses and crimes, have passed into history. These *mangngol,* or courageous warriors, are still remembered nostalgically by the old men. Such a man was Bakidan of the region of Buaya, for example, whose reputation as a fearless warrior, a wise interpreter and administrator of custom law, is well known in northern Kalinga. Bakidan has a place in recorded history. Dean C. Worcester, first Commissioner of the Interior in the Philippines, credits Bakidan with saving his life and that of his party in 1905 (Worcester and Hayden 1930:428–434).

Another feature of most regional gatherings is the recital of a prominent man's accomplishments, *i-iyab* or *manyamyam.* These sessions spring also undoubtedly from the past, permitting, as they do, even a man who might not have been a headhunter to gain recognition in Kalinga society. The accomplishments recounted are essentially economic — a man boasting about his many rice fields or swiddens; or his fine, expensive house; or again about his wealth in livestock. A man might also boast about his illustrious ancestors and fine children who are brave and industrious. In rare cases in the past, there occurred the combination of the two avenues to Kalinga success in one man, that is, the fearless warrior and the man of outstanding economic resourcefulness. The fortunate man who, in addition to such a combination, also possessed the ability to interpret custom law properly and to enforce it when needed, became the undisputed leader of his region. The fame of regional leaders often went beyond their home regions, but there is no evidence that such leadership ever operated in uniting two or more regions into one political unit. Indeed, the regional leader or leaders were not political figures; they were men of high prestige who were consulted for all important regional problems and were asked to settle personal disputes which involved two or more kindreds. Extra-regional troubles in the past were apparently resolved only by resorting to the vengeance pattern, but intraregional problems were brought before these "arbiters," and indeed they still are. Influential leaders settle problems according to the well-established body of custom law, but they also have "an ear out" for public opinion in each case. The Kalinga are a proud people and any unfair pronouncement is challenged even though made by powerful leaders. Hence, influential leaders among the Kalinga undoubtedly have interpreted custom law and administered justice in a manner that would be acceptable to the local population.

With the disappearance of headhunting, the avenues toward influence and distinction in Kalinga society shifted to the second alternative — economic resourcefulness. Influential leaders at present come from the well-to-do group, the *baknang*. In former times, this class was weakly developed, if indeed it existed at all, and certainly subordinate to the warrior group. As modern developments hastened the disappearance of headhunting, the baknang class began to emerge. In the south among the pagan peoples of Benguet, Bontoc, and Ifugao, and even at Lubuagan, this class has deeper historical roots.[20] At Lubuagan, for example, there are well-established families or bilateral descent groups with a fairly long history, long enough so that they comprise an incipient aristocracy, the *kadangyan*. This group is absent in the north and while the term is familiar to these Kalinga they will not apply it to any of their own family groups. Among the Northern Kalinga there are only two economic classes, the poor, *kapos,* and the well-to-do, baknang. Some deference is shown by poorer individuals to those of greater wealth, but there is no clearcut distinction between the two classes. Every kindred has well-to-do and poor families. Socio-economic mobility is flexible and there are numerous cases of individuals from poor families who have risen to positions of wealth and influence. In some instances, such individuals were even children of mistresses. The deferential behavior is probably a recent phenomenon and attributable to Ilocano influences. The Kalinga are thus an essentially classless society where status and influential positions are achieved rather than being determined by family connections. Any visitor among the Kalinga is impressed by their independence of temperament. It is this characteristic which undoubtedly appealed to early Americans who found such behavior compatible with their own love for individual freedom and independence.

The absence of bilateral descent groups among the Northern Kalinga and the incipient development of these units in Lubuagan suggests that descent groups might be correlated with societies having a more stable economy. Thus, bilateral descent groups are fairly important socio-economic units among the irrigated rice farmers of Ifugao (Lambrecht 1953, 1954) and Sagada (Eggan 1960:29–30).

The weak development of class stratification among the Kalinga is associated, as could be expected, with dry rice farming. Where more complex social structures are evident in the Mountain Province they occur in connection with wet rice cultivation or are definitely recent. In the latter category belong the positions of peace-pact holders, for example, which are clearly associated with bilateral descent groups but of shallow historical depth. In all Kalinga regions, informants were able to name the original pact-holder for each one of the peace pacts of that region, and by far the majority of the dates initiating a pact are in the present century.

Influential leaders among the Kalinga at present come from the well-to-do class. In Lubuagan the term pangngat is used both as a term of address and reference for these individuals, but among the Northern Kalinga the term, while known, has little currency. Instead, among the latter, influential regional leaders are called lakay or capitan, either in address or reference.

Pangngats (lakays, capitanes) are well-to-do individuals, but a man of means is not necessarily a member of this distinguished group. An informal, tacit acceptance of the individual by the regional population is the only road to pangngathood. This is a long process. There is no formal vote taken; people "just know" who has arrived at the point where he may be considered an influential regional leader. A man of wealth who wants to enter this privileged class must speak up in regional festivals and he must argue wisely, eloquently, and at length, the cases of his home region at peace-pact meetings. No man is barred from speaking at Kalinga gatherings, but public reaction to any comment or speech, whether favorable or unfavorable, is unmistakable to a Kalinga spectator. A man who speaks often and who receives the respectful attention of an audience may be said to be along the road to becoming a pangngat. If in addition such an individual begins to be sought for his advice in time of trouble, and the news gets around that he gives wise counsel, another step in the right direction may be said to have been taken. As a man of means becomes mature, continues to speak eloquently and wisely at gatherings, counsels often and in keeping with the fundamentals of custom law, sooner or later people will begin to address him as pangngat, lakay, or capitan. When this happens the individual is a member of this informal but influential fraternity.

The pangngats do not meet as a formal body, and certainly they cannot be considered in any sense a council. They do often discuss regional problems but such discussions occur informally at regional festivals where men of influence lounge around together, squatting and chewing betel nut and discoloring the ground about with their spittle as they talk for long hours. In discussing regional troubles and cases which have been brought before them, each leader presents his views, usually by citing precedents from similar cases previously settled but always injecting his own opinions. At such times the regional leaders sample public opinion which will be considered carefully by each one when called upon by relatives in trouble.

In settling actual cases, the regional leaders operate more as arbiters than as formal judges. Any trouble such as theft, physical injury, or adultery, is taken immediately by the injured party to a pangngat who is related to his kinship group. In the meantime, the offender has done likewise, consulting a man of influence who is related to his kinship group. The immediate reaction of the regional leaders is to advise moderation and caution against hasty, unreasonable action. Each leader will look into the case at once, calling upon the older and most respected members of each kinship group. Eventually the two pangngats involved in the case will meet. In such a meeting the highest qualities of diplomacy are exercised. Each regional leader is careful not to offend or arouse the ire of the other and the use of personal compliments is profuse. Preliminaries may take several days. In the meantime, some regional festival, such as a wedding, a sickness rite, or a funeral will have taken place. Each of the leaders involved will have had an opportunity to discuss the case, listening attentively to the opinion of other leaders. On the basis of such discussions and on precedent from other cases an "amicable settlement" will be made.

Probably in no case involving a dispute does one of the kinship groups get off scot free. Each group pays, even though it may be simply a *molta*. (A molta is a kind of token payment to defray the expenses of a feast or to provide wine or a pig.) The feast itself is celebrated to bring together the principles of the dispute and their kinship groups, along with the regional leaders.

Interregional contact of influential local leaders is brought about in peace-pact meetings. On these occasions, such leaders from each region lounge together with their compatriots in one area of the assemblage. Occasionally one or more of these men may circulate about the throng, greeting and shaking hands with acquaintances. But when the discussion gets underway, influential leaders address the people from the area where their co-regionists have assembled. A few chairs are placed in an area most favorable for listening to the discussion and for watching the dances that provide a periodic and pleasant interruption to the discussion. These chairs are for the visiting peace-pact holder, one or two influential pangngats from neutral regions not represented among the pangngats of the two principal regions, and a few non-Kalinga visitors. The latter comprise local school teachers, perhaps a lowland Filipino official, and on rare occasions an especially appreciated visitor — an American.

Peace-pact meetings give an opportunity for regional leaders to employ their most eloquent and flowery speeches. What goes on in these gatherings has important repercussions in the home region. If the representatives of a region defend their cases forcibly and win concessions, the home region is gratified. The regional pangngats who have comported themselves favorably add to their status at home. Such recognition is not always restricted to seasoned regional leaders, however. A young man who has not previously distinguished himself may make an impressive speech which is instrumental in placing his home region in favorable circumstances. The news travels home and his region becomes aware of a potential leader. Thus peace-pact meetings, like regional festivals, help to elevate the status of individuals who speak up.

Since peace-pact meetings are broadly interregional, including people from regions other than the two principal ones involved, the performance of regional leaders registers widely. In recent years, as Kalinga have entered modern Philippine politics, these meetings have become extremely important as campaigning arenas. Kalinga candidates for municipal and provincial offices realize the importance of being present in such meetings. Anyone who wishes to speak may do so, and one does not have to restrict his speaking to the cases of the principal regions involved. Indeed, speakers tend to digress widely, for peace pacts clearly serve an entertainment function just as important as the avowed one of settling regional differences.

Regional leaders maintain a higher standard of living because of the aid that they have furnished or can potentially supply. Thus, an influential leader can request anyone in his hamlet or other hamlets over which his influence extends, to perform services for him. Such help is frequently demanded for a variety of tasks from simple errands to such complex and heavy work as the construction of a house. He does not pay for these services, except to provide food for the workers while they are engaged. In return, he himself is obligated to extend services whenever called upon. The service that he performs is of a different kind than that which he receives. His services consist primarily of dispensing legal advice and getting individuals and families out of trouble. It is important here to emphasize that the masses of a regional population are not "vassals" and the pangngats "lords." The services demanded by regional leaders and performed for them are of a sporadic and temporary nature. A regional leader realizes that to take all of the able-bodied individuals of a household or a hamlet at one time or even to use the services of one individual over an extended period of time would destroy the subsistence pattern of Kalinga society. Further, no one regional leader's economic resources are so bountiful that he can support more than his household for very long. It is also important to point out that all Kalinga value their personal independence and would rebel against long-term service for another. The *poyong* are sometimes called servants, but we have noted that such individuals are more like adopted children since they are entitled to a share of their master's property and that they have the same kinds of rights and privileges as other Kalinga. Thus the social and economic differences between a regional leader's family (or the families of the baknang class collectively) on the one hand, and the rest of the Kalinga population on the other, are not extreme. It would be a mistake to consider the Kalinga either as a feudal society or a society in which there is sharp difference between the wealthy and the poor.

The Kalinga had known about the municipal form of government existent among lowland Filipinos long before it was finally established in the Mountain Province during the American period. Thus, the Spanish designations for municipal officials such as *presidente* (president), *consejal* (councillor) and *teniente* (lieutenant governor) had already been current among the Kalinga. The early American lieutenant governors recognized the influence and importance of regional leaders and brought them into the orbit of governmental activities. Leaders with the most prestige and influence were given the title of "presidente" and paid a small salary. The presidentes proved invaluable to early American administrators. A diary (Wilson 1957) maintained by Walter F. Hale, first lieutenant governor of Kalinga, during 1909 and 1910, indicates the cooperative activities between himself and these regional leaders and reveals the respect and admiration he had for these men. Later, when the Kalinga Subprovince was divided into municipal districts, some of the more important regional leaders were appointed as municipal officials with Spanish designations. The title "presidente" was given to the municipal head, the seat of the government was called the presidencia, and the region or barrio where municipal headquarters was established became known as the *población*. Other native leaders were given positions as vice-president and councillors *(consejal)*. The latter, located in the presidencia, represented the different areas of the municipality or barrio and corresponded to the traditional Kalinga regions. In addition, the regions or barrios had an official designated as the barrio lieutenant (teniente). The barrio lieutenant had direct contact with the settlements and presented the problems of the latter to the presidencia through the councillors. Some of the larger towns or hamlets of the region or barrio also appointed vice lieutenants. The chain of command thus pyramided upwards from vice-lieutenants, barrio lieutenants, through councillors to the presidente and from thence to the seat of the provincial government in Bontoc. The only non-Kalinga in the municipal government and until recently the only literate official was the secretary-treasurer. The latter was appointed by the provincial governor and was usually an Ilocano.

While the native municipal officials in other areas of the Mountain Province were apparently figureheads controlled by more powerful leaders behind the scenes (*see* Keesing 1934:109–110), this does not appear to have been the case in Kalinga. Former municipal officials were members of the baknang class and were often pangngats. They are respectfully addressed as *pasado* (from Spanish "past," hence former municipal office holders).

The municipal officials have remained substantially as they were in the latter part of the American period. At present, all of the municipal officials except the secretary-treasurer are elected. The latter is still appointed by the provincial governor although at present he is usually a Kalinga. Literacy is now a requirement for all municipal positions, a factor which has eliminated a few older pangngats from municipal offices. The drive for education, however, is so strong that virtually all influential individuals at present are literate, speaking and writing English with great fluency and having a good speaking knowledge of Ilocano as well. The barrios themselves have also formed councils with the barrio lieutenant as the presiding official, vice-lieutenants as councillors, and a secretary-treasurer who is in charge of barrio funds and records the minutes of meetings. (*See* Appendix for a list of the 1960 officials of Balbalan Municipality and the barrio of Mabaca.)

The subprovince of Kalinga contains the bulk of Kalinga population, but there are substantial numbers in areas adjacent. In Madukayan, a barrio of the municipal district of Natonin, Bontoc, live a group of Kalinga migrants from the Tanudan valley (Kalinga Subprovince) with a population of 359 reported in the 1948 Philippine census (Scott 1958a: 318–319). These Kalinga moved into the area at least as early as 1900. Elsewhere Kalinga migrants have in more recent years established residences in Apayao and the Cagayan Valley (Cagayan Province). Others live on a less permanent basis, usually as wage workers, in Baguio and in mining communities in the southern part of the Mountain Province.

The Kalinga have a mania for organization — school teachers organize elementary school children into all kinds of work and study committees, and the region sponsoring a peace-pact celebration has committees for a variety of tasks including entertainment, butchering, and clean-up. These committees all have chairmen who must make verbal and usually written reports of their work and the funds expended. There are also a number of clubs for both men and women. One of the most surprising experiences for non-Kalinga visitors to the regions of Mabaca is to see at the end of a long and arduous hike over precipitous mountain trails a sign at the isolated house of Lino Taway: *Mabaca Women's Club — Mrs. Lino Taway, President.* At Limos (Pinokpok District) I was asked to photograph the members of a similar women's club who all posed in bright native Kalinga costumes. The president of the club gave me a

Attractive young presidents of woman's clubs are not a Western prerogative, as demonstrated by Petra Gupa-al, head officer of the Limos Woman's Club, northern Kalinga.

written account of the club's activities and asked me to submit it along with the photograph to one of the Baguio newspapers for publication.

The drive for organization among the Kalinga may have its roots in the ambitions of warriors and pangngats to exhibit influence and power. Every organization, whether a temporary committee or a permanent club, has a leader who delights in planning programs and assigning tasks. There is, however, no record of organizations as such in the past; tasks which needed to be performed were accomplished by the kinship group, either by households or larger segments of the kindred. Non-kinship organizations such as associations or sodalities of a more formal and enduring type, were absent in traditional Kalinga culture. The mediums were and are independent curers and religious practitioners without organization. There were no organizations for occupations such as blacksmithing, pottery making, or basket weaving. Why then the sudden urge for organization? My guess is that the suppression of headhunting left unfulfilled the Kalinga's need to express leadership. The lieutenant-governors early in the century and later the school teachers — all Americans — were themselves organization minded and undoubtedly helped to reinforce the urge for organization. Thus organizations permitting expression to individual leadership qualities are partial answers to the need of Kalinga individuals to bring attention upon themselves. Another avenue of individual expression is political participation, which is discussed more fully in the concluding chapter.

Notes to Chapter 2

1. The problem of territorial expansion and warfare among swidden farmers has been recently elucidated by Vayda (1961:346–358).
2. Compare, for example, the settlements in the Lubuagan region. Mabilong, one of Lubuagan's fifteen towns, has 254 houses and a population of 1,248 (Table 3, page 15).
3. The term "family" without qualification designates the nuclear family.
4. In Lubuagan, *obog* has taken on a specialized meaning as "the habitual sleeping place of boys"; elsewhere among the Kalinga, obog simply refers to a sleeping mat.
5. The kinship circle or kindred of the Lubuagan Kalinga is more narrowly defined *(see* below).
6. See Goodenough (1955) for a distinction between bilateral kin groups of the type surrounding any particular individual or sibling group (our "kinship circle" or "kindred") from the type consisting of a group of relatives descended from a common ancestor (our "descent group").
7. For a recent classification of kin groups with specific reference to bilateral societies see Murdock 1960:1–14. cf. Coult 1964, Davenport 1959, Firth 1957, Goodenough 1961.
8. The initiator of a peace pact and his/her descendants may also be considered a descent group, but enforcing the pact is the obligation of a pact-holder and his/her kinship circle or kindred.
9. That is, for the Kalinga, it may well be that formerly in the area of Benguet and Bontoc subprovince descent groups were associated with societies practicing the cultivation of root crops in swiddens.
10. After reading this paragraph, Professor Eggan commented that the Northern Kalinga achieve discrete groups by endogamy and control of swidden territory, hence structurally these groups are equivalent in some ways to descent groups. Goodenough (1955:81–82) suggests an association of a descent group with

land tenure in early Malayo-Polynesian society. This suggestion has been challenged by Frake (1956:170–172) who offers a suggestion similar to the one proposed in this chapter, that private ownership of land and functionally associated kin groups developed among those Malayo-Polynesian groups who adopted wet rice cultivation or who found themselves on islands where the amount of cultivable land was limited. See reply by Goodenough (1956:173–175) who accepts Frake's suggestion in part, but concludes that under some conditions swidden farming might exert pressure for private ownership of land. In support of this belief Goodenough points to his own field work among the Nakanai of New Britain Island in Melanesia, a group which jealously guards its *"title* to swidden lands, even though [the group] is happy to have others use them."

11. Parents occasionally arrange marriages between their children who are second cousins, apparently in order to keep valuable property in the control of the kinship group. One of my informants in Lubuagan was contracted to his second cousin, but he broke the engagement because he wanted to continue his college studies in Baguio.

12. Lubuagan informants report that this terminological usage also characterizes the Kalinga regions in Tinglayan and Tanudan municipal districts, but I have not recorded kinship data personally from these areas.

13. Barton (1949:167–168) believes that the Kalinga peace-pact institution developed out of the *aboyog*.

14. With the possible exception of the Poswoy region; here, after a curing rite for a married couple (sabblay), the inhabitants of the hamlet in which the couple live are supposed to observe a "rest day" *(see* below).

15. The term *ngilin* also refers to the time when restrictions are observed and may be applied to the ceremony when such restrictions are lifted *(see* below). The Ibaloy (Leaño 1958:84) and Sagada (informants' statements) also use the word ngilin in this meaning.

16. The Ibaloy of Benguet believe that sour fruits are harmful to pregnant and menstruating women. "It is believed that [eating sour foods] would clot the blood and prevent its flow" (Leaño, 1958:57).

17. Our information on birth and observances taken during the first months of a child's life is most complete for the region of Poswoy, but similar practices were reported for Lubuagan.

18. The initial morph, *mang* or *man* means "maker" or "performer." Thus *mandadwak* means the maker or performer of the ceremony *dawak*. The extra *da* is a common Kalinga feature of reduplication in derived words.

19. Efforts were made as early as 1927 to outlaw boasting about war exploits in public gatherings. In that year several *presidentes* of Kalinga and northern Bontoc (now also part of the Kalinga Subprovince), themselves famous warriors, incorporated into law regulations which forbid the practice of certain customs and the use of certain words bound up with headhunting, the taunting of youths because they have not yet killed, and the boasting of war exploits both informally and ceremonially (ordinances of the Provincial Board, No. 41, 1927). These regulations are generally ignored, however, yet the importance of these boasting sessions has diminished because headhunting and killings have become unpopular as a means of achieving distinction and status.

20. Cf. Keesing 1949:594–598.

3. | Agriculture, Property Ownership, and Inheritance

AGRICULTURE associated with rice, whether wet or dry, is the most important single economic activity of the North and South Kalinga at present. The Kalinga do not subsist entirely on a rice diet, however; meat from livestock and hunting and vegetables and fruits are all important subsidiary foods.

While swidden farming is undoubtedly old, irrigated rice farming appears to be new. Older inhabitants of the Lubuagan region readily admit that rice paddies are recent in the area; and among the Kalinga of the Saltan and Mabaca River valleys, rice terraces were introduced in the memory of living men. Indeed, rice fields are still being newly constructed everywhere in the Kalinga area. Significantly, the Kalinga usually employ Bontoc or Kalinga farmers from the upper Chico to construct their rice fields, pointing to the source of this method of growing rice. Further evidence for the recency of wet rice among the Kalinga is the paucity of ritualistic activity associated with irrigated rice farming. We shall see in the chapter on religion that most of the religious observances associated with farming are in connection with the cultivation of upland rice.

Minor Economic Activities

The Kalinga engage in a number of minor economic pursuits besides agriculture. These activities are known to all so that they cannot be considered occupational specialties, even though some families may pursue a particular one such as weaving or blacksmithing or pottery-making more zealously than others. There is also a tendency for some of these minor industries to be distributed areally, yet full-time specialization in

Irrigated terraces are well established in the Lubuagan (southern Kalinga) rice fields.

one industry does not characterize one group of Kalinga over another or even one family over others in the same region.

The Northern Kalinga, particularly of the Banao region, are well known for excellent manufacture of spears and headaxes which other mountain peoples trade for or buy from the Banao people.

Iron for spears, knives, headaxes, and farming tools is obtained from other items traded into the area. In the past such tools were made from old Chinese cast-iron kettles which had been damaged and could no longer be used for their original purposes. At present, iron from American materials, particularly from discarded automobile springs, is used for making steel implements. Smithing procedures are well developed. Bellows of either bamboo cylinders or stovepipe flumes, a wooden box, and carabao hide provide a forced draft to produce the high temperatures needed to forge iron into steel implements. Soot is worked into the iron by pounding alternately with a stone hammer or another stone, or a steel anvil, and then plunging the material into water. Virtually all Kalinga areas have some knowledge of smithing, but the northern Kalinga area is especially well known for the development of this industry. Blacksmithing is an exclusively male industry among the Kalinga.

Bark cloth is used for blankets, short jackets for men and women, the woman's wraparound skirt, and for wrapping babies. It is made from the bark of a tree called *sopot* in north Kalinga dialects.[1] The sopot tree, a species of mulberry, is planted purposely for making cloth, and it grows rapidly. The trunk of a young sopot tree, approximately three to four inches in girth and four to six feet high, will produce a piece of rectangular cloth four by six feet. The bark of the tree is removed and pounded on a

Presenting distinct contrast is this example of terracing started only recently, in the Salegseg region of northern Kalinga.

board until the desired size is achieved. The cloth is then dyed, either yellow, with a plant dye called *lagtang,* or red, with the seeds of a plant called *anosi* or *kanosi.*

Cotton garments are no longer woven by the Northern Kalinga; it has been found easier to buy clothes from the Southern Kalinga or from Ilocano traders. Indeed, as early as 1885, Schadenberg (1889) reported little weaving in the northern Kalinga areas. In the south, Kalinga women still do considerable weaving and supply themselves as well as other Kalinga with cotton cloth. The piece of cloth woven is about ten inches wide; a single piece about ten feet in length serves as a gee string, while the usual *ka-in* or wraparound skirt, is made in a rectangular piece with three such widths sewn together. Blankets are made simply from more pieces of regulation width, sewn together. Weaving is done on a simple backloom which appears to be the same type everywhere in the Mountain Province. Kalinga weaving is rather coarse and does not wear well. It does not compare favorably with Bontoc or Sagada weaving. While the same kind of cotton yarn of Ilocano manufacture is used, the weaving of the latter peoples is much tighter and the garments have a more lasting quality.

Pottery is also made in virtually all Kalinga settlements. It is made from a grayish clay, moulded by hand, dried for two or three days, and

Women of southern Kalinga still use the backloom to weave cotton cloth for their families and for trade. The Northern Kalinga buy cloth or garments from the Southern Kalinga or Ilocano traders.

then fired in an atmosphere of free oxygen. The finished product is reddish black in color. Small pottery jars stacked one on top of another to as many as five or six pots high on the tops of women's heads are a characteristic sight in a Kalinga village. Ordinarily water is transported in such jars, but occasionally also soups and other liquids.

Baskets and other carrying devices are made throughout the Kalinga area. The Mabaca region is especially well known for excellent baskets of all sizes for transporting and for winnowing rice. The carrying packs — *pasiking* — are made in several different sizes. They are used mainly by the men since ordinarily the women transport loads in baskets carried on the head. Materials used for baskets are rattans, *owoy,* and other vines and grasses known as *gapak, balneto* and *owoygayang.* One or more of these materials is also intricately woven in plaits to form various types of containers and carrying devices.

Other items of Kalinga manufacture and use consist of the sugar cane press — *kalay.* The gears or grinders are made from a hardwood tree called *gasatan* (described in Scott 1958:326). Other items: raincoat of palm leaves sewn together — usually of two types: 1) *ana-ao,* large leaves of palm; and 2) *linas,* smaller and thinner leaves of palm. Brooms called *tabagan* or *talagadaw* are made from a grass called *bananito* (Sp. *bayoneta (bayonet)*) while the bindings are of colored rattan. The *buyo* bag for carrying betel nut, tobacco, and other accessory items is made from red cloth bought in Chinese stores. The ends of the bag are tied to a cloth strap hung around the neck, each end is decorated with many rings called *sikalang,* made from melted coins. The bag itself is called *pangyu* or *tayay*. A kind of tub is made from carabao skin — rawhide. Palay is placed on this and threshed, before pounding in the stone mortars.

Shields are called *kalasag* and are made from either the *sablang* tree (a tree with beautiful red blossoms which bloom in March), the *dapdap* tree, or the *polay* tree. These woods are light, yet do not often crack when dry. Sablang was preferred for shields actually used in tribal wars in the past, as it is most resistant to splitting. The other woods are used to make shields to be used for training young warriors. Two types of shields have been noted — a long one with three rather high prongs tapering down to two prongs; and the other not tapering, with shorter prongs and smaller as a whole. The first type is usually blackened, or, rather, smoked, to harden the wood and undecorated. The other is painted, usually orange, and decorated with intricate black designs. Both types are stitched with rattan just before the beginning of the prongs in order to strengthen the prongs. There is a swelling or protrusion at the center to protect the fingers that grip the shield.

Water and soup or other liquids are ordinarily carried by the women in small pottery jars stacked high on their heads, a system leaving the hands free for livelier young burdens.

Headaxes are of two types — a narrow type, called the *sinawit* which is the one most generally thought by the Kalinga to be a headaxe; and a second type, more squat in size, used as a working tool for clearing swiddens and for other tasks — *gaman.*

The bolo (English?, Kalinga *badang*) now commonly carried by Northern Kalinga and other mountain peoples is generally agreed to be of recent introduction. Some Kalinga believe that it was introduced at the beginning of the American occupation about 1900. The Kalinga report that the headaxe is a more handy tool, especially since the pointed end, or "ear," is useful in helping to ascend slippery paths, and is more versatile in farming and everyday tasks. Spears *(sangay* or *tubay)* are of many types and are essentially similar among all Mountain Province peoples. The Kalinga prefer the more simple type with small tangs.

Perhaps the most characteristic possessions of the Kalinga are the highly prized heirloom jars, plates, and beads made of agate and porcelain. These possessions have been handed down from generation to generation, sometimes for as long as four hundred years. They were originally obtained from Chinese traders, either directly or through Ilocano traders. Kalinga generally call heirloom beads *onggoong;* jars are called *gosi;* and plates, *maokong.* Most common types of agate beads are ranked into three: *masilap* (most valuable), *abali* (next in value), and *kinawayan* (lowest in value).

Hunting

Hunting is an important occupation among the Northern Kalinga. Wild pigs, deer, and wild chickens, as well as a number of different kinds of birds, are plentiful.

Wild pigs and deer are hunted with dogs. The dogs are especially trained for hunting, and at least four different breeds are recognized. Of the male dogs, breeds called *basiwal, sawal,* and *lomangday* are considered best; of the female, breeds known as *bayangyang* and *sobat* make the best hunters. While these breeds are considered good hunting dogs, a hunter examines the nipples of an individual animal to determine whether it is a good hunter. Well-separated nipples are recognized as signs of a good dog. Several dogs are used, and it is good to mix up the breeds in a hunt. When dogs smell the odor of wild pig or deer they bark and eventually track down the hunted creature and corner it against a cliff or a brook.

The spear is used in hunting with dogs. The dry season is best for this kind of hunting because when the forests are not wet, it is easier for the dogs to follow the scent. Also the dry season is a time of relative leisure; rice fields have been planted, and the growth on swiddens has been cut and dried before burning. Although high-powered rifles are prohibited by law, many Kalinga now have them. Hunting by rifle is done at any time and without the use of dogs.

Formerly all hunters observed traditional omens religiously, but at present, such observance is not frequent. Before going on a hunt, a hunter must listen to the *idaw,* or omen calls. While idaw is believed to refer specifically to a small reddish bird slightly larger than an English sparrow, in general it refers to calls or sounds made by a number of different birds or fowl. Some of these omen birds are: *Sikot, kolipag, balniban,* and the wild chicken, *agitalon* (northern Kalinga dialects). If the sound of the idaw (any general omen bird-sound) comes from the left side (or if the bird itself flies from the left side) this is considered a bad omen, and the hunter must postpone his trip for a day or so. If the sound comes from the right side, or if the bird itself comes flying across the hunter's path from the right side, this is a good sign, and the hunter may proceed with confidence that he will have a successful trip. It is said that some hunters may play a trick on the omens; that is, even if the sound comes from the left, they may circle around so that the sound comes from the right!

Other omens foretelling good or bad luck in hunting are the following. In Mabaca if you dream of rice cake mixed with coconut oil or if you dream of drinking wine then you will catch a fat wild pig. Generally in the north, dreaming of a dead person is considered to be a sign of good luck in hunting. If you or a companion sneezes while hunting, stop for a few minutes before proceeding on the hunt; if the sneezing continues for some time, postpone the hunting until the next day. A complete rainbow is a good sign, but not an incomplete one. Falling rocks or a landslide *(dapo-og)* is an evil omen; postpone hunting for at least a day. A snake *(olog)* seen when departing for a hunting trip is bad; postpone the trip.

Wild pigs *(baboy)* are always black, they are smaller than tame ones and the meat is considered to be better than that of domestic pigs. The snout is longer in the wild pig and tusks are huge. The deer *(ogsa)* of the Mountain Province is uniformly the same, a small animal slightly larger than a goat when fully grown.

The following birds are hunted or trapped for food: *Kalaw,* a bird with a large horn-like bill; *tiktik,* a kind of grouse; *balog,* a big fowl like a chicken; *balniban,* a kind of dove or pigeon; *sagola,* a bird the size of a domestic pigeon, white or gray in color; *agitalon,* a wild chicken, like a domestic one but gone wild; *ot-ot,* a kind of dove with a red bill.

Traps are used for catching wild pig, deer, and the birds above. Traps are rather intricate and will not be described here. In order to insure that traps catch their prey, the following rituals are observed. When the traps are set, the trapper returns to his house and prohibits anyone not of the immediate family from entering the house. Knotted runos, *pordos* or *poldos,* are placed on the door indicating that entrance into the house is prohibited. The prohibition follows the general pattern observed when the house is closed to visitors at the time of a birth, or when rice grown in swiddens is being harvested.

A man who has set out traps is prohibited from eating taro *(lidoy)* leaves until he has removed the traps.

The following are considered amulets or good luck charms for the hunter: lemon fruits, *dilayan;* rattan vines, *sang-o;* teeth of crocodile, *sa-ong;* a kind of ginger, *dotol.* Carrying one of these items on one's person is believed to reward the hunter with success.

Supplementary Foods

Rattan shoots, *pa-it,* young fern shoots, *latong,* water lily roots, *pikaw,* water cress, *kris,* are among the principal wild vegetables eaten. A variety of wild fruits such as guavas, *iba, boyoba,* wild "yams," *obi,* and a red fruit, *pinit,* are also popular. An extremely hot pepper called *sili* (Mexican Spanish, *chile*) is popular with the Kalinga, particularly in the north, as a seasoning for foods. Every Kalinga village or hamlet has groves of coconuts, and the coconut palm always marks the site of a settlement. Fresh coconut is a favorite in-between-meal food and is mixed with diket rice cakes.

Camotes, taro, Indian corn, and sugar cane are grown in swiddens, usually after the first or second planting of rice. Sugar cane stalks are eaten as candy and the fresh juice is used to sweeten coffee and other foods. The most important use of sugar cane juice and the reason for which it is principally grown is for *basi* (Ilocano), or *bayas* (Lubuagan Kalinga dialect), a kind of wine. While old wine, that is, wine a year old and older, is preferred, the need for wine in ceremonies and festivities is so demanding that basi of only one month or at most three months old is most commonly used. Kalinga wine, except the rare aged variety, is extremely sweet. The wine is stored in the large heirloom Chinese jars.

Taro roots and leaves are important foods, but they are forbidden under certain circumstances. Thus, for example, a pregnant woman must not eat gabi leaves, nor must a man who has laid out traps. In Lubuagan, the man who performs the circumcision operation must refrain from eating gabi roots or leaves.

A variety of small fish and mussels are caught in small brooks in basket traps. In larger rivers (such as the Saltan, Mabaca and Chico) the *palilong,* a sucker type of fish, which is a favorite with all Kalinga is caught. It is four to six inches long and is boiled without cleaning. The water in which the fish are boiled is relished as a broth. Also caught in these larger rivers is a squat fish about one to one and a half feet long, called *ikan*. Palilong and ikan are caught with a small hook tied usually to the end of an umbrella rib. Boys and men dive into the water or immerse their heads and upon seeing a school of these fish simply hook them by making quick runs of the hook through the school of fish.

Eels are also speared in the larger rivers. These were tabooed food to the Kalinga until recently and are still avoided by the medium. The eating of eel as well as dog is considered to have been learned from peoples to the south. Both are considered real delicacies at present.

The betel nut preparation popular among the Kalinga is called *boyo* or *moma*. The ingredients of boyo are as follows: the betel nut — *bowa* (the nut of the areca palm) lime — *opol* (this is the shell taken from river beds and burned into a fine, powdery ash), and the piper leaf — *lawod*.

Betel nut is prepared for chewing as follows: the nut is split into four pieces; lime is spread on a piper leaf and the leaf and lime are wrapped around the nut and the preparation is then ready for chewing.

Coffee was introduced during the initial American period and is now extremely important. All hamlets have groves of coffee trees and coffee is served to visitors and guests at feasts.

Tobacco is grown by all Kalinga. It is chewed or smoked in long cigars by both sexes; even ten-year old children smoke or chew.

Sweet potatoes and root crops are not as important in the diet of the Kalinga as among the Bontocs, Kankanay, and Ibaloy in the southern part of the Mountain Province. The diet of the Kalinga, particularly in the north, is more diversified. A meal usually contains rice, but in addition at least three or more other types of food mentioned in this section are served.

The Cultivation of Rice

The Kalinga are, above all, growers of rice and the larger part of their economic activity is involved with rice. Potentially the northern Kalinga country would be a fairly rich area if its water resources were developed, as they can be by constructing irrigation canals. On the lower Saltan River area the valley widens out and there is much level land although at present rice is grown almost solely in swiddens. If irrigation canals are constructed from upriver, a task which does not seem to be formindable, much land can be made to produce large quantities of rice. At present, swidden farming is not very effective, and the rice yield is low in most of the area.

Both the Northern and Southern Kalinga raise two crops of rice in irrigated terraces, *payaw*. The seeds of the first crop, a large-grained rice

The pounding mortar, the rice bowl and the carabao hide, where the un-threshed rice is kept, are all part of the vital preparation of rice after harvest. This major item of woman's work is shared by old and young.

called *oloy* or *onoy,* are planted in special plots in the fields in early December. *Daykot* or *dikit,* a glutinous rice made into cakes on cere-monial and festive occasions, is planted at the same time in the fields but in smaller portions. Early in January the seedlings of onoy and dikit are transplanted. With two weedings and constant observation to see that the water is continually flowing in the rice paddies, they are ready for harvesting in late June or early July.

The second crop is called *oyak.* The seeds of this crop are planted in June in gardens near houses (*payotok,* Lubuagan; *pinal,* northern Kalinga, "planting seeds in gardens"), and the seedlings are transplanted in the fields in July. With one or two weedings they are harvested in December.

Onoy and dikit seeds are planted in the rice fields since they require plenty of water. For swidden farming, onoy and oyak need not be started in special plots since they are planted at the beginning of the rainy season and thus grow well.

Swiddens are planted in May at the beginning of the rainy season, and the rice harvested, with usually only one weeding, in November and December. The same varieties of rice are grown on swiddens and rice paddies, that is, onoy, oyak, and dikit. Apparently onoy is the oldest form of rice known to the Kalinga, since most of the ritual devoted to rice cultivation is associated with this particular type of rice.

Importance of Rice

The importance of rice in the lives of the Kalinga should not be minimized. A discussion of the activities engaged in during the year always highlights work associated with the cultivation of rice and particularly with cultivation in swiddens. In the yearly round of Kalinga activities presented below, Kalinga "months" can be seen to differ from region to region both in the designations used and the time period they cover. The list presented here was compiled from the reports of the residents of the hamlet of Bolo, Salegseg region (northern Kalinga).

SEASONAL ACTIVITY

Time of year	Name of equivalent "month" and seasonal characteristics	Primary activity
January	*Loya* "ground is muddy"	Transplant the first crop, *onóy*
February	*Opók* "warming oneself"	Selection of swidden sites.
March	*Kiyáng* "waters get low, can walk across rivers"	Cutting growth in swiddens, hunting.
April	*Ladáw* "blooming of the ladaw tree"	Débris in swiddens permitted to dry; hunting and peace-pact celebrations.
May	*Kitkití* "time for burning swiddens"	Burning of swiddens; hunting and peace-pact celebrations.
June	*Panabá* "time to plant swiddens"	Planting time for swiddens; harvest of onóy in fields; prepare second crop, oyák.
July	*Adáwoy* "blooming of a tree called adáwoy."	Transplanting seedlings of oyák.
August	*Akál* "height of rainy season"	Weeding in rice fields and swiddens.
September	*Mamagitóng* "typhoon time"	Leisure before harvest and trading time.
October	*Walo* "time of hail"	Trading time.
November	*Pobokáo* "windy time"	Start harvesting swiddens and second crop, oyák.
December	*Kíling* "harvest time"	Harvest completed; Onóy seeds are planted in special plots in the rice field.

A thirteenth month is recognized in some parts of Kalinga. In Poswoy it is simply referred to as a division or interim period, *soldak*. Apparently this "month" is used to make the correction necessary in any annual calendar system based on lunar months. Soldak in Poswoy is fitted in between December and January, that is, between the "months" of Kíling and Lóya.

Daily activities, aside from working in the swiddens and rice fields, also emphasize the importance of rice in the life of the Kalinga. At any time during the day, women may be seen threshing, winnowing, and pounding rice while men are transporting rice on the balanced pole from distant granaries.

The Cultivation of Dry Rice

Rice grown on swiddens — (oma). The techniques of growing rice in swiddens are discussed with reference primarily to the Northern Kalinga, but significant differences are mentioned which appeared in the course of field work between the southern and northern Kalinga swidden cultivation.

The initial task of clearing and preparing the swidden is called *tolba*. The work unit in clearing and preparing a swidden is the extended household (*see* section on social organization) although other close relatives and those living in the same hamlet may also give assistance. The work group varies from about ten to thirty adults of both sexes.

Before clearing starts, however, the plot must be selected and certain rituals observed regarding its actual use.

In selecting a plot, primary attention is given to soil conditions and the nature of the cover vegetation. Generally a plot must have lain fallow for six or seven years, but soil conditions and the vegetation may either shorten or lengthen this period. Thus, an area grown over with *cogon* and *ak-aki* grasses is not considered a suitable plot in which to make an *oma*. Tree forest is best and bamboo is also good. Generally a woody forest is considered good because it will burn quickly and produce the ashes which are thought to enrich the soil. Gravel is an indication of poor soil, although a number of large boulders in a field is not considered to affect the fertility of the soil. Generally a dark or black soil is preferred.

Once a plot is selected, the man who is to cultivate it goes alone to the spot. He listens to the *idaw*. He takes along bamboo stalk-clappers *(pantangkog)* to inspire favorable bird sounds and to repel bad or unfavorable ones. The belief is that the omen birds listen to the pantangkog and will respond favorably. Practical and doubting Kalinga say it is to "drown" unfavorable sounds! In Lubuagan, finding a bird's nest in the forest which

The implements needed for constructing and planting a swidden (plot), are simple and basic, and include the axe that was traditionally used in headhunting.

is to be made into a swidden is a bad omen. Throughout the Kalinga area earthquakes generally are bad omens, and the worker must return and try his luck at a later day.

If all omens are favorable, the man works for only about an hour, just cuts a little grass, and then goes home to come again after three days with some helpers. Helpers include his extended family and also others from the hamlet in which he lives. Only three types of tools are employed for cutting brush, felling trees, and preparing the field for burning. These are the long-handled axe *(wasay)*, the squat type headaxe *(gaman)*, and the bolo.

Generally about two or three hectares a season are cleared by northern Kalinga dry rice farmers. The amount of time it takes to clear a plot this size, of course, depends on the size of the labor force and the nature and extensiveness of the vegetation cover. Generally, however, the cutting and slashing *(manggoma)* go fast, and usually a swidden of two or three hectares is cleared in one to three days. Extremely big trees, particularly of hardwood like the *kalay* tree, are ringed and left to die. Kalay is a hardwood tree from which rice mortars and pestles are made.

After the plot has been cut, the man who is to cultivate it leaves a tied runo to indicate that this is his field. The plot is then left to dry *(malango)* for about a month. Cutting of the vegetation growth, that is, the initial preparations *(tolba)*, takes place in late March or April. During late April and most of May the plot is drying; in late May, just before the rains begin, it is burned *(sogob)*.

Cleaning *(malasang)* takes about four to seven days after burning. The tools used for this purpose are: 1) long-handled axe; 2) headaxe; 3) grub hoe *(landok)*; 4) bolo, and 5) carrying baskets *(balokó)* used by the women. Two or three days after cleaning, the swidden is ready for planting.

Planting is called *manósok,* and is done with a pointed stick about three feet high and about one and a half inches in diameter *(gadang),* and a bamboo container for seeds about two feet long and about two inches in diameter, pointed at the end *(kolong).*

In the Lubuagan region old men begin the planting; in northern Kalinga generally, old women start planting with a prayer. Among Northern Kalinga two methods of planting are employed in the swidden: In the first method, men drill holes with the digging stick and women follow with the bamboo seed container, dropping the rice seeds into the holes (about two to three inches deep). In the second method, both men and women drill the holes and plant. The second method is reportedly used when the swidden is steep and hence, the first method cannot be used conveniently.

Planting a swidden of two or three hectares is usually accomplished in one day.

After rice (mixed with millet — *sagob*) is planted in the swidden, climbing beans *(antak* or *longa)* are planted. Along the edges where trees have been left standing (i.e., not burned off) in the swidden, another variety of a climbing bean *(kolda)* is planted. In between rows of rice a kind of pea *(koldis)* is planted with plants about four feet apart because this plant is a woody shrub and needs space. Around large boulders watermelon *(asimon)* is planted.

In the second or third year the swidden is planted with "mongo peas," *(balatong)* a small black or greenish pea which is extremely important to the Kalinga diet. Indian corn and sugar cane are also crops to be raised after the second or third year in the swidden.

At the end of planting onoy (not oyak) in the swidden, an old or mature woman, but not necessarily a medium, smooths the soil at the end where the last seeds were planted and recites a prayer. This ritual is called *kopilopit,* "closing the evil." This is a practice of the Northern Kalinga; it has not been observed or reported for the Lubuagan region.

After the seeds have been planted, if the swidden is near a pasture where carabaos graze, it will be fenced with bamboo. Otherwise, a flimsy token fencing of bamboo or runo stalks called *bakóko* will be constructed. This is believed to keep wild pigs out of the swidden.

Only one weeding is performed in the swidden, *mambolat* (in rice fields weeding is called *mangga–at*). The only tool used is the grub hoe. Weeding is done only by women. Rice in the swidden is harvested in November and December. The swidden is visited (*mambiling*) periodically, however, to determine that rice is coming out well and that wild pigs or insects are not bothering it. Shortly after the rice begins to grow, a shelter *(sigay)* is erected. This is a hut in which to rest or sleep if the swidden must be guarded against wild pigs.

All Kalinga areas growing the variety of rice called onoy have a ceremony when the plants in the swidden do not germinate properly. In Mabaca this ceremony is called *salipit,* in Poswoy, *mampisik.* Despite differences in detail there is an over-all similarity in ritualistic observances in all Kalinga areas where dry rice is grown. The ceremony is performed by a medium who sacrifices chickens or a small pig, offers rice cakes, and chants the prayers appropriate for the ceremony. The heads of the chickens and the head of the pig sacrificed to "make rice grow" are left in the field with the heads pointing upwards.

It is difficult to obtain information about the gods to whom prayers are offered. Poswoy informants recognize a god or goddess of rice called *Daladaw* (they are not sure of the sex although they are inclined to believe that it is male). One informant believes that generally all prayers in connection with rice cultivation are offered to: 1) the departed spirits of grandparents, and 2) to a vaguely defined god Daladaw of the rice. In other areas of northern Kalinga, there was a belief in a "good" god or goddess that reigns over rice; but most thought it was simply *Kaboníyan,* the benevolent god of the Kalinga and other Mountain Province peoples. Kaboniyan is never invoked specifically, however, and he does not "punish"; but Daladaw in Poswoy and the god of rice elsewhere in Kalinga do inflict illness and keep rice from bearing if taboos are violated. The same informant who believed that prayers are addressed to the two categories above believed that there was a man and wife (god and goddess) who reigned over matters connected with the cultivation of rice.

Harvest of rice in the swidden is called *manáni* or *manámi* in northern

Kalinga dialects. Immediately before the harvest, men gather *anós* or *gapák,* a kind of bamboo fiber, for bundling *palay* (general Philippine word for mature stalks of rice). Old women gather ritualistic materials; for example, different species of fern leaves, *lamot,* especially varieties known as *itan, do–ot,* and *sokag,* and also get a special oiled stone, *batbato,* and a bamboo knife. All of these items are placed in a basket and an old medium sets it in the middle of the swidden. The immediate area around the basket is not harvested until the whole plot has been harvested. Prayers are said by the old medium as she places the basket in the middle of the swidden; they apparently are directed to the two categories of spirits as above.

In the northern Kalinga areas, a group of old women begin the harvest by taking four bundles of palay (one *iting).* It is interesting that in Lubuagan (and apparently in all regions south of the Pacil river) old men gather the initial four bundles of palay. (*See* also above where the old men plant first in Lubuagan, whereas planting in the northern Kalinga area is begun by old women.) As the women gather the four bundles they recite prayers, again to spirits of grandparents and also to the rice deity, according to Poswoy informants.

After the initial ritualistic gathering *(inapolan)* all the harvesters join in to help. No conversation, singing, whistling, shouting, or laughing is permitted until the plot is half-harvested. After this the harvesters may talk, and in Poswoy and also in other northern Kalinga areas the group sings the *gosombi,* "just to comfort everybody." Gosombi is an epic tale and recounts in song form the story of a valiant hero, *Gawan,* and a heroine, *Gamilayan.* Whistling and shouting are not permitted at any time during the harvest, in Poswoy it is said, "Daladaw will punish." Anyone carrying chickens must detour widely around the harvesting party, and visitors are not permitted in the houses of the harvesters. People not actually engaged in harvesting are also prohibited from entering the swidden while harvesting is in progress. There are also food restrictions on the harvesters: chicken, dog, carabao, and birds are not to be eaten, pork is the only meat permitted to the harvesters. Harvesters are also prohibited from cutting their hair and shaving during this period. These prohibitions are similar for the northern Kalinga regions and in Lubuagan.

After the harvest everybody is fed in a *palanos.* A palanos is a feast which is essentially social in character and the animals slaughtered for the occasion are not considered as sacrificial offerings. A harvest group, a work party, or the visit of friends are occasions for a palanos. It is a time when the host shows his generosity and exhibits his wealth by providing a lavish feast.

The only tool for harvesting is the harvest knife. This is a small metal knife with a straight blade called *oko*. The lowland type knife (Ilocano, *lakom),* with a small bow-shaped blade running at right angles to the handle is coming increasingly into use. The Northern Kalinga maintain, however, that any knife, even a pocket knife, will do as a harvest knife.

A good yield of rice in a swidden was given as fifty cavan per hectare. This appears to be rather high and may be a boosted figure in keeping with Kalinga pride. The figure is for onoy; the yield in the swidden is about half that of the first crop of onoy.

The palay is dried on an upright framework and in the shelter for approximately one week; then it is temporarily stored in the shelter. Soon after, it is tied neatly in bundles of four (one bundle is called a *botok;* four of these tied together are called *iting).* The bundles of palay are then stored in the granary.

When the rice has all been stored in the granary, a ceremony called variously *tolgad, olgad,* or *manaldak* in northern Kalinga dialects *(mamaltok,* Lubuagan) is performed by old women. These are any old women and not necessarily mediums, who know the prayers which are said on this occasion. Again prayers are made in general to the departed spirits of grandparents and also to the deity of the rice. Sometimes, as in Poswoy, the deity is specifically named (Daladaw); elsewhere it is thought of simply as Kaboniyan, although apparently the name is never mentioned. A pig is butchered, and the blood of the pig sprinkled on the granary hut.

It is interesting that in the Lubuagan region the ceremony in the rice granary when the rice has been stored is performed by old men. The old men are not mediums; they simply know the prayers. Chickens and pigs are sacrificed.

After the harvest ceremony in the rice granary, restrictions on visiting and food prohibitions are lifted, and the household functions normally again. Generally these restrictions do not last very long — planting is usually done in one day, harvesting may take three days at most, and storing the rice in the granary is only a day's work. The same may be said of restrictions at other times, such as those applying to the birth of a baby or those invoked when traps have been set out.

The Cultivation of Wet Rice

The irrigated rice field (payaw). The irrigated rice field receives little attention ritually among the Northern Kalinga. The Lubuagan region devotes greater ritualistic attention to rice grown in the irrigated terraces, but not nearly so much as the regions further south: Bangad, Sumadel, and Tinglayan. Ritualistic activities thus are most complex in the Kalinga regions closest to the area of elaborate irrigated rice terraces among the Bontoc and Ifugao. Progressing northward, ritualistic observances devoted to irrigated rice diminish until there is hardly any ceremonial activity associated with the practice in the northern regions. Conversely, there is a correlated increase of ritualistic attention given to rice grown in the swiddens. This phenomenon appears to demonstrate the recency of irrigated rice cultivation in the Kalinga area and also point to the source of this technique of farming. It is also clear from the greater ritualistic attention given to upland rice techniques that these have deep historical roots among the Kalinga.

In all areas of Kalinga, varieties of the first rice crop (onoy) grown in either the irrigated rice field or the swidden, involve greater ritualistic observances. Indeed, no specific rituals connected with oyak, the second crop grown in either the swidden or rice paddies, have been observed in northern Kalinga. Our information is not adequate for southern Kalinga agricultural practices to demonstrate whether this statement would hold rigidly there, but the casual questioning of southern Kalinga individuals indicates that the second crop, is not as important ritualistically as the first crop. The reason for this differential practice is not immediately apparent. One explanation is simply that the varieties of oyak may be new in the mountains and hence ritualistic observances have not been developed in connection with their cultivation.

Selection of a place in which to make a rice terrace involves careful reconnaissance. For the areas north of Bangad, the choice of a plot is usually made with a friend or a hired man from Sumadel, Bugnay, or from one of the Bontoc barrios. Northern Kalinga readily admit their own ignorance of places to make rice terraces and recognize the ability of Kalinga in southern regions and Bontocs to make good selections. The availability of water, i.e., the presence of a spring which flows permanently, is a primary consideration. Understandably, therefore, selection is made in the dry season, for at that time, many streams which run full at other times may become a small trickle or completely dry. Once a plot has been selected, the Kalinga make ritualistic observances almost identical with those made initially in the selection of a swidden site. The general pattern of ritualistic observances for making a new rice terrace (called boká) for both the northern Kalinga and the Lubuagan region is similar. The two areas differ only in that the Lubuagan Kalinga ritual observances are more detailed. In both areas a man alone goes to the plot playing the pantangkog, observing taboos, and listening, as previously outlined, to the sounds of the idaw for making a selection of a swidden plot. If the sounds are good, the man cuts a bit of the grass in the plot and returns home. In Lubuagan he comes back to the plot three days later with a chicken which he sacrifices on the spot. He then returns home, and after another three days, returns with a pig which he also sacrifices on the spot. After this he may bring helpers, both men and women, and work until the terrace is completed. Upon completion, both chickens and pigs are sacrificed and the blood sprinkled around the field. Afterwards there is a general feast *(palanos)* for everyone who has assisted in making the rice field.

The Northern Kalinga have simplified this pattern of ritualistic observance. After the initial observance of taboos and listening to the idaw, the Northern Kalinga man returns to the plot on the third day with workers, and works until the terrace is completed. Only when the terrace is completed are chickens and pigs sacrificed and blood sprinkled around the field as above. A palanos is also celebrated at the end for all the workers.

Undoubtedly much of the ritual associated with making a rice terrace among the Northern Kalinga is influenced if not completely borrowed from those Southern Kalinga and Bontoc men who construct or help make rice terraces. During the time that a rice terrace is being constructed, the Bontoc or Southern Kalinga helpers remain for several days working and living in the homes of their Northern Kalinga employers. There is opportunity at this time for much exchange of ceremonial information and since the workers come as technical experts, the ritualistic observances they suggest are considered a necessary part of the construction of rice terraces.

The tools used for making a rice terrace are the following: for the initial task, a long handled axe, a headaxe, a bolo, a crowbar *(salówang)*, a *kalóp* (a wooden flat board, used as a shovel), a hoe, and a carrying basket. Men and women work together, but most of the carrying-off of dirt is done by women.

In both Lubuagan and the northern Kalinga areas, there are prohibitions on visiting in the house at the time the seeds of onoy and diket are planted in seed beds. There is no comparable ceremony for the planting of oyak seeds in either the swidden or the gardens in June to be later transplanted in the rice field. Generally in all Kalinga areas the house members are prohibited from eating certain foods, particularly taro, eel, and dog.

Other than the ritualistic observances in making a rice field, and the food and visiting restrictions at the time of planting the first crop of rice, onoy, and diket, there are no other observances of a ritualistic nature associated with the growing of rice in rice terraces among the Northern Kalinga. The Kalinga generally, but particularly the Northern

Kalinga, handle irrigated rice cultivation very practically. In Lubuagan, however, food and visiting restrictions are repeated at the time of transplanting the onoy and diket, when the first crop of rice is harvested, and again when the rice is put into the granary.

The following ritualistic practices were observed in Lubuagan in connection with rice grown in the irrigated terraces. In the transplantation of rice (onoy and diket) the field supervisors, a woman medium and the women transplanters, appeared in the rice field for a few minutes on the initial day of planting. While the medium sacrificed chickens in the field, the field supervisors passed out ten rice seedlings to each woman planter who set out the plants. This was the extent of the transplanting on that day; all the workers then ate the chickens which were boiled in the field. The medium placed the heads of the chickens along the edge of the rice field, beaks pointing upward. After eating the chickens, the workers all went home. On the following day, planting began in earnest and continued until the field was transplanted.

Two other occasions for ceremonial ritual are reported from the rice fields in Lubuagan. When rice has taken root, chickens are sacrificed by old men in a ceremony called *omapoy*. Again when the rice bears fruit, old men sacrifice chickens and on this occasion pigs as well. This is true again when the harvested rice is placed in the granary.

None of the above practices were observed among the Northern Kalinga, and informants claim that no ceremonial rituals are or were ever performed on such occasions for rice grown in irrigated terraces.

Supervision of planting and harvesting of rice grown in irrigated terraces is also more rigidly prescribed in Lubuagan. In the Lubuagan region, rice fields are divided into three divisions: the lower and middle fields are called by a single term, *sadog;* the upper field is called *sosong.* The three divisions are important in the sequence of planting and harvesting and in water use. For each field or division there is a supervisor, a position inherited within three bilateral descent groups. The first born takes over the position, unless the heir is clearly incompetent, in which case the position goes to a brother or sister, or if the heir did not have siblings, to the nearest relatives of the person who had held the position before. These positions are recognized as belonging to specific family lines and if at all possible the position goes from father (or mother) to first-born son or daughter. There seems to be no sex preference; if the firstborn happens to be a woman, she inherits the position, although her husband or a brother may perform the prescribed tasks for her. The family heads in charge of Lubuagan fields at the time of my work were as follows: 1) for the upper fields, Kisob; 2) for the middle field, Kotong (a woman); 3) for the lower field, Awos. All three inherited their positions from their fathers who held them until the time of their death.

About forty years ago, when the agricultural ceremonial cycle was still operating with some vigor in Lubuagan, these "supervisors" set the time for planting and harvesting and saw to it that the rituals associated with the cultivation of rice were performed. At present, the rigid adherence to rituals has lapsed, and planting and harvesting times are determined by individuals. These supervisors still allocate irrigation water, however, and settle disputes (with the aid of pangngats) arising from controversies over water and land rights.

While there are no longer specific dates for planting and harvesting in Lubuagan, such procedures are probably much as they were in the past. Owners of the upper field plant first and harvest last. This is because the temperatures are lower in the upper field and the rice takes longer to mature. Owners of the middle field follow. The last to plant but the first to harvest, because of milder temperatures, are the owners of the lower field. Difference in elevation between the lower and upper field is approximately 1,500 feet, the middle field lying only about five hundred feet above the lower one. The Lubuagan region is bowl-shaped; streams run eastward down the sides to the Chico River which at this point flows almost due north. Elevations range between 3,000 and 1,500 feet. The most densely populated area is at about 2,300 feet.[2]

The northern Kalinga regions do not have supervisors like those of Lubuagan. Planting or harvesting now or in the past was never done on days specifically set by recognized "supervisors" whose positions were inherited in specific descent groups. Local leaders, the *lakay* (more rarely called pangngats) settled disputes regarding land or water rights. The positions of lakay are not inherited, but "achieved" among the Northern Kalinga by the possession of a number of traits and/or accomplishments. Formerly a "war record" was one of the important roads to becoming a respected leader; since the end of headhunting, it is wealth, ability to talk, and wise and fair counselling that receive the greatest emphasis in attaining positions of leadership.

Maintenance of rice fields — Most of the northern Kalinga rice fields are prepared for planting by turning the soil with a wooden spade, sharpened stick or pole tipped with iron. The field is then tramped into proper condition by barefooted individuals. In the Lubuagan region, carabaos are commonly used to prepare fields for planting. A crude wooden plow with an iron share is hitched to a carabao. After it is plowed, the soil is further broken by dragging with a harrow which usually is a heavy board into which wooden pegs have been driven. Trampling the soil is also accomplished simply by driving from two to six carabaos around and around until the soil is the proper consistency for planting. All the work in fields to which carabao cannot be transported is performed by human beings; this is especially true of the northern Kalinga regions where the rough terrain discourages the use of animals.

No fertilizer, except the decaying straw of the previous crop, is added to the rice field. Transplanting and weeding are the work of women. There are only two weedings during the growing season of each crop. While women weed, men repair terrace walls, ditches, and flumes. Irrigation involves the inundation of, first, the highest terraces; then each tier in turn is flooded by making openings in the retaining walls. A constant current is maintained which prevents the formation of stagnant pools. The fields are used continuously; rainfall and the flow of streams from higher reaches of the mountains to the fields, trickling from one terrace into another, apparently supply all the minerals needed to maintain fertility. While some fields have a greater yield of rice than others, and the Kalinga realize that this is due to differences in soil fertility, it is surprising that they make no effort to enrich the soil of the rice fields. There is, of course, a paucity of large domesticated animals which could supply manure, but there are numerous caves where there are rich deposits of bat guano. The Kalinga appear to be unaware that bat guano is an excellent fertilizer and can be utilized with little investment of time and energy.

A shelter or hut is erected in the fields where workers rest, tell stories, and eat lunch during harvest. The shelter also provides the place from which various clattering devices lead into the fields. These contrivances are employed to frighten birds and animals that prey on the rice. The most common type of device consists of a number of dry bamboo poles cut at the top into strips. The poles are tied at intervals to a long rattan line which leads from the shelter into the field of maturing rice. A boy or man sits in the shelter and occasionally pulls on the rattan line which sets off a clatter as the bamboo strips strike together, causing the flight of birds and animals.

Domesticated Animals

There are few animals in the mountains of north Luzon. I saw only two horses in my travels among the Northern Kalinga, one was owned by the Roman Catholic priest and the other by the board member, Mr. Simeon Bogacon. These horses are typical of the Philippines, small and wiry and said to be best adapted to the islands. The two horses in northern Kalinga were used only in the immediate area of the Balbalan municipal headquarters or población. It is impossible to take a horse over most of the rugged trails in the Kalinga country, inasmuch as these trails are suited only to foot travel and best adapted to the bare feet of the mountain peoples.

Carabaos among the Kalinga are used primarily for food. Some Kalinga keep a few cattle, but cattle are subject to a variety of diseases, and hence carabaos, obviously hardier animals, are preferred as a source of beef. Pigs and chickens are fairly numerous and are common sacrificial victims on ceremonial occasions as well as the source of meat for festivities of all kinds.

Property Ownership and Inheritance

Barton (1949:84–136) has provided an extensive discussion of property, ownership and inheritance practices in the Lubuagan region which hold in general for all Kalinga. What follows is a summary of the more important and general patterns, reference to differences between north and south, and comments on significant aspects.

The most valued possessions of both the Southern and Northern Kalinga at present are irrigated rice fields. Also important are house sites, either with dwellings on them or where future houses might be erected. Because of recent population increases, especially in the south, house sites which were formerly rice terraces are now sacrificed to provide room for dwellings to house new families. Livestock in the form of carabaos and pigs may be listed next in valued possessions. Animals are primarily important as sacrificial victims, but their possession also brings prestige and status.

In a special category, but extremely important as an index of wealth and prestige, is heirloom property, consisting, as I have said, of Chinese jars, plates, gongs, and beads inherited from past generations. Since these items are not of local manufacture, they have acquired a value far in excess of their actual worth. A single agate bead of the type called *sang–al* is reckoned to be equal in value to a mature carabao, and a necklace in which lesser-valued agate beads of *masilap* and *abali* are strung with those of sang–al might be worth as much as a dozen carabao. Since a fully grown carabao sells for one hundred to one hundred fifty pesos in the Mountain Province, the price of these beads when translated into Philippine currency is enormous.[3] Chinese gongs, jars, plates, and bowls are also given a correspondingly high value. Heirloom items are exchanged among the Kalinga themselves and rarely go beyond the boundaries of the subprovince. These items are not valued by Christian Filipinos, and the few Americans who have visited the Kalinga either find the heirloom articles unattractive or are appalled by the value assigned to them by the Kalinga. Indeed, the Kalinga are perfectly willing to retain

Heirloom Chinese plates, highly treasured by the Kalinga, are displayed along a wall in a southern Kalinga dwelling.

these heirloom articles for themselves, since the equivalent value in Philippine currency would not give them as much distinction and status among their own people as the articles bestow.

A special shelf or shelves *(pagod)* is erected along part of the wall in every home to exhibit Chinese plates and jars inherited in the family or acquired by trade from other Kalinga. It is a source of pride and prestige to a family to be able to have two or three such shelves running on two sides of the room filled with heirloom possessions. Since all Kalinga display their Chinese pottery, it is immediately evident which family in a town or village is most wealthy. There are, of course, other evidences of affluence, but Chinese vessels are usually a quick method of determining wealth and prestige. The wealthiest families have a special room where such items are displayed, and the room itself is reserved for entertaining guests. Mere quantity in the numbers of plates and jars displayed is not an index of wealth; there are different types, some more valuable than others. Rare types have the most value, but color, design, and form all play a part in setting generally recognized gradients of value on Chinese plates and jars. Indeed within a region, any adult knows the individual pieces owned by various families and is able to indicate the value of each plate and jar.

Curiously, items of Kalinga manufacture are not excessively priced and never achieve the status of heirlooms even when old. Thus, headaxes, spears, shields, blankets, and women's wraparound skirts are all moderately priced. Headaxes and shields are given to American friends as gifts, and Kalinga seem frankly amused that such items are cherished by Americans.

Swidden plots fit into a special category as property. Hill farms in the past were simply considered unowned. A man staked out an area of forest land and followed the procedure outlined above for clearing the plot. After cultivating it for a year or two, he abandoned it to revert back to the jungle and regain its fertility. If another man subsequently wanted to expend the energy to clear and construct a plot in the same location, no objection was raised. After all, in the sparsely populated areas where swidden farming was practiced, there were usually plenty of potential swidden plots, and any man who wanted to do the heavy work of clearing, burning, and planting was welcome to any plot. There has not been much change in this attitude in recent years except for those plots which can be converted into rice fields. It is now customary to ask the permission of the man who first cultivated the plot or, if he is no longer living, of his descendants. This is usually granted unless the original cultivator or his descendants want to use the land. Despite increased population, there is not an overwhelming demand for hill farms, and there is usually enough land for those who want to go to the trouble of constructing a swidden. Indeed, the pressure for hill farms may not be greater today than formerly, since the danger of headhunters in the past made it imperative to cultivate lands close to the settlements. Today, under more peaceful conditions, it is possible to go to considerable distances from a settlement to make a swidden.

Prior water rights to a rice field are theoretically held by the man who has constructed the first irrigated terrace watered by a stream or spring. In practice, however, no one is denied the use of water. Terraces higher on the mountain receive water first. The water then trickles successively to the lower terraces. If disputes arise, regional leaders, pangngats and capitanes settle the problem by taking into consideration the needs of all who draw from a common stream or spring. When streams and springs are flowing regularly, water may trickle into all the fields; but when the flow becomes scanty, water is apportioned for specified amounts of time so that there is an equal distribution. Considerable difficulty arises over the use of water where streams have a scanty flow during the dry season. Perhaps no problem causes more bickering and occasional fighting and killing than the use of water. As may be expected, disputes over water are most frequent and most pressing in the south where the people are dependent primarily on rice grown in the irrigated terraces. The designation of specified individuals to settle the problems that we have noted in Lubuagan indicates the crucial importance of water allocation in the south. There are no special individuals charged with settling water problems in the north; regional leaders take on these responsibilities along with other regional problems. Even so, regional leaders in the north are called upon to settle water disputes more than other kinds of problems, and their ability to compromise and their skills of diplomacy are most severely taxed over these disputes. Greater intraregional antagonisms in the south are clearly attributable to disputes over water. Conversely, greater regional cohesion and more peaceful conditions prevailing in the north are directly related to the fact that irrigated terraces are new and swidden farming still important. It is clear that as irrigated terraces increase and populations expand, disputes over water in the northern Kalinga regions also will become a serious problem.

Two categories of property are recognized everywhere among the Kalinga, inherited property *(tawid)* and acquired property *(ginatang,* Lubuagan or *ngining-ak,* north Kalinga).

With regard to inherited property, Kalinga custom law emphatically holds that such property is kept in trust by parents for their children. The Kalinga feel most strongly that the interests of children should be safeguarded, and this sentiment is especially marked with respect to inherited property. Strong sanctions are brought to bear on one who would sell, trade, or otherwise dispose of his inherited possessions. Property is owned separately by husband and wife and passed on to children when the latter set up individual households upon marriage. Since residence is predominantly matrilocal, the land and the house site are conceived as owned by the wife. The husband has assisted in the construction of the house and makes repairs as needed, but the house is not considered as jointly owned. Once children are born, the husband's attachment to the house becomes more secure, but should any trouble arise and the couple separate, the house and house site revert back to the wife and her parents. In patrilocal residence, the reverse is the case, house and house site are then owned by the husband and his parents. Cases of separate residence are rare, and always in such cases the house site has been provided by the parents or the relatives of one of the spouses and hence belongs only to one of them. Rice fields, as we have noted, are the most valued pieces of property. Such land is worked jointly and its products shared with their children, but if the question of the disposal of a rice field arises, the spouse who owns the field must decide it. In practice it is customary for the wife and husband to discuss the matter, but the final decision rests with the owner. Indeed, the spouse may prefer to consult his or her relatives and exclude the marital partner from the consultation, and the latter may thus have no part in the decision reached.

A man and wife maintain separate ownership of all other types of inherited property as well. What has been said about houses, house sites, and rice fields applies equally to heirloom possessions and livestock inherited from parents or relatives.

Property acquired after marriage is usually considered joint property unless it can be clearly demonstrated that one's spouse had no part in its acquisition. It would be difficult to establish the latter since additional property is usually acquired from the produce of rice fields and swiddens which are worked together and hence considered joint property. For those individuals who work for wages it is of course possible at present to acquire individual property, but this was not so in the past when rice fields and swiddens provided the primary subsistence foods as well as the chief means of acquiring other commodities either by trade or sale. Traditional attitudes are still predominant among the Kalinga, however, and individual incomes have not substantially changed the manner in which disputes over the ownership and inheritance of property are settled. There has, however, been some change of attitude toward acquired property. Apparently because abundant inherited property was associated with prominent families, there was until recently a negative evaluation of the *nouveau riche* families who acquired their wealth after the development of new economic opportunities such as wage-work and trade. This attitude was especially strong in the south where, as we have noted, there was an incipient development of an aristocratic class, the kadangyan, based on wealth handed down along particular family lines. The term kadangyan was apparently never used seriously in the north, and the distinction between privileged and non-privileged classes was not clearly delineated. In my own travels in the Kalinga country, I noted aristocratic snobbery only in Lubuagan; in the north, those who had become well-to-do by initiative were not censured and were respected as fully as those who enjoyed prominence because of inherited wealth. It is understandable that distinguished families and entrenched wealth should be correlated with a well-established economy and one which provided a surplus of economic goods. Swidden farmers cannot be expected to furnish these conditions; they rarely achieve a level beyond subsistence. With the diffusion of irrigated terrace farming, some of the Kalinga were achieving a position of economic well-being; but this process has been arrested by wage-work and trade and the associated equalitarian notions about class divisions that came in with American control. Moreover, Kalinga culture, again especially in the north, was already geared toward rewarding individual aspirations and achievement. At present, the Kalinga are eager participants in an economic order which has some of the same characteristics as the American economic system.

Acquired property consists of essentially the same kinds of items as inherited property. Heirlooms, houses, house sites, and rice fields are sold only as a last resort and then reluctantly by inheritors of wealth. This is, of course, because an individual realizes that he is depriving his children of their inheritance when he sells property he himself has inherited. In transactions involving inherited property, negative feelings toward the buyer are also generated. These feelings, in part at least, have contributed to the attitude that acquired property is not quite respectable. A Kalinga usually hesitates to buy inherited property, realizing that his action will arouse ill feeling toward himself from co-regionists. This reluctance to buy inherited property persists even though Kalinga custom law provides for gifts to the relatives of the seller in sales of valuable inherited property.

In recent years, many Kalinga who have the means to purchase rice fields have preferred to buy irrigated land outside of home regions rather than to arouse the ire of co-regionists by buying local rice fields. Other Kalinga who derive income from wage-work or trade satisfy status drives by building elaborate lowland type residences on their own inherited land. Such an action does not deprive anyone of inherited property and often provides compensation to co-regionists who are employed in the construction of the house. One may, of course, freely add to other types of property: cattle, carabaos, and pigs which may be bought outside the home region. In the north, a man may also work hard and devote considerable time to clearing a mountain side for a house site or making a rice field. The Kalinga, therefore, tend to explore other methods of acquiring wealth rather than the purchase of inherited property which exposes them to the possibility of dispute and costly settlement.

Despite complications, rice fields and heirloom articles do occasionally change hands, most often probably as the result of fines or payments imposed by regional leaders following a dispute, but occasionally also as economic ventures for profit. In the transfer of such properties the kindred of the seller must be compensated by gifts. This practice is partly to "clear the title" and prevent disputes, but also to assuage the conscience of the seller who is disposing of the inheritance of his children. Compensating relatives in this case also reflects a basic Kalinga principle or value: that of considering the kinship circle or kindred as a unit. This principle asserts itself constantly among the Kalinga and other mountain peoples: in the collective responsibility of the kindred for revenge, in the payment of weregilds, and in the fulfillment of the responsibilities involved in the peace-pact institution.[4]

Despite the occasional sale of inherited property, the Kalinga usually see to it that their children receive a good inheritance. Not only is it in keeping with Kalinga values to give generously, but the number of sacrificial animals offered and the elaborateness of the feasts prepared during a parent's illness or at his death are commensurate with the size of the inheritance. Parents give generously because they want their sons and daughters to propitiate the spirits when they are ill and to continue to do so for their comfort in the spirit world after death. Sons and daughters, on the other hand, are fearful that the departed spirits will punish them with illness and death or that they will be adversely criticized by the regional population for not providing generously when close relatives are ill or have died. Thus the cycle moves on, one generation attempting to control and use the other, motivated in its actions by gain or profit and fearful both of the spirit world and of public opinion.

Everywhere among the Kalinga a son or daughter takes possession of his or her inherited property after marriage when a new household is established. The best fields, the choicest house site, and the most precious of the heirloom possessions go to the first married, whether son or daughter. There is some tendency, especially in the Lubuagan region, for a mother to give her property to daughters and the father to sons, but in most instances son and daughter inherit from both parents. Subsequent children get less property, but no one is completely deprived. Parents are careful to see that all children receive something if only to satisfy public opinion which is especially alert to injustices to the inheritance rights of individuals. Adopted children, servants, and the children of mistresses all are entitled to property and if they are slighted, some relative or even an unrelated regional member will bring the matter up to influential leaders. Litigation procedures are costly, and a controversy over inheritance is sure to be decided in favor of those who have been ignored or who have received a meager amount. Parents try to be as fair as possible and are guided considerably by regional customs and public opinion.

House sites are ordinarly reserved for daughters, since parents have working relationships with them and anticipate these relations to continue in the form of extended households. As I said before, this custom is not rigidly followed, and parents do occasionally provide a house site for sons near the parental home. The last to marry, whether son or daughter, inherits the parental residence and whatever property has remained undivided.

Cultivated swiddens are allotted in the same fashion as other property. A former swidden lying fallow is not given; it is the property of the incipient descent group which farmed it first. Permission to re-use the swidden after it has regained its fertility is sought among close relatives of the original user. Such permission is apparently always granted unless the first cultivator or his nearest of kin intend to re-use the plot. The feeling that no plot of land should lie idle if there are people who want to make use of it seems general throughout the Kalinga country. The question of who has priority rights to a swidden evokes the same response everywhere: "If a man wants to exert the effort of clearing and burning, he is welcome to any plot." There is the feeling, undoubtedly coming from the past, that hillsides and mountainsides are public domain much as are forest and pasture lands. Ownership is associated only with irrigated rice fields. Only with swiddens that can be converted into rice fields is there an assertion of ownership by reference to the original cultivator of the swidden.[5]

At the moment of death, a parent may alter or reverse his allocation of inheritance property. This is done to favor the relative who has slaughtered the most animals and who has made the most elaborate feasts during his illness. The parent in taking this action has, of course, a purely personal motive: that of binding this relative to provide a lavish funeral feast and so insure the parent's safe entry into the spirit world. The expectation of a large inheritance, on the other hand, prompts relatives to vie with one another in providing large numbers of sacrificial victims for the illnesses of a relative who possesses a large estate. This is quite aside from the fear of disease-producing and death-inflicting ancestral spirits and of censure by public opinion. These sacrifices, therefore, are acts performed primarily, if not wholly, for personal gain.

Since property is customarily divided when children marry and set up their own households, single children acquire inheritance property only upon the death of a close relative. If such a child died before his parents, there is nothing for him to leave except a few personal belongings. Illness and death rites for propertyless unmarried individuals are a simple affair — that there are rites at all is due to fear of ancestral spirits who may punish the nearest of kin or because of the fear of public censure.

A surviving spouse does not inherit from his or her deceased mate since the latter's property is for children of the union. In the event that there are no children, brothers or sisters or other lateral descendants of the deceased have priority rights to the property. As long as there are children, the surviving spouse holds the property of the former partner in trust for the children but has no right beyond suggesting and advising to determine its division. Such advice is seriously considered, however, by regional leaders if disputes arise over the inheritance property of one's spouse. In such cases regional leaders guard against the distribution of property to a deceased's lateral relatives and their descendants who might deprive young children of their rights. The advice of the surviving spouse is helpful in these cases since he is likely to be neutral, having little or nothing to gain from the division of property.

The regulatory laws governing the economic system are extremely complex and well developed among the Kalinga. Hence only a small portion of what appear to be the most important aspects of economic regulation has been included in this study. The Kalinga are a legal-minded people, and through the years have accumulated a remarkably uniform set of regulations for adjudicating a variety of transgressions and offenses. These are not restricted to economic activities, although they are perhaps most numerous in this area.[6] The body of regulations together constitute the custom law of the Kalinga. These laws are, of course, all verbally transmitted from generation to generation. Interpreters of the regulations are regional leaders with an extensive knowledge of these "laws," who pass judgment in terms of precedent when infractions are brought to their attention. Although Barton's (1949) study of Kalinga custom law is excellent, so vast and complex is this important area of society and culture that there is need of a fuller study. The Kalinga and other mountain peoples of northern Luzon have in fact developed a set of regulatory devices or "laws" which is perhaps the most complex of such systems among non-literate societies.[7]

Notes to Chapter 3

1. I regret that I was unable in every case to identify the crops, plants, animals, and birds with scientific and English names. I have no training as a botanist or zoologist and the time spent in the field did not permit me to collect specimens and to have them properly identified.
2. After reading this paragraph Dr. Harold Conklin of Yale University suggested the inclusion of a groundplan indicating the divisions mentioned here as well as other aspects of the irrigation system. Unfortunately my stay in Lubuagan was too brief to become acquainted with the geographic features of its rice fields. The inclusion of such a sketch or map would indeed be helpful.
3. Recently in the barrio of Uma (Lubuagan Municipal District) a few enterprising Kalinga have started to manufacture beads from old combs and phonograph records which are remarkably like the actual heirloom beads. These items are purely for the tourist trade; no Kalinga, except perhaps a child, would wear them. Since these beads are excellent imitations of the actual ones, an American

tourist is as pleased with such a necklace as if it were the real thing and it costs only a trifling amount.

4. The circle of relatives who receive gifts in the case of a sale are also the ones assessed to provide gifts in case of a purchase. The practice is identical to that followed in receiving weregilds and providing for weregild payments.

5. Compare Frake 1956:170–173, Goodenough 1956:173–175.

6. The body of Kalinga regulations governing the cases that come up before adjudicators in a peace-pact meeting is also extensive and complex.

7. See Barton's exemplary study of Ifugao Law (1919).

4. | Religion

RITUALISTIC PERFORMANCES, the spirits or deities recognized and named and those invoked — all these show extreme variation among all the Kalinga areas and from one region to another. Indeed, even within the region there is variation in these religious features of Kalinga culture. This variation results primarily because the isolation of regional populations has retarded diffusion. An additional cause of variation is the continuous desire of the religious practitioners or mediums themselves to make innovations. Among the Kalinga, each medium has her own spirit helpers and endeavors to bring novel techniques into her performance of rituals in order to set herself apart from other mediums.

General Characteristics, Concepts and Practices

Despite variations there are common patterns, in both religious concepts and practices, not only among the Kalinga but among the pagan peoples of northern Luzon generally. As among non-literate peoples everywhere, religious beliefs and practices are closely related to the form of subsistence, social organization, and values. *Cause* and *effect* in this relationship is perhaps impossible to determine, but the correspondence of religious beliefs and practices with subsistence and other social and cultural features is interestingly reflected in the populations of the Mountain Province.

Disease, crop failure, death, and all misfortunes are attributed primarily to the machinations of spirits. Other causative agents, such as sorcery and the violation of taboos, are also offered to explain a particular illness or death, but generally any misfortune is thought to be brought

[*159*]

about by spirits. These spirits may be those of deceased individuals, particularly of close relatives, or they may be any of a host of malevolent spirits. The former are generally known as *anitos,* a designation used by virtually all mountain peoples for the spirits of departed ancestors.

When an individual dies, his soul or spirit must be properly dispatched to the afterworld and the prescribed funeral rituals carefully observed. The place of the afterworld is not too clearly conceived; some believe that the spirits of the dead simply hover about the neighborhood, others believe that there is a separate abode for them somewhere in the sky. Life on earth does not appear to affect existence in the hereafter except for suicides and those who have died in accidents or who were killed in warfare. These spirits are vengeful and might cause illness and death unless properly propitiated. But there are no "rewards" or "punishments" in the hereafter for the kind of life people have led on earth. Everywhere among the mountain people there is a belief that the spirit of the dead remains near the corpse until after the funeral and watches carefully to see that all the ritualistic observances are made. Should anything be neglected, the spirit will take vengeance on his own relatives by sending illness or death. While the deceased's spirit is most potent during the period immediately following death, it is still likely to inflict illness or death at a later period if demands are neglected. Requests for things that an ancestral spirit needs come in the form of dreams, but sickness in the family may also be a sign that the spirit of a dead ancestor wants something. In the latter case, the medium interprets the message and indicates the object or objects desired by the spirits. Requests are usually for the sacrifice of animals but sometimes for specific items like a blanket, tobacco, and other utilitarian items which are then placed on the deceased's grave.

The non-human spirits who bring illness, death, or other misfortune are variously designated and not too clearly conceptualized. Some of them are good spirits although perhaps a majority are malevolent. Various precautions are taken to avoid the machinations of these spirits, and the main task of religious practitioners is to placate and propitiate them by prayers and the sacrifice of chickens and pigs. Some of these non-human spirits are more powerful than others and are more active in their efforts to inflict harm on the living. For the weaker spirits or the good ones, the mountain peoples have little concern; their preoccupation is with those which are powerful and hence a source of evil. These malicious spirits must be constantly propitiated by elaborate and costly sacrifices.

The machinations of anitos or ancestral spirits appear to be emphasized in the south, particularly among the Ibaloy (Barton 1946:9–10; Leaño 1958:226 and Sagada [Eggan 1959]). Among the Northern Kalinga and the Tinguian (Cole 1922:295–314) non-human malevolent spirits appear to be most important as causative agents of illness, death, and misfortune. The Southern Kalinga, that is, in the Lubuagan region, appear to stand about midway in this respect. While the religion of the Ibaloy and Sagada might be considered a form of ancestor worship, at least in part, such a characterization would not be appropriate for the Northern Kalinga. The main preoccupation of the Northern Kalinga mediums is with malevolent spirits, and the anxieties of the living are toward the machinations of those spirits which are evilly disposed. Except for funeral ceremonies and the observation of taboos during the mourning period, offerings are not made for the dead among the Northern Kalinga.[1] For the Tinguian, Cole *(ibid.* 294) specifically denied that the religion of these people could be considered ancestor worship. It is possible that the importance of specific family lines among the southern groups might be correlated with this difference in religious emphases. Elsewhere we have noted that bilateral descent groups are present in the south, but not among the Northern Kalinga. The social units of the Tinguian have not been clearly defined, but Cole's brief description (*op. cit.* 359–360) indicates that social organization, while more complex, is similar to that of the Northern Kalinga. Given a belief in the power of ancestral spirits it seems reasonable to expect that such spirits would be accorded greater attention where specific family lines are singled out. Just as adult members of important families exerted control over their relatives, so also they would be inclined to do so after death unless they were constantly appeased. The correlation here suggested is of course a highly conjectural one, but the crucial contrast between the two areas is the presence of bilateral descent groups and the emphases placed on ancestral spirits in one but not in the other.

In the central and south portions of the Mountain Province, sorcery is frequently reported as a cause of illness and death (Leaño, *ibid.*; Barton *ibid.*) but the Kalinga are skeptical about it and have little or no anxiety over witchcraft. Cole (*ibid.*) does not consider sorcery an important concern of the Tinguian, and Keesing (1962b) in an article on the Isneg of Apayao makes no mention of sorcery or witchcraft as an important source of anxiety among these people. Poisoning is, however, greatly feared and Kalinga attitudes toward poisoning often take on a magical significance that is closely related to the concept of witchcraft. Thus it is believed, for example, that injury, illness or death can be brought to an individual by "poisoning" his clothing or other items which are constantly in contact with him. The most frequent method of poisoning is by introducing a poisonous preparation made from putrefied roots into drink or food. While this would be considered an act of true poisoning, the precautions to ward it off are magical. Throughout the Kalinga country, individuals carry various kinds of amulets and preparations which are supposed to detect the poisoning of food or drink. A common preparation is the mixture of coconut oil and a certain type of root. The preparation is called *somang* or *soblay* in the northern Kalinga dialects. Soblay is carried in a small bottle and when food or drink about to be eaten has been poisoned, oil oozes out of the bottle thus alerting the carrier. Some informants report that the possession of preparations like soblay magically breaks the container of food or drink that has been poisoned. Old, childless women are especially feared by the Kalinga as potential poisoners. Such women are said to seek revenge for their condition and will entice a traveler into their homes to poison him with food or drink.[2]

The violation of taboo is everywhere a cause of illness, death, or misfortune in the Mountain Province and may be associated with ancestral or malevolent spirits. The omission of necessary details in the performance of the ceremonies, or the disregard of prohibitive regulations during birth and early childhood ceremonies, or at times of planting, harvesting, and other important occasions may all be occasions of evil consequence. The spirits who reside in the *podayan,* a small shelter at the entrance of a village are easily offended if villagers do not pay proper respect to the guardian stones called *bayog* contained therein. *Sang-ásang,* considered to be the powerful guardian spirit of the village and formerly associated with warfare, lives in the podayan. If this shrine is violated, the guardian spirit of the village will take vengeance by sending some kind of calamity, hence proper respect must be displayed. A small glass of wine or an egg in a bowl should be offered periodically to the village guardian spirit.[3]

Almost all the mountain peoples venerate a creator-deity or culture hero or both. The names *kabonìyan* and *lomáwig* or closely related cognates of these designations are reported in all of these groups. Virtually everywhere among the Kalinga there is simply one such creator-god called kabónyan or kabonìyan.[4] This deity is directly appealed to only in rare cases, such as when a man has lost a loved one through death or accident, or has suffered a sudden calamity such as the destruction of his rice fields by a storm. On such an occasion a man might exclaim: "Kaboniyan, look thou upon me and have pity for see what has been taken from me!" Kabonìyan is not invoked by the mediums, however. Each medium has her own spirit helpers to whom she appeals when performing a ceremony. The Kalinga and other Mountain Province peoples appear to propitiate only those spirits which can harm; since kabonìyan does not inflict injury, bring sickness or misfortune, there is no need to placate or appease him. In their attitude toward spirits and deities, the practical, self-interested characteristics of the mountain peoples are again highlighted: "why exert time, energy, and use up one's economic resources in sacrificial feasts for benevolent spirits and a good deity? Those ancestral and malevolent spirits who bring about illness, death and misfortune are the ones who need to be compromised."

Categories of Ritualistic Activity

The areas of human activity emphasized by ritualistic activity are much the same among all of the Mountain Province peoples. They center about the life cycle, agriculture, and headhunting. Ceremonies for the last category have diminished, lapsed, or have been reinterpreted in some groups into rituals that emphasize community welfare. This is true, for example, of the *Begnas* ceremony of Sagada and other neighboring peoples ([Eggan 1959] Scott Field Notes). This is a clear example of cere-monial reorganization. Formerly the Begnas ceremony honored the return of a successful headhunting party with rites which centered about the disposition of enemy heads. At present, the ceremony is given three times a year. Instead of human heads, heads of pigs, dogs and chickens are used, and the ceremony is performed for the benefit of the whole com-munity [Eggan 1959]. Headhunting ritual is still vividly remembered by the Kalinga, but the energy for the hunt and the celebrations has been rechanneled into the popular peace-pact activities.

Ritual associated with the life cycle and agriculture still goes on but such rites have diminished in intensity and frequency as the result of non-traditional governmental and missionary influences. Mountain peoples still do, however, highlight those stages in the life cycle of the individual which are potentially dangerous. Among the Kalinga, as we have seen, special rites, the kontad series, bridge the child over the period when it is most vulnerable to the machinations of the spirits. The child is unable to protect itself at this time so parents and close relatives must observe the taboos which if transgressed would harm the child. They bribe and buy off by sacrificial offerings the malevolent and ancestral spirits who may take advantage of the child's vulnerability. While these rites are specifically of the Kalinga they are much the same in all groups. Marriage rites emphasize prestige and status drives practically every-where, but there is recognition, too, of the entrance of the individual into a new life and a new set of relationships. Finally, the ritualistic activities associated with death stem out of kinship ties between the liv-ing and the deceased, but the relatives who conduct the ceremonies also have practical and mundane interests in performing these rites. The bountiful and lavish offerings express not only an affectionate attach-ment of living relatives for the deceased but there is also the desire to impress others by the very elaborateness of the ceremony. In this final aspect, the Kalinga are perhaps most obviously "worldly" and exhibitionistic, emphasizing more than other groups the prestige features of all of these ritualistic events.

The ritualistic activities that are observed in connection with agriculture vary to the extent that basic subsistence patterns differ. These activities also reflect historical circumstances; that is, the persistence of certain practices fitted to earlier forms of subsistence and agricultural techniques. Thus, the ritualistic attention given to the planting of taro at Sagada and Bontoc ([Eggan 1959]; Jenks 1905) appears to indicate a shift from the primary cultivation of wet taro (now insignificant in the diet of these people) to irrigated rice. Among the Kalinga we have noted that the cultivation of dry rice receives emphasis although wet rice is now of equal or even of major importance. Indeed, among the marginal groups in the Mountain Province, there are also ritualistic observances devoted to hunting and collecting which appear to reflect greater dependence in the past on these subsidiary sources of food.[5]

The concepts associated with headhunting, despite obvious differences in ritualistic practices, again appear to be much the same. Headhunting apparently satisfied primarily prestige and status needs of the mountain peoples. The conversion of the rituals formerly associated with headhunting into community welfare interests indicates that a secondary aim of headhunting rituals was to fortify magically the village or region against enemy attack. Community solidarity was, of course, reinforced by headhunting activities, and it is natural that with the cessation of these activities, reorganization of the rituals would suggest the emphasis of community well-being in such reorganized ceremonies. A further function of headhunting activities, especially for swidden farmers, was undoubtedly the maintenance of territorial space (compare Vayda 1961). Such a function is now obviated since Philippine governmental regulations of land tenure now determine limits of territorial expansion. Less clear as a possible alternative or subsidiary function of headhunting was its relevance to fertility. Early writers (Worcester 1912:833–930; Folkmar MS 1906; Barton 1949:236) were convinced that "bringing home a head brings general welfare, increases the fertility of fields, domestic animals, and women, and brings abundance of life generally" (Barton *op. cit.*). Informants emphasize the prestige element for headhunting activities, but there is also a commonly held belief that spilling human blood is a cure for childlessness. Another motive for headhunting is the one of "evening the score." Thus, it was incumbent upon a young man to secure an enemy head when a near relative died, whatever the cause of death may have been. This act "evened the score:" "we lost one and the enemy lost one."

Chanted Myth-Prayers

Ritualistic performances are conducted by men in Sagada, Bontoc and the Ifugao and by women among the Kalinga, Tinguian, and Isneg.[6] Despite the sex difference of the religious practitioners, the petitioning or placating of spirits is similar among all the mountain peoples and consists of two aspects: 1) sacrifice of chickens, pigs and carabaos;[7] and 2) prayers. These prayers are chanted or sung, and report the experiences of the medium in the spirit world or may report the activities of deities or culture heroes in the past. There are aspects of both imitative and sympathetic magic to the prayers: just as things were done in the past or just as spirits and deities behave, so also must mortals conduct themselves. Such behavior will cure the sick, bring general well being to everyone, securing bountiful harvests, and multiplying animals and humans. Every ritualistic event performed by a medium has lessons for everyone — even the curing rite of the Northern Kalinga prescribes proper behavior for the congregated relatives. Ifugao prayers are perhaps more properly myths, since they appear to be restricted to a reporting of the activities of culture heroes in the past (Barton 1956). Such prayers appear to have little direct relationship to the ceremony being performed. Kalinga ritualistic performances have a more direct bearing on the occasion. The Kalinga medium's spirit is transmitted to the spirit world to seek comfort for the anxieties of the relatives or in the curing rite to find the spirit or soul of the patient and bring it back. Yet the Kalinga medium departs to some extent from activities that have specific relevance to the occasion by reporting her encounters with mythological deities or spirits in the spirit world. We include below an outline of the Northern Kalinga curing rite which reveals some of these characteristics. While there is considerable variation among the prayers sung by mediums, and each medium has different spirit helpers, such prayers and the activities of the mediums in a ceremony do adhere to a similar pattern. Thus, ritualistic performances all have the following salient features:

1) The medium begins her chanted prayer by invoking the deities or spirits collectively as *Apo!* (sir, master, or lord).

2) The medium lists her qualifications as the performer of the ceremony.

3) She names her spirit helpers, usually three or more. She reports that the sacrificial victims are being offered for their needs.

4) The medium is possessed by her spirit helpers. She is in a dazed, partly unconscious state. Other mediums may explain her chants if they are unintelligible. (Possession only occurs in an actual ceremony.)

5) The medium goes into the spirit world to retrieve the spirit of the person (in a curing rite) or to communicate with the spirit world and try to answer the demands and questions of those who have come to attend the ceremony.

6) The medium describes her experiences in the spirit world. She recovers the spirit of the patient (in curing rites) and begins her journey back to the land of the living.

7) The spirit or soul is returned to the patient and the medium regains consciousness.

8) Medium and her medium helpers entertain the spectators by various skits.

9) Medium gathers all of the things used in the ceremony, puts them in a basket and leaves the house without looking back.

The above outline has some of the same features covered by Ifugao rituals as listed by Barton (1946:4–6). Kalinga ritualistic performances also have many of the characteristics possessed by the Tinguian rituals. The name *dawak* is shared by Northern Kalinga and Tinguian for the designation of the portion of a ceremony where the medium's spirit helpers are named, invoked, and possession takes place (Cole 1922: 315).[8] Dawak is a general term among the Northern Kalinga for the curing rite, and mediums are designated as mandadawak, or the "performers of dawak." The Tinguian have considerably more ceremonies than the Kalinga but both groups emphasize sickness rites. The chants of the Tinguian mediums called *diams* (Cole 1915:5–6; 26) are similar to those of the Northern Kalinga. The diams which Cole designates as "stories dealing with the relations between certain persons and the natural spirits or those of the dead" are especially like the Northern Kalinga ritual chants (compare Cole *ibid.* 27; 183–189 with the dawak ceremony presented below). Tinguian mediums and their activities also correspond (compare our description below with Cole 1922:301–304). Practices differ considerably from those of the Ifugao, Sagada, and Bontoc. The religious practitioners of these groups are perhaps more properly called "priests," and several of them are involved in a ceremony. Kalinga ceremonies are performed by only one woman medium, occasionally by two or three, but never with as many as fifteen priests as among the Ifugao (Barton 1956:5).

The chanted or sung myths employed in rituals comprise a most important and widely distributed literary form among the mountain peoples. Cole (1915:5) called them "explanatory myths," so designating them because they are used to support or rationalize a ceremony (cf. Barton 1956:3 for Ifugao). They are usually chanted only by mediums, and generally occur in rituals, although there are some exceptions. Among the Northern Kalinga some women, not mediums, chant special mythical folktales at harvest time or at night for diversion. These mythical folk-songs are called *gosombi* and are sung as solos and only by certain women. Barton *(op. cit.)* reports that similar myths among the Kankanay are narrated for diversion and do not occur in ritual contexts.

Folktales and Legends

Folktales or legends about the mythical period constitute another form of oral literature that is widespread among the mountain peoples of northern Luzon. Such stories are related rather than sung, usually or perhaps always by men gathered in regular lounging places such as the stone platforms *(dapay)* of Western Bontoc *(see* Scott 1958c:66) or any place where people come together — on the trail, in the field houses, or in bonfire gatherings around the village. Nonformalized locations for story-telling characterize the Kalinga and Tinguian (compare Cole 1915:5) and perhaps the Isneg of Apayao; these people do not have the formal lounging places of Bontoc and Sagada. These folktales or legends are not narrated in connection with ceremonies, but do report the activities of the deities and culture heroes who also sometime figure in ceremonies. Commonly these stories are about the creation of the world, or its modification, or the creation of man and the invention of death. In these tales the deities or culture heroes, Kabonían and Lomawig, often figure; but there is also a variety of other mythical, essentially benevolent deities who are the subject of such folktales or legends.

Chants or Songs Associated With Headhunting

In the past there was undoubtedly among all groups a set of chants or songs which were associated with headhunting (compare Cole 1922: 371–378). Two types of headhunting chants are current among the Northern Kalinga, one called *asassay* or *kayayyogan,* sung by men only, and another called *kalommatik,* sung by old men and old women. These are both group songs and were formerly sung in the celebrations which followed the return of a successful headhunting expedition. To these songs may be added the boastful recitals of headhunting exploits by those men who have actually taken heads. These are recited as solos and are highly individualized with many improvisations of incidents and details. In the Lubuagan dialect these headhunting recitals are called *palpaliwat,* and among the Northern Kalinga, *pokaw*. These recitals formerly occupied a central place in the dancing and feasting that followed the return of a headhunting party. Such recitals are now given at the end of peace-pact celebrations.

With the above may be included the Kalinga boasting sessions of accomplishment called *i-iyab* (Lubuagan) and *manyamyam* (northern Kalinga). These recitals are chanted by prominent individuals of the baknang or kadangyan class who on festive occasions boast of their economic wealth. Like the accounting of war exploits, these recitals are highly individualistic and, depending on the inventive abilities of the boaster, are likely to vary greatly in detail, style and degree of elaboration. As far as I know such boasting recitals of economic accomplishments have not been reported for groups other than the Kalinga.[9] Given the importance of headhunting and wealth among all mountain peoples in northern Luzon, boastful recitals of the kind found among the Kalinga would seem likely to be characteristic of these other groups as well. Further research will undoubtedly reveal that they occur among the other pagan peoples of the Mountain Province.

Other Songs

A variety of songs for entertainment and diversion form still another part of the rich oral literature of the mountain peoples, and the Kalinga have their share of them. Some of these songs, perhaps the majority, are sung during ceremonial occasions and are considered to please and secure the good will of the spirits. These songs also provide pleasant diversion from the discussion of cases in peace-pact celebrations and help to entertain the large numbers of people who attend ceremonies.

A list of the songs current among the Kalinga, but generally represented among other mountain peoples of northern Luzon, has been included in the appendix. As has been noted, some of these songs are sung by either sex, but only as solos; others are group songs sung either by men alone, by women alone, or more rarely by men and women together.

Most popular of these songs is the pan-montane *salidomay* or *diwas*. Some of the melodies of the salidomay are known by all the major ethnic groups of the Mountain Province. While the melodies appear to be limited in the songs of this group, there is constant improvisation of words to fit the occasion, as for example in the case of serenading a girl friend, the words are made to suit the appearance and personality of the girl. The singer attempts, at least, to adjust the choice of his words to conform to the time, circumstances, and the person or persons involved.

Dances

Each ethnic group has its own characteristic dances as well, but because of present opportunities for observing one another's dances, young people are familiar with the whole dance repertoire of the Mountain Province. The general term for dance among the Kalinga is *tadok,* and this name is often applied to the dance most common in an area; but there are three fairly distinct dances among the Kalinga. With the Southern and Eastern Kalinga, the most popular dance form is the *palo-ok* or *pattong.* As many as eight men beat copper or bronze gongs *(ganzas)* with a small cloth-wrapped stick and dance in a line.[10] Women may also dance, in which case they join the file of men at the end of the line but without instruments. The men crouch at times, twist their hips and jerkily straighten up, all in unison and keeping in step with the music. Old and middle-aged women, teen-agers, and even girls three or four years old join the line which moves along in a circle. Women and girls rest their

Bronze *ganzas,* or gongs, provide music for the dances at peace-pact meetings of both Northern and Southern Kalinga. For the *salidsid* dance of the Northern Kalinga, either six or twelve musicians beat distinct rhythmic patterns on the surface of the gong with the flat of the hand. For the *palo-ok,* danced at all Southern Kalinga festivities, as many as eight men provide the accompaniment on the gongs, and for this dance strike the *ganzas* on the underside with a stick.

palms on their hips or extend their arms outward, palms and fingers outstretched. This is the dance most popular south of the "pacil line" (that is, the Pacil River) which is recognized as the cultural border between the Northern and Southern Kalinga.

While the Kalinga north of the Pacil River are acquainted with the palo-ok and join such dances at peace-pact celebrations, their own favorite dance is called the *salidsid*. The orchestra in the salidsid is a set of six ganza players or double this number. Each ganza player beats a separate pattern on his instrument (as is true of the palo-ok players); hence, it is necessary to have a set number in order to produce the proper harmony. The members of the orchestra kneel on a line, each player places the ganza against his thighs and secures the handle of the instrument inside his belt. The ganza is inverted and the top of it is struck with the palms of both hands. The dancers are a man and a woman, but a married couple may never dance together. The dance is begun by the man who is given a piece of cloth or blanket about the size of a bath towel or a wraparound skirt, called the *ayob*. While he moves to the open area reserved for the dancers, a scarf has been handed to a girl or woman who is to be his dancing partner. When the male dancer has seen that the scarf has been given to his partner, he snaps his ayob which is a signal for the dance to begin. The woman moves into the circle having tied the scarf about her hair. Her arms are at right angles defining an arc, while her fingers are open. The man advances toward her, she comes toward him and both pass to either side. The man prances around in a circle with the woman following. Occasionally he moves backward and then forward with much stamping of the feet. The woman follows at a short distance with more sedate steps, while the man employs highly exaggerated knee action steps. The piece of cloth is held at arms length, or it is brought to the side, or again it is wrapped around the waist. Finally, the man extends his right hand toward the woman and she does likewise but she moves her hand in a circle and avoids taking his hand. This may be repeated several times but eventually she accepts his proffered hand, whereupon the dance ends and the cloth and scarf go to another pair of dancers. Another version to conclude the dance is for the man to spread out the ayob in front of the woman who, if she wishes to terminate the dance, simply throws her scarf into the ayob. The prancing of the salidsid dancer is highly suggestive of a rooster circling about a hen. It is an extremely spirited dance and improvisations frequently made by the male dancer always evoke laughter from the attentive audience.

Occasionally, the same dance may be performed by six or ten pairs or a single man may dance with as many as six women. This version is called the *goyyabba* and is danced without the ayob and scarf.

The inverted rice mortar on the right holds a small Chinese bowl containing an egg as offering to the spirits, thus beginning auspiciously the *salidsid* dance — which can never be performed by a couple who are married to each other.

The salidsid is danced in all ceremonies and is the favorite in peace-pact celebrations involving regions of northern Kalinga. In any festive occasion, the first to dance are the principals of the occasion, except that in funerals the surviving spouse or nearest close relative cannot dance. For other ceremonies of the life-cycle series, the father or the groom begins the dance with a prominent woman of the community, not a near relative, as his partner. In peace-pact celebrations the peace-pact-holders, if of opposite sex, begin the dance; if both are men the guest peace-pact holder dances with the wife or nearest relative of the host pact-holder. The dancers that follow are chosen in terms of relative importance and prominence. The task of selecting the dancers falls to the barrio lieutenants who must exercise great care in the choice. It is important to select important individuals first, and care must also be exercised that visitors from other regions are given preference over local people.[11]

The third type of Kalinga dance was observed only among the Northern Kalinga and it may be restricted to this area since it is a version reported to have come from the Tinguian. This dance is called *Inilawd* and is similar to the salidsid, but both the man and the woman hold a cloth the size of a woman's wraparound skirt. The orchestra consists of only two gongs, one beaten with a stick and the other with the palms of the hand. Cole's description of the most common of two types of Tinguian dances called *tadek* appears to be identical with the inilawd. It is obvious that *tadek* and *tadok* are cognates, the latter employed throughout the Kalinga country for the most common dance of an area; hence, the palo-ok is called tadok in Lubuagan and the Northern Kalinga refer frequently to the salidsid as tadok.

Formerly men who returned with heads from a headhunting expedition also participated in a dance which in pantomime described the actual killing of an enemy warrior and the manner in which the head was severed. The dancing was marked by grotesque posturing and a peculiar falsetto type of chanting. During the dance the warrior brandished his headaxe and shield to show how he had killed. Headhunting dances and celebrations are now a thing of the past, but the memory of the festive occasions when men returned with the heads of the enemy is still very much alive.[12]

The palo-ok for the Southern Kalinga and the salidsid for the Northern Kalinga are a part of virtually every ceremony whether of a secular or a religious character. They also occur on all festive occasions including peace-pact celebrations and Roman Catholic Church-sponsored festivities in the población of Lubuagan and Salegseg. These dances are also popular where large numbers of Kalinga are resident off the subprovince in the mining communities and in Baguio. Along with other similar dances by the other groups of the Mountain Province, these symbolize the strong sense of panmontane unity which is growing among the younger generation of mountain natives.

Musical Instruments

In the use of musical instruments the Kalinga also show their affinity to other Mountain Province peoples. The Kalinga have a rather wide range of instruments which they share most closely with those of the Tinguian described by Cole (1922:440–442). Curiously, the drum made out of a hollowed log and covered over with cow's hide, deer, or pig's skin was not encountered among the Kalinga. This instrument, however, is widely represented among the central and southern groups of the Mountain Province and is a common instrument of the Tinguian. Only the ganzas or gongs are used for providing musical accompaniment to dances; other Kalinga instruments are for serenading and for diversion usually in the evening when the busy Kalinga household has some degree of relaxation.

The Kalinga Medium

The only professional position for men or women among the mountain peoples is that of the medium, *mang-alisig* (Lubuagan), *mandadawak, mang-anito* (northern Kalinga). This position is nowhere a fulltime occupation nor are there organizations of mediums with graded or specialized functions except incipiently among the Ifugao. Each medium, when she has learned the myths and the chants, embarks on her profession on a par with the others and retains her independent status. Mediums are most numerous among the central groups of the Mountain Province, particularly the Bontoc and the Ifugao. These groups have a long history of wet rice cultivation, and the activity of the mediums reflects this basic economy. The ceremonies of the Tinguian also involve the activities of mediums, but here the primary concern is with health and well being. Among the Kalinga and the Apayao there are fewer mediums, ceremonies are less elaborate, and the mediums emphasize curing and headhunting rituals. We have already noted that religious practitioners are men among the Bontoc and Ifugao, whereas among the Tinguian, Kalinga and Apayao (Isnegs) they are women. Ifugao rituals appear to be an outlet for masculine exhibitionism; to a lesser extent this is true of the Bontoc, but especially of the Tinguian, Kalinga, and Apayao men who achieve distinction in warfare or as mediators of troubles that arise from the infractions of custom law.[13] Thus, if the Ifugao are geniuses of ritual activity over which "priests" preside, then the Kalinga and their neighbors excel as political manipulators. The profession of a medium is not closed to men among the northern groups, but these peoples feel that such positions are properly for women. Among the Kalinga, mediums are perhaps accorded the least distinction anywhere in the Mountain Province. Men frequently refer to them deprecatingly as "quack doctors," and informants are inclined to mask their importance, yet will seek their services in time of illness or death.

Individuals cannot become mediums by choice; they must be "called." The Kalinga have a variety of symptoms which they interpret as summons to join the profession. Among the most important are disturbing dreams, trembling fits, illness or nausea following the eating of certain kinds of foods, eel and dog among others. A Kalinga woman may resist the "summons" initially but if the symptoms persist she will seek out a medium and become her assistant serving as a kind of apprentice. Over a period of several months, even over several years, she will learn the myths, the chants, and the names of a variety of deities and spirits. Much of this information she will have already acquired from being present at ceremonies where mediums officiate; hence ritualistic performance would not be completely new to the novice. Under the instructions of an experienced medium, the novice will begin to summon spirits into herself. Sooner or later if she is qualified and destined to become a medium, she will experience possession, and out of a maze of spirits and deities who pass before her subconscious, some will appear more frequently and occupy her thoughts more persistently. Out of these she will eventually concentrate on three or four who will become her spirit helpers.

A Kalinga medium wears a turban, *bayóbong,* made out of barkcloth and during the performance of a ceremony she carries a Chinese plate which she rings with a bamboo stick as she chants. Other common items which form a characteristic part of the medium's ritual paraphernalia are the following: headaxe, coconut shells, tools such as grub hoe and bolo, various types of ferns and hibiscus flowers. At the end of her ritualistic performances all these articles will be carefully collected and placed in a basket. While not all the items in each medium's ritual collection are the same, some, such as the barkcloth turban, the Chinese plate with bamboo stick, and the basket which contains these items are standard. A medium sacrifices a chicken in most rites but for the major ones, for example, those involving serious illnesses and funeral rites, the sacrificial victim is one or more pigs. Ritualistic activities are conducted inside a dwelling. The medium's paraphernalia is deposited on a runo mat which serves as a kind of an altar before which she sacrifices and chants her prayers. Occasionally she may move about the room with the items but they are always returned to the mat. Kalinga ritual paraphernalia do not

Until recent years, the only semi-professional position for a Kalinga woman has been that of medium. Here a medium from the region of Poswoy wears the turban characteristic of her calling.

include wooden idols or sorcery boxes as among the Ifugao. Compared to those of the southern and central groups and the Tinguian, the ritual paraphernalia and the activities of the Kalinga medium are enormously simple, although they bear an obvious affinity to the Tinguian.

The Kalinga medium has no set fee for her services. As payment, she may receive the choicest part of the meat of the sacrificial victims, beads, money, clothes, or tools such as a headaxe, knife, or grub hoe. Such payment is never high and personal profit appears to have no part in the Kalinga medium's dedicated service.[14] She is obligated to answer a request for her services regardless of when or by whom she is asked. A medium sincerely believes that she has been selected by certain spirits or deities to perform the ceremonies and that failure to carry out these responsibilities will have serious personal consequences. It is obvious, of course, that mediums derive considerable personal satisfaction from being the focus of attention in ceremonies, but the profession is a demanding one. Kalinga mediums not only perform their share of women's work around the house and in the fields, but they also devote long and sleepless hours to ceremonies.

The activities of Kalinga mediums are similar to classic shamanistic performances the world over (compare Lowie 1954:161–64; Nadel 1946:25–37). Illness is believed to be the result of a temporary loss of the soul; restoration brings about a cure. Souls are "stolen," most generally, by the spirits of dead ancestors of the patient, although malevolent spirits may also steal a soul. If a soul is kept permanently, the victim dies. It is the task of the medium to bring the soul back and hence cure the patient. When called upon to treat a patient, the medium first determines whether the illness is caused by the spirit of an ancestor or ancestress (anitos) or by other kinds of spirits. The medium sacrifices a chicken or pig, examines the liver of the animal and determines whether it is an auspicious time to enter the spirit world. If the sign is favorable, if the liver is not spotted or marked, she chants her prayers and summons her spirit helpers. As she chants she appears to become sleepy and on the verge of falling asleep, yawning periodically. During one of these yawns *(manowob)* the name of the relative whose soul is causing the illness is emitted from her mouth. Upon regaining full consciousness the medium will instruct the relatives how to placate the deceased relative and hence bring about recovery. If the soul has been captured by malevolent spirits, the activity of the medium follows the course as outlined in the following dawak ceremony: [15]

Dawak — The Northern Kalinga Curing Rite
(An abbreviated free translation of the chants and
explanatory comments about the associated ritual)

Chants:

1) *Mambáli*

"Apo! The highest — calling on the most highest! We pray that the whole family may have good health — especially the sick person."
[Medium wears a *bayóbong* (turban of barkcloth), carries a Chinese bowl and taps it with a bamboo stick.]
"You spirit of sick person do not stay away — return to your place — we are now making dawak and we are killing a pig and I have already prayed for your return. If you are lingering in the shadow of death come back to life again."

2) *Dawák* proper

"I'm going to cure for the relatives of the sick person because it is the purpose of the Dawak and to prove to the people that I am a man-dadawak and have the power to cure."
[The medium is partly unconscious — her spirit is about to be dispatched into the spirit world.]
"My spirits are: Nagpiliyan, Nagpilitan, and Dagowalo. They are three female goddesses living in the above, their home is in the atmosphere. They are my helpers."
"We are now making this sacrifice and I hope you will pity us, especially the sick person — give her or him good health by not tempting her/him to death. We are now sacrificing the needs that you want."

3) *Mangípos*

[The medium chants that she is now preparing to enter the spirit world to seek the spirit of the patient. When she locates the spirit she will grab it, then she will fall down "for spirits always struggle."]

4) *Mamóso*

[The medium holds the pig, she blows on the pig, then on the sick person, chanting the while.]

5) *Dísag*

[The medium chants that she has entered the atmosphere and is searching for the spirit of the sick person.]

"I have found a footprint of the patient's spirit and I see my relatives and I'm trying to overtake them in order to obtain information about the patient's spirit."

"I have located the spirit of the patient. It is shedding tears, I'm pleading with it to return through *Lobawan* [a barrio of the spirits]. I've got the spirit and I'm returning and passing by *Binang Kawan* [a village] the other side of *Nansigloan* [meeting of rivers] because the water is very high."

"Let us hurry because evil spirits might catch up with us and we will be careful in crossing the river because there are crocodiles and *gilgila* [an evil water spirit]. A couple has escorted us, Magalita and Dolamigan, both good spirits. I'm offering them *boyo* [betel nut quids] for their help. I tell them that the people on earth [*gawa-an* — mortals] have sent me to bring back the spirit of the patient."

[Medium describes *Mambootan*, a barrio, as the happiest place she ever saw, but next to it is the barrio of *Nanlogawan* and here she saw headless people.]

[The medium regains consciousness and restores the spirit to the patient.]

6) *Innáy*

[Medium chants a song about the beauty of a good spirit and imitates her. Medium says she is going to put on a beauty contest to display her beauty. As she walks about the room chanting, she reports that she has more beauty than anyone there, and is the best-dressed woman on earth.]

7) *Manggóygoy*

[The medium entertains the audience by rocking a coconut shell as if it were a baby — she chants the while.]

8) *Indomdombáy*

[The medium chants a lullaby — reports that when the child grows bigger, she will teach him to court. The child is *Tawi,* a good spirit. Medium rubs her mucose on the coconut shell, saying this is the proper way to oil the skin of a baby.]

9) *Mangngíngding*

A blanket is prepared to cover the patient to prevent malevolent spirits from seeing him. Chanting the while, the medium dances around the patient with each of the following: 1) pine wood torch, 2) headaxe,

3) coconut shell, 4) tools (like grub hoe, bolo, etc.), 5) chicken, 6) pig's head.

The medium then throws the coconut shell outside and shouts five times asking the spirits to come and join the feast. She requests a member of the household to name the names of all members of the family of the patient.

10) *Mangwagawák*

[Medium chants about the meaning of dreams and their consequences.]
"If you dream of the bird *konlipag,* this is bad, request the services of a medium from some faraway place."
"If you dream about seeing yourself in a mirror, this is also bad."
"If you dream about dressing yourself, also bad."

The medium gathers all the things she used in the dawak, ferns, flowers, bolo, headaxe, and the like, and puts them in a basket. Someone helps to put the basket on her head and she leaves without looking back.

The chants of the curing rite outlined above consumed approximately two hours of recorded time. In an actual ceremony, these chants would be sung over a period of four to six hours as time is taken out for various kinds of accessory activities. A medium and her helpers usually perform their rites at night, but the preparations and the feast that are part of the curing ceremony ordinarily start in the afternoon of one day and go on to about mid-morning of the next day.

In a public or semi-public ritual, mediums do not restrict themselves to the immediate purposes of the ceremony. They are also entertainers. They may dance, sing (besides the chants), or admonish the people about proper behavior. The audience often asks them questions about the spirit world or about specific messages of the spirits. The ceremonies in which mediums perform are not solemn occasions; there is much joking among the spectators, and the mediums themselves are often engaged in conversation and in humorous bantering.

Illness and Death Rites

Life-cycle ceremonies and those ritual observances made in connection with agriculture have already been described. The rituals associated with headhunting will be discussed in the next chapter. Here we want to present additional data and practices associated with such fundamental events as illness and death. The rites differ in detail from region to region but the broad patterns are similar among both the Northern and Southern Kalinga. The foregoing description is specifically for the region of Poswoy.

An individual who is not feeling well is advised by his family to stay home and refrain from work. If he is still ill the next day, a medium is called. The latter sacrifices a chicken or a pig and examines its liver to determine the cause of illness (a medium can tell from the condition of this organ whether "anitos" or "demons" are responsible for the illness). The medium then decorates the four corners of the house with different kinds of ferns. The door is decorated in the most elaborate fashion in order to discourage the evil spirits who may seek entrance into the house to harm the patient. Rice cakes mixed with coconut milk, called *sinonglag,* are served to invited relatives, and betel nut preparation (called by its ritual name, *gongway*) is placed in a small Chinese plate outside for the spirits. The curing rite, dawak, is then performed by the medium and her helpers.

During the night, the men play the *tongngatong* which consists of six or more bamboo tubes of various lengths. The cylinders are struck on a stone platform and produce sounds suggesting the music of a xylophone or a marimba. Approximately ten days later if the patient has shown no improvement, another dawak is performed by the mediums.

Several pigs and even carabaos may be sacrificed on the occasion of a curing ceremony. One of the mediums takes on the role of supervisor and instructs the relatives about the preparations which are needed to appease the spirits. If the patient is a prominent person the entire regional population will be invited and the occasion becomes a grand prestige affair. Outside, gongs are played and people dance the salidsid. Dancing is sporadically interrupted by playing the tongngatong and clappers *(patangkog).* These activities begin in mid-afternoon, continue through the night, and terminate about mid-morning of the following day. While dancing and the playing of instruments go on outside, the mediums are busy with the dawak in the house where the patient lies on a mat. The entire affair, the dancing, the music and the chants of mediums, are all performed to placate the spirits who indeed, are believed to join in the feast and to enjoy the festivities along with the mortals.

If the dawak is unsuccessful and the illness continues, the aid of an herb specialist may be sought. Such an individual, called *mandadagop* in some of the northern Kalinga dialects, may be a man or woman. Not everyone can be a mandadagop; he or she must be a person who has dreamed about the curative properties of certain kinds of plants and the manner in which they are to be used in the treatment of specific kinds of illnesses. These plants are called *balat* and are considered to be the special property of the dreamer. Only the mandadagop who has received specific instruction in a dream about these plants is entitled to employ them and only when administered by such an individual are they effective. Food restrictions and taboos accompany the administration of balat, and the mandadagop instructs the patient and his relatives about the kinds of observances to be made. Such restrictions consist of abstention from chicken, carabao, cow meat, crabs, shrimp and sugar cane. While the patient is taking balat, the house is closed to all visitors except the mandadagop and household members.

The mandadagop is not a medium. He has no spirit helpers, nor does he chant or sing or "enter the spirit world" to communicate with either ancestral spirits or "deities." He is simply one who dreams about the curative powers of specific plants and the manner in which they are to be employed in curing specific types of diseases.

The mandadagop is given *pisok* which is a gift of insignificant value: a knife, a bolo, or a few coins amounting to no more than a peso. Failure to give pisok may cause the mandadagop to have the same illness which his balat will cure. Mandadagop never refuse to treat a patient when asked, and they are always given something for their services.

The Kalinga also hire the services of herbalists and curers from other groups, particularly from the Ilocano. Such "doctors" are paid a fee and are distinguished from the Kalinga curers and mediums. In Poswoy, non-Kalinga medical practitioners who are not mediums or modern medical doctors are called *mallawos*.

To cure persisting and nagging illnesses, the Kalinga try all kinds of medicines. They frequently buy herbal or other medical preparations, usually of Chinese provenience, in Baguio and other towns in the Mountain Province. Medicines dispensed by the few modern medical doctors available to the Kalinga are so popular that a number of unscrupulous Filipino doctors have supplemented salary incomes by selling medicines given to them as free samples.[16] Roman Catholic and Protestant clergy charge a nominal price for medical supplies from their dispensaries in order to prevent the use of them by individuals who do not actually need medication. The Kalinga, like many other non-literate peoples, consider medicine a "cure-all" and will take as much as they are given. They tend also to disregard dosages. If one pill is prescribed they reckon that two or more will hasten the cure. But if the medicine is available, persons who are really in need of medication are never turned away by the missionary dispensaries simply because of the inability to pay.

Although medicines are sought, visits to modern medical doctors and to hospitals are avoided until all other forms of treatment have been explored. The procedure is usually as follows: a dawak ceremony by a medium; native medicines prescribed by a mandadagop; herbal medicines secured in Ilocano or Chinese shops; modern medicines obtained from a doctor or from missionary dispensaries; and finally, as a last resort, a visit to a modern doctor or the hospital at Lubuagan.

In Poswoy a ceremony called *songngá* is performed in cases where the illness of the patient is so grave that death is considered imminent.

The medium sacrifices a chicken or a pig and pours the blood of the victim on the patient "to wipe out the fingerprints" of the malevolent spirits. A feast is prepared and served to the nearest of kin and neighbors. Music, songs and dancing are forbidden during the songngá, just as such entertainment is prohibited during a funeral in Poswoy. Since a cure is not expected, the ceremony and feast are primarily to uphold the honor and dignity of the patient's family and near relatives. Neglect of an individual at the time of death is considered a serious offense, and public censure would be extremely severe on a family that did not continue to make sacrificial offerings.

Funeral rites have been discussed in some detail in the life-cycle section of Chapter II; only a few additional particulars are included here.

Until the deceased is buried, members of the kindred are forbidden to eat the meat of pigs slaughtered during the funeral. Immediately after burial, the house where the deceased was watched, as well as the yard about the house is swept clean, and another pig is butchered. The meat of this pig may be eaten by all except the surviving spouse of the deceased who cannot eat any kind of meat and is also forbidden to eat certain kinds of fish and root crops for another month. The spouse is also forbidden to prepare his own meals for the same length of time. At the end of this period, the sacrifice of a chicken lifts the food restrictions.

The death of a prominent adult binds members of his kindred in other types of mourning restrictions *(mangngíngo),* for one to one and a half years. During this time these relatives must wear a strip of black or brown cloth, they must not dance or sing songs like the adí, dangnó or salidomáy. The surviving spouse should not remarry for a year and must not oil or cut the hair for the same length of time.

Kalinga Deities and Spirits

Kaboníyan is the most important benevolent deity of the Kalinga. Kaboníyan is conceived of as a male and stories about his creative powers and his miraculous feats are related everywhere. He is said to have made man and woman out of clay and breathed life into them so that they lived and began to populate the earth. The number of people increased so rapidly that Kaboníyan had to invent death in order to control the population. He is credited also with making the mountains and rivers of northern Luzon.

Kaboníyan is apparently never invoked directly nor are sacrifices made specifically to him in any ceremony.[17] The chanted prayers of the mediums in the kontád, sickness and death rites, are addressed either to their own spirit helpers and/or to spirits called collectively *kadódwa,*

dódwa or *mandódwa* and this may include both benevolent and malevolent spirits.[18] Spirit helpers of the mediums are never the same for any two mediums. The medium whose chants of the dáwak I recorded indicates *Nagpiliyán, Nagpilitán,* and *Dágowalo* as her spirit helpers, but other mediums will have other spirit helpers. In chanting the dáwak reproduced above, she began her prayer with the pan-montane expression Ápo (lord, master). It is taken for granted, of course, that the sacrificial victims and the wine served in any ceremony are to be shared by mortals and spirits good or bad, ancestral or natural.

A medium when performing a ritual in a swidden or a rice field will sometimes invoke *"bákbakot"* for a good yield or an abundant harvest, but this term simply means woman or old woman and in this context, according to informants, the medium is simply invoking the female deity of the rice field without specifying such a deity by name. Only in Poswoy was I able to obtain a specific name for a rice deity, Daládaw, which was given to me by a medium. I suspect that Daládaw was simply the name of her own spirit helper, and that there is not a specific rice deity and for that matter, specific deities are not addressed in ceremonies for sickness, death and headhunting.

Only with Kaboníyan, then, is there common agreement about a name and associated positive attributes of a benevolent deity. There is more agreement about the names and attributes of malevolent spirits. Hence, there is a general belief among the regions of northern Kalinga that the term Ngílin refers both to the restrictive period during pregnancy and to a malevolent water spirit which hungers for and devours human embryos unless specific counter measures are taken. The Ngílin in Poswoy is believed to be a pigmy or dwarf although this characterization is not accepted everywhere. Informants in other regions simply indicated that the Ngílin was a water spirit but could not tell what it looked like.

A class of malevolent spirits about whom there appears to be general agreement as to their designs and attributes are the Álan. These are ghouls that devour corpses and thus prevent the satisfactory dispatch of a deceased soul or spirit into the afterworld. The sacrifices and offerings made during a funeral are made primarily to placate or to ward off these spirits. There is no general agreement, however, about the appearance of the Álan. In the north the Álan are conceived to be giants, and in Lubuagan they may take various forms either of men or animals.

Other names and attributes of malevolent spirits common among the Kalinga, but about whose form or appearance informants were not able to provide information, are the following:

Sil-ít, the god of thunder. It may punish individuals or damage swiddens and rice fields unless properly propitiated.

Bolaláyaw, the god of lightning, causes illness and damage to rice fields.

Ángton, a malevolent spirit or deity of food, makes people gluttons.

Sangásang, a guardian spirit of the village, is resident in the shrine called *podáyan* located at the entrance of each hamlet. Formerly warriors deposited heads taken from the enemy in a basket fashioned on top of a bamboo stalk *(sokólang)* at the podáyan as an offering to the sangásang. At present, betel-nut offerings are made at the shrine. Failure to make these offerings or defilement of the shrine will anger the sangásang who will punish the village by sending illness or some other form of misfortune.

Anito, as among other mountain peoples, refers to ancestral spirits as distinct from nature spirits. This term may be recent, however. Mr. William H. Scott of Sagada who has travelled extensively in northern Luzon reports that the word refers to a ceremony in many parts of the Mountain Province. He suggests that the present meaning might have been introduced by this generation who are in need of terms to discuss "classes" of pagan spirits. There is, for example, no general term for nature spirits, although Alan is sometimes used for malevolent non-ancestral spirits collectively. The generalizing terms which exist in the Mountain Province languages tend to be either of Spanish, English, or Ilocano derivation.

It is clear from the Kalinga's inability to provide a list of benevolent supernatural beings and the rather ineffectual nature of their one "all good" god that the supernaturals are very much feared. The primary religious occupation of the Kalinga is to compromise this evil supernatural environment. The chanted myth-prayers of the mediums and the lavish feasts which are to be shared by mortals, departed souls, and nature spirits all reinforce the view of supernaturals as malevolently disposed and the constant need to appease them. Kalinga ceremonies are designed to secure health, safety from the enemy, bountiful crops, success in hunting, and the benefits of general prosperity by their performance at times which are considered especially auspicious or threatening. We will return to the central theme of Kalinga religious activity once we have considered the nature of Kalinga ceremonies.

The Significance of Kalinga Ceremonies

As is true with peoples everywhere, those areas of life in which problems cannot be resolved by simple or practical techniques become sources of anxiety or concern and the foci of religious preoccupation for the Kalinga. Viewed in this fashion the intensity of religious activity forms a gradient which reflects basic Kalinga anxieties quite accurately.

Thus the concern over health and well being receives primary attention. In the development of an individual, the vulnerable periods are approximately the first year of life and the times of illness. The restrictive observances called Ngílin are taken to safeguard a pregnant woman and her unborn child. Once the child is born the special ceremonies of the Kontád guide it during the period when it is most vulnerable to the machinations of the spirits. In between the Kontád rites and the death observances, illness is treated by the general curing rite, dáwak or posípos, but each region has its own special ceremonies for particular types of illnesses. Given the view of the supernatural world as evilly disposed to the living, death rites are naturally emphasized. The spirit of the deceased must be sent off graciously, otherwise it, in league with other spirits, might wreak its vengeance on the living by sending illness or other misfortunes. Thus there is a widely held belief that when a grandparent dies he or she will take along one or more of his grandchildren. While children may be in greater danger, no member of the kindred is exempt, and all relatives attend the funeral and observe traditional precautions during and after. The concern of the relatives is emphasized by the lament of the widow in Lubuagan and southern Kalinga regions. She sits wailing and sobbing beside the corpse, begging the spirit of her late husband to hurry on to the spirit world and not send illness or death to herself or their children.

Formerly headhunting and warfare also loomed as important events and sources of deep anxiety. Religious activity equal in intensity to that accorded sickness and death rites were devoted to this complex. With suppression of headhunting and the decrease in interregional feuding and killings, such rituals have almost completely disappeared. The peace-pact institution with its emphasis on hospitality to visitors and the popularity of the peace-pact celebrations are now substituted for the anxieties and ritual activity which formerly surrounded headhunting and warfare. In the process, social and recreational outlets which were formerly confined to specific regions have been extended interregionally over wide areas of the Kalinga Subprovince. In the past, such purely social activities were largely restricted to intra-kindred activities and regional marriages. At present, the palános or pa-ínom, a hospitality feast to honor regional visitors, is given primarily on occasions when an individual or a group from another region arrives for a visit.

Agricultural ritual, a focal area of religious activity in such intensive terrace irrigation areas as those of the Ifugao and Bontoc, receives comparatively slight attention among the Kalinga. Everywhere in the Mountain Province the primary and almost exclusive ritual crop is rice. Because of the density of the population and the pressure on cultivable rice fields, the southern groups do not always have sufficient rice for their needs.

Moreover, these people must exert great effort to grow it, constructing plots that are level, reinforcing retaining walls, and guiding water in ditches and bamboo flumes in just the proper amount to insure a steady flow. If these tasks are not properly performed, and if there is too much water or not enough, or if there is a landslide, the long and tedious labor might have been for naught. The anxiety over the cultivation of rice is thus a nagging and persistent one and to reduce such anxiety, the Ifugao and Bontoc have understandably developed a complex system of religious observances and rituals.

The Kalinga do not have the deep concern over rice production that exists among the southern groups and hence have not developed a complex set of rituals to go along with rice cultivation. Rice is important to the Kalinga and its cultivation is not devoid of ritual observances, but such activity does not compare in quantity or intensity with the elaborate rites of the Ifugao or Bontoc. Moreover, rice in swiddens receives greater ritual attention; irrigated rice, except in areas nearest the Bontoc and Ifugao, is almost completely ignored ritually. This distribution of ritualistic practices alone, were it not for other evidences, indicates the recency of wet rice among the Kalinga and the source of its diffusion (*see* Chapter III). Other reasons for a more casual attitude toward the cultivation of rice are evident considering a number of factors. Kalinga populations do not approach the density of the Bontoc and Ifugao areas; hence, the pressure on land is not as great. The Kalinga ecological environment is also more favorable for the exploitation of other food sources. Lower elevations and a tropical vegetation produce more abundant and greater varieties of both wild and cultivated fruits and vegetables. Hunting is also more rewarding; there are more deer, wild pigs and chickens, and various types of birds in the tropical or semi-tropical forests of the Kalinga country.

The production of rice is not, therefore, a pressing concern of the Kalinga, and there is no need to emphasize agricultural activity with elaborate ceremonial rites. In a recent publication, the late Felix Keesing has summarized the Isneg's ceremonial preoccupation in terms that are also appropriate for the Kalinga. The Isneg of Apayao are neighbors of the Kalinga immediately to the north. Keesing (1962:15) reports:

> The Isneg approach to the supernatural, when compared to that of the terracing groups, brings to mind the anthropologically familiar contrast between the Navaho and Pueblo peoples in the American Southwest. Where the terracers and the Pueblo maize cultivators focus their major hopes and anxieties upon the annual crop cycle and related phenomena, the Isneg and Navaho appear absorbed with health and curing, with survival of their small and scattered living groups in vast, relatively empty spaces, and in the face of marauding enemies. As with Navaho "sings," the Isneg

healing rites not only succor the sick or wounded, but also reinforce the health and power of the well persons who are participating. The great festivals *(sayam)* may bring several hundred persons into face-to-face interaction.

There are no community welfare ceremonies like the *Begnas* ceremony of Sagada (Eggan MS 1959) at present among the Kalinga, although the earlier headhunting ceremony, *sagáng,* appears to have been such an event. In former times the *Begnas* ceremony was undoubtedly a celebration for a victorious return of a headhunting party. With the suppression of headhunting in the late 1800's, Eggan reports that the ceremony was reorganized to emphasize community welfare. We have noted above that suppression of headhunting among the Kalinga resulted in the development or elaboration of the interregional peace pacts, and the periodic renewal celebrations of the pacts have become popular interregional social events. Ceremonial reorganization in these two examples has taken different forms although the original ceremonies were at least in purpose much the same.

Ceremonies among the Kalinga clearly underscore the events which concern the people most and cause the most anxiety. The more anxiety-producing an event is, for example serious illness or death, the more elaborate the ceremonial activity. Another indicator of the importance of an occasion or an event is whether or not there is consultation of omens before the event takes place. Some such events as the initial work in making a new swidden or rice field, preparing to go on a deer or wild pig hunt, and the escorting of the groom to the home of his bride have already been noted. Other times when omens are carefully observed are the following: before taking a long trip beyond one's home region; before departing on a headhunting trip; before the burial of a deceased adult relative; before opening a new peace pact or renewing an old one; before departing to make the initial arrangements in an interregional marriage contract; and before selling a valuable Chinese jar into another region. All these events are of primary importance, and omens must be observed to insure their success. Also, upon beginning any important task or journey one or more men beat the bamboo clappers (patanggok) in order to inspire favorable idáw sounds.

The Kalinga are beginning to lose faith in omens, however. Opportunities for travel and the need to meet schedules have necessitated violations in strict observance. Repeated experiences where events did not turn out as indicated by omens, whether favorable or unfavorable, have made the Kalinga skeptical. Impressive incidents which are indicative of catastrophic consequences, such as earthquakes and landslides, still guide the conduct and actions of Kalingas, however. It is unlikely, for example, that a Kalinga will disregard the ominous and foreboding signs of a severe earthquake or landslide just before beginning an important task, no matter how strongly he may be influenced by Christian or Western concepts.

The Nature of Kalinga Religion

Kalinga religion is based on a view of the supernatural world as antagonistic to the world of the living — the two worlds being regarded as opposed to each other. Supernaturals, whether the souls of spirits of the dead or spirits of beings who were never mortal, are malevolent and punitive. Kaboníyan, the culture hero, is an exception — a good god who never punishes. Yet the propitiatory activities of the Kalinga ignore Kaboníyan and consider him inconsequential or at least ineffective. A few isolated cases suggest that he is on rare occasions petitioned for help (compare Barton 1949:20) but the prayers, sacrifices, and anxieties of the Kalinga indicate an overwhelming preoccupation with spirits of the dead and other malevolent spirits. The spirit helpers of the mediums help to cure when petitions and sacrifices are offered to them, but they are not benevolent beings.

Thus, the supernaturals, with Kaboníyan excepted, must be constantly appeased and pacified. Failure to offer prayers, wine, and sacrificial victims causes them to respond with vengeance, sending illness and death and destroying swiddens and rice fields. Supernaturals are regarded as the enemy, much in the same manner as non-kin beyond the borders of the regional unit. The difference is that supernaturals are propitiated, but the human enemy, at least in the past, was controlled by defensive warfare or by periodic offensive retaliatory forays. It is significant, however, that intraregional disputes and conflicts suggest the pattern followed with supernaturals. Kindreds or, more narrowly defined, relatives of an individual who transgresses against another, pay weregilds to the latter's relatives and then cap the settlement with a feast. With the cessation of headhunting and warfare, the described practice of settling disputes in the home region has been extended to interregional conflicts through the machinery of the peace pact. The feast which terminates the establishment of a pact between two regions or the renewal of such a pact resembles the palanos. Both types of events are similar to sacrificial feasts given on the occasion of a curing or funeral ceremony. The guests at the latter are invisible members of the spirit world; in the palanos they are visibly present, the offended kindred; and in the peace-pact celebration, they are members of a former hostile region. In all cases the guests are potentially dangerous, and only tactful and generous treatment of them by the hosts will keep them friendly and willing to compromise.

Kalinga hostilities are directed outside the kindred. Within the kindred group there is remarkably little conflict. A child is made aware of his large number of relatives as soon as he becomes conscious of his external surroundings. Formal visits such as the omóy pasíbit, omapó, balón di babát and mamilók impress upon the child at an early age the host of bilateral relatives who are concerned about his well-being. Virtually every important ritualistic event reinforces this bond so that an individual soon develops a strong loyalty to his group. In the northern Kalinga regions where the kindred, in theory at least, is believed to embrace the entire regional population, kindred loyalty binds everyone together.

Kindred relations are marked by considerable freedom of action, with acceptance and tolerance of one another. These characteristics are instilled in a highly permissive childhood training period, but the permissive development goes on relatively unchecked into adulthood. Transgressions occur within the kindred, but these are usually resolved quickly, openly, and without leaving deeply rooted grudges.[19] Moreover, since a large segment of an individual's kindred takes the blame for an action, these relatives act as a buffer for him by sharing the unpleasant task of paying fines and otherwise making adjustments. The Kalinga grows into old age, then, with deep loyalties to and trust in his kindred. His suspicions and fears are directed instead at the supernatural world and at non-kin who are spatially removed.

Kindred loyalty and trust as they operate among the Kalinga have largely eliminated suspicion and distrust within the group. My own Pueblo background made it difficult to accept this state of affairs among the Kalinga for a long time. I kept looking for the kind of damaging, backbiting gossip (although rarely in the open) which characterizes intragroup relations among the Pueblos. Factional cleavages among the Rio Grande Pueblos often align non-relatives together and may throw siblings in rival factions. Among the Hopi, the core of a faction may contain a matri-lineage or a segment thereof, but it may place one's father, or a father's sister, in a hostile camp. In both Pueblo cases, spouses may be thrown into separate factions. Such alignments, despite an early permissive childhood training period, engender distrust and suspicion among Pueblo individuals.[20] While a Hopi tends to be loyal to his siblings and maternal first cousins, he becomes confused and distrustful when a beloved father or an affectionate father's sister suddenly appears in an opposing faction.

No society is entirely free of conflict among closely interacting kin and the Kalinga are no exception, yet the relations among parents, parents' siblings, and their children are remarkably free of friction. The spouses of these relatives are, of course, also included in the kindred (*see* discussion of the kinship circle or kindred in Chapter II).

It is important here to indicate another contributing factor for the rarity of intra-kin conflict. Kalinga settlements (except for some of the south Kalinga towns) are small and dispersed and until recently were moved frequently within the region. This type of settlement pattern, which has nevertheless allowed for periodic interaction of kin, undoubtedly fosters greater tension-free relationships among close relations.

From my Pueblo experiences I had also expected to find evidences of witchcraft and sorcery among the Kalinga. While they are aware of it and there is an occasional reference to a person practicing sorcery in the densely populated south Kalinga regions, the Kalinga have no anxiety about it.

Among the Pueblo and elsewhere, witchcraft appears where close neighbors are distrusted and feared. The Kalinga vent their hostilities on the enemy, or did until recently, while most of their fears and anxieties are bound up with supernaturals. Intra-group wrongs and offenses are immediately challenged and brought up openly before regional leaders and resolved as kindred or kindred segment responsibilities. These factors undoubtedly explain why witchcraft, which is born of fear, distrust, and suspicion of closely interacting individuals (often near relatives), has not been a problem among the Kalinga.

Religious values reflect conditions in the Kalinga temporal life in a remarkably accurate fashion. Perhaps all traditional religions of fairly homogenous societies mirror the world of the living in this way. Such key concepts as vengeance, appeasement, and generosity which operate in the everyday life of the Kalinga also characterize the behavior of supernaturals and the latter's relations with mortals. Supernatural spirits, like mortals, are considered vengeful, inflicting illness and death when not properly propitiated. Appeasement of spirits may be compared in mortal existence to the payment of fines or weregilds to assuage an injured party. Generosity is demonstrated to spirits by the lavish feasts prepared for them which they are believed to share with mortals. Whether the Kalinga believe that spirits can be generous is not apparent, but they obviously hope so. Generosity is a trait they exploit to extreme degrees among themselves, however. It is keynoted in the gracious hospitality extended to visitors and the palanos feast given to honor them. A related concept, that of indebtedness, is maintained with supernaturals and the living. Prayers and offerings obligate the supernaturals to the living while generous hospitality and gifts bind the living to one another in a mutual system of obligations.

Western and Christian Influences

Western ideas and concepts did not forcibly affect the Kalinga until the closing periods of the last century. During the initial Spanish missionization period in the seventeenth century, some of the ancestors of the Kalinga surely received Christian indoctrination in the Cagayan missions, but as refugees they undoubtedly quickly divested themselves of such training. The event that brought about important changes among the Kalinga was the Spanish trail from Abra across the Cordillera Central and thence into the Chico Valley. This trail was built to supply the military posts which were established to control the periodic raids of the mountain peoples. Contact between Spanish soldiers was probably infrequent, but the trail opened up opportunities for trade and travel and brought the Kalinga in contact either directly with the Ilocano or with groups such as the Tinguian who were in contact with the Ilocano. The Ilocano language undoubtedly become established in the mountains as a lingua franca at this time, and with it, Spanish terms diffused into the Kalinga language and other mountain vernaculars. Notions about Spanish rule and political divisions present among the Kalinga also diffused, and most important of all, the popular tool for interregional understanding and friendship — the peace pact — was born. All of these factors facilitated the dissemination of Western and Christian concepts during the first decade of the American period when roads and trails were constructed throughout the mountains of northern Luzon.

American control brought political divisions modeled on the Spanish colonial pattern and a representative form of government. The early lieutenant governors working through local leaders introduced Western notions of law and order and suppressed headhunting and warfare. The latter had already started with the peace-pact system but American endorsement of the system, as well as the training of a native constabulary force, accelerated the establishment of law and order. Schools were started and training in health and sanitation was begun, so that by the end of the second decade of the century, a fairly effective foundation for an American version of Western civilization had been laid. The number of American or foreign personnel was small — there were probably no more than a half dozen Americans in governmental service in the Kalinga Subprovince up to the outbreak of World War II. At first, lowland Filipinos occupied important subprovincial and municipal posts, but these were slowly replaced by Kalinga. At present, positions in the government and in the schools, except in missionary establishments, are virtually all in the control of the native population. (*See* Chapter I for a more detailed discussion of the American period.)

Western influence and genuine enthusiasm combine in celebrating the peace pact, as shown by this sign celebrating the arrival of the delegates from Asiga in the hamlet of Allangigan.

Since the third decade of this century, three religious denominations, one Catholic and two Protestant, have served the Kalinga population.[21] The number of actual converts is minimal — the Kalinga have not embraced Christianity in vast numbers. The reason for the few converts is primarily the problem of establishing an effective missionary program in an extremely rugged area where the settlements are reached only by precipitous trails which are almost inaccessible during the rainy season. Missionary personnel is also entirely inadequate in numbers to serve such a mountainous population. Almost the whole of the Kalinga area, for example, is served by two Roman Catholic priests resident in Salegseg. One priest, the rector of the mission, administers to the población and nearby hamlets, while his assistant serves other hamlets in Salegseg and hamlets in the regions of Poswoy, Ababaan, Daoangan, Balbalan proper,

Banao, Mabaca, and Buaya. This is an area of approximately one thousand square miles interlaced with rugged mountain ridges and deep gorges. The hamlets are dispersed in the sides and pockets of the mountains, and the trails leading into them are so steep and in such poor repair that the priest, like the natives, must take off his shoes to reach the settlements. In addition, the lower elevations of the area are infected with the malarial mosquito. While the disease may now be averted by taking malarial pills at regular intervals, the many demands made on the priest for administering to the sick and the dying and for conducting religious services cause him to forget to take the pills regularly. Both priests at Salegseg during my study had contracted the ailment early in their missionary work and were often incapacitated by malarial fever.

The priests have trained native catechists for each of the regions of their district who provide instruction in Catholic doctrine in the local hamlets and thus relieve the clergy of some of the routine work. Nevertheless, the sacraments must be administered by a priest; hence, there is need for periodic visitation to isolated hamlets. When the rector's assistant leaves the mission post for his round of visits, he is gone from two to six weeks.

The missionary efforts of both Protestants and Catholics are frustrated by meager personnel and by a rugged, mountainous terrain. Most of the Kalinga converts come from the mission schools where Christian indoctrination is carried on over longer periods of time and under more intensive circumstances. Kalinga do not object to missionaries and are friendly to all denominations whether Protestant or Catholic. Most Kalinga who profess to be Christians are Roman Catholics. This is because the clergy of this denomination, represented by the Belgian Fathers, have staked out the heart of the Kalinga region for missionary work. Some Kalinga have also become affiliated with the Episcopal mission at Balbalasan and the United Brethren Church at Lubuagan and profess to be members of these denominations. (For additional information on the activities of the missionaries, see Chapter I.)

Although the number of actual converts to either Catholicism or the Protestant denominations is small, Western and Christian concepts have diffused widely among the Kalinga. The cessation of headhunting and the termination of the rituals involving this sport are evidence of this diffusion. Other changes attributable to Western influences include the omission of many of the ritual steps in the Kontad, marriage and death ceremonies. The enthusiastic involvement of Kalinga in provincial and municipal elections and general politics is also indicative of Western influences. We have also noted the eager participation of the Kalinga in organizations and committees, triggered no doubt by missionaries and early American school teachers. Schooling is highly valued, and higher education is a desideratum of almost every Kalinga. Finally, of dubious value but nevertheless stemming from American contact, is the desire for Western products even though they may be inferior to their own natively manufactured items. A particularly glaring example of this is the corrugated tin roof which is rapidly replacing the old cogon grass roof. The latter sheds rain as effectively and keeps the house cooler, but a tin-roofed house marks the residence of an influential and sophisticated man!

Western and Christian influences are effecting important changes among the Kalinga, but indigenous values persist. Difficult to eradicate is the Kalinga's urge for revenge and retaliation. A Catholic priest in Lubuagan remarked that while the Kalinga had made great strides in acculturation, they could not pluck revenge from their hearts. The pre-occupation with this deeply imbedded trait was borne out by a young Kalinga College student in Baguio. The youth organized a group of his co-regionists to fight a gang of lowlanders, members of which had insulted him. The young Kalinga remarked: "I thought I was a good Christian, but the need to 'even the score' is a part of all Kalinga. Until we have revenged an insult or injury we will not stop!"

Notes to Chapter 4

1. The Kalinga do believe that persisting sorrow or thoughts about the loss of a parent, son or other close relative is a summons to join the deceased one in the spirit world. In such cases, which are reported to be rare, the bones of the deceased are exhumed and washed in order to placate the spirit of the departed relative.
2. The people of certain regions are considered to be especially prone to poisoning others, although in general the Kalinga of one region will always suspect the worst of the inhabitants of another region. On one occasion, in the spring of 1960, my Salegseg guide and I decided to make a shortcut to Limos via Poswoy and Ababaan rather than take the regular trail to Balbalan and thence down the Saltan River to Limos. We were warned in the village of Obol (Salegseg) and again in Capas (Poswoy) not to accept food or drink in any of the villages of the region of Ababaan for we would surely be poisoned. The huge meal we had been served in Capas and the water in our canteens sufficed until we reached the home of the school teacher, Gupa-al, in Limos where a lavish feast was prepared for us.
3. An interesting anecdote about the Roman Catholic priest resident in the poblacion of Salegseg for many years is related by the Kalinga. The veneration accorded the guardian stones in the podayan so infuriated the priest that on one occasion he kicked and scattered the stones in the shrine. He purposely defiled the sacred stones to show the Kalinga that no evil consequences are likely to ensue from such an act. Soon afterward, the priest became very ill, so ill indeed that he was unable to prevent a ceremony performed for his

recovery by the Kalinga of the region who had an affectionate regard for him. The medium chanted her songs, sacrificed a chicken and performed her rites despite the priest's weak protestations to stop the rites. The priest recovered and while he attempted to convince the Kalinga that his illness had no connection with his defilement of the sacred shrine, the Kalinga feel otherwise. No doubt the priest, who was also extremely fond of the Kalinga, accepted the ceremony as a sincere expression of their affection for him.

4. Lomawig is reported in Tinglayan by Folkmar (MS 1906). Undoubtedly the veneration of Lomawig has diffused from Bontoc where this deity is the most important culture hero and prominent in all the folktales and legends (Jenks 1905).

5. Among the Kalinga and the Isneg of Apayao, considerable use is made of ferns and other wild plants in rituals associated with swiddens (compare Vanoverbergh 1941).

6. The southern Kalinga mediums are also predominantly women although a few men also take up the profession. The regions nearest Bontoc, for example, Bugnay, Butbut and Basao have more men mediums than do those of Lubuagan and Dalupa-Ableg. The latter are along the Pacil River, the boundary between the Northern and Southern Kalinga. Whereas men are not barred from becoming mediums, among the Northern Kalinga and Tinguian (Cole 1922:301), few men ever take up the profession. I did not meet a single male medium among the Kalinga although I became acquainted with a number of women mediums.

7. Carabaos are proper sacrificial victims for all ceremonies among the Northern Kalinga but are not used for such purposes among the Ifugao (Lambrecht 1932:18), and in Sagada carabaos are butchered only for food in marriage celebrations (Eggan 1959).

8. This appears to be "true possession," *(see* footnote 15 below).

9. Boasting recitals associated with war exploits have been reported by Eggan (1959) for Sagada, and Reid (1961:14) for Guinaang and Bontoc, while Worcester (1912:833–930) and Barton (1949:157–159) describe Kalinga recitals, but none of these writers mention boastings about economic wealth.

10. *Ganzas* are heirloom possessions handed down in families. They obviously came into the area through trade, probably with the Chinese, as they are not manufactured in the Philippines. The ganzas are shaped like a tambourine, about ten to twelve inches in diameter, with the sides varying from about an inch to two inches in height. The handles of the gongs, by which they are carried in the left hand and beaten with a stick held in the right hand (as with the Palo-ok), were formerly human jaw bones. Human jawbone handles are still in the possession of many who own ganzas but they do not ordinarily use them unless they are certain that only regional members are present at the dance.

11. As an American visitor in a peace-pact warm-up celebration between Poswoy and Dalupa-Ableg held in the latter region, I was honored as the second dancer by being paired off with the Poswoy pact-holder, a spry old woman of about sixty.

12. Headhunting was still important among the Northern Kalinga during the first decade of the century. There are, therefore, still a number of older men alive who actively participated in the sport and who delight in relating their experiences. Worcester, who witnessed an actual headhunting celebration among the Northern Kalinga about the turn of the century, gives an eyewitness account of the feast and provides excellent photographs of dancing warriors (Worcester *op. cit.*). Ritual headhunting and the festivities connected with it still go on sporadically in other remote areas of the Kalinga country. One of the Roman Catholic priests of Natonin (Eastern Kalinga) related that several heads had been taken in the spring of 1960 and the related rituals performed.

13. Among the Ifugao, the activities of mediums are much more specialized than among the other mountain peoples, and their practices (*cf.* Lambrecht 1929:41; 1955; and Barton 1946) are similar to the activities commonly associated with priests. While the political organization of the Ifugao appears to be simpler that of the Bontoc (Jenks 1905; Keesing 1949) or the Kalinga, the religious activity of their mediums or priests is exceedingly complex (*cf.* Barton 1946:10).

14. The payment made to the medium for her services is minimal, but the number of sacrificial victims slaughtered and the feast prepared for kindred members and visitors are enormous. In illness and death ceremonies the costs of the offerings are paid by those relatives who will inherit or who have inherited the most property from the patient or the deceased. Any occasion where sacrificial victims are offered are prestige feasts as well. Hence, all members of the patient's kindred, including the spouses of such a group, are eager to make the occasion a memorable one and try to evoke the admiration of the entire regional population.

15. The chants of the dawak were recorded on tape, but only an abbreviated translation was obtained. It had been my intention to work with the medium and the interpreter at a later date and secure a word-by-word translation, but unfortunately the opportunity never presented itself. I have also listened to other chants, but in remote hamlets where I could not take a tape recorder.

   Possession takes place only on ceremonial occasions; the medium who chanted the curing rite went through the "dawak" portion without a change in voice or personality. Possession was not actually observed, but the description related by informants indicates "true possession." The medium becomes partly unconscious, the pupils of her eyes move about wildly, arms and legs become taut, and she loses contact with those about her. Finally the medium speaks in a strange voice, the "voice of spirits," and begins to describe her experiences in the "spirit world." Sometimes her speech is unintelligible and an assistant interprets for her. When she "returns" from the "spirit world" she recovers from her trance and once again she is normal, yet unaware of what she has said or what she has done during the time that her spirit was wandering in the "spirit world" (Compare Cole 1922:303).

   The medium who sang the chants of the dawak presented here explained through an interpreter the entire ceremony which I have indicated by inserting explanatory comments. It is important to emphasize that each medium presents her performance of a ceremony in somewhat individual fashion, yet the general pattern here presented would not differ substantially from the curing rite of the dawak given by other mediums.

16. There is a high rate of turnover in medical doctors provided by the Philippine government to serve the Kalinga. The hospital at Lubuagan usually operates with two doctors, another doctor serves the Eastern Kalinga from Natonin, and another the Northern Kalinga from Salegseg. Like the few Roman Catholic priests in these remote and mountainous areas, these doctors suffer hardships in reaching patients in the isolated hamlets. Unfortunately, these doctors lack the dedicated devotion to their work which the priests have and tend to shirk their responsibilities by remaining in the home stations as much as possible. Eventually the remoteness and hardships become too difficult to bear and they request transfer.

17. Barton (1949:20) cites a Lubuagan informant's account of a prayer which petitions *Kaboniyan's* help to cure an illness, but adds another informant's correction that the prayer should actually state: "Kabunian, who is the greatest, the wisest and strongest of all and who stops the cruelty of the anitu, stop those bad spirits and defend this person." This correction indicates that Kaboni-yan may prevent malevolent spirits from causing illness, but he himself does

not cure and by implication does not inflict illness. My informants denied that Kaboniyan was ever directly petitioned for curing or preventing any kind of misfortune.

18. William H. Scott of Sagada suggests that these terms may be related to *dowa* (two) and hence carrying a meaning of "one like" or "a double."

19. This statement will not hold for Lubuagan where urban-like settlement patterns have disrupted kindred solidarity patterns, and occasionally serious rifts are said to develop between close relatives.

20. Initiation of Hopi boys (aged six to nine) into the Katcina cult also adds to the confusion and distrust of closely related kin and neighbors. At this time boys discover that the Katcina are not really supernatural beings, but are merely portrayed by men from their own village.

21. In 1959 another Protestant denomination, the Philippine Lutheran Mission, was added.

5. Headhunting, Warfare, and the Peace-Pact Institution

WE HAVE NOTED the regional character of Kalinga populations. This is most pronounced in the rugged mountains of the present municipal districts of Tinglayan, Lubuagan, Tanudan, and Balbalan. Adherence to well-defined territorial regions is conditioned partly by the presence of well-marked geographical features such as gorges and mountain ridges, but also by the desire of the population for social cohesion. Kalinga regional populations are endogamous, and individuals within a regional unit are closely linked by kinship ties. Formerly each region presented a united opposition to other regions through periodic headhunting forays or retaliatory attacks to avenge a killing, injury, or other wrong inflicted upon it by another region.[1]

In the foothills and plains of the present Pinokpok and Tabuk municipal districts, Kalinga populations are not restricted to territorial regions as in the more rugged terrain. For about a century and a half this northeastern area was an unoccupied buffer zone between the aggressively proselytizing Spanish missionaries and lowland Christian populations on one side and the hostile mountain populations on the other. It was an area, which if settled might have been preyed upon by either group, by the mountain peoples for heads and by the Christian populations for workers to serve as carriers or in other roles equally hard and uncompensated. In addition to such dangers the area was also more heavily infested with the malarial mosquito than either the mountains or the Cagayan Valley. Within the last half century, with the establishment of peace and some successful results in malarial control, Kalinga populations have begun to move into this formerly unoccupied territory. Some of these migrants remain covered by peace pacts instituted in former home regions and where new peace pacts have been made, such pacts cover variously a single community or at times a whole series of settlements, but they do not extend over specifically defined territorial regions, as among the Kalinga of the mountainous terrain.

The regional, endogamous character of Kalinga populations in the rugged mountains may also not go back very far into the past since interregional cultural and linguistic differences are not extreme enough to indicate long separation of these units. It is likely that territorial consciousness began as recently as the early decades of the eighteenth century when the first Spanish missions were established in the Cagayan Valley. Historical records indicate that large numbers of former foothill or lowland dwellers fled into the mountains to escape the oppressive activities of Spanish missionaries. While there were undoubtedly already people in the mountains, the refugees swelled the population, and presumably closely related kin groups settled together, forming the nuclei of the present regional population units. In time these regional populations developed subcultural characteristics and dialectical differences, but American control at the turn of the present century put an end to further interregional differentiation with the suppression of headhunting. While some of the early lieutenant governors actively tried to stop headhunting, their efforts were not alone responsible for the disappearance of the practice. American control acted rather as a catalyst, bringing about changes which made headhunting unpopular and encouraged interregional mobility. The construction of roads and trails, trade and wage-work opportunities, the opening up of educational institutions, all brought about interregional activity. The instrument which afforded interregional travel with guarantee of personal safety was the peace-pact institution, in the main a Kalinga invention. This device will be described in some detail in this chapter, but to understand the Kalinga peace-pact system, it is important first to characterize Kalinga headhunting and warfare activities as they are remembered by older Kalinga who were active participants.

Headhunting

Headhunting (*Kayaw,* Poswoy dialect; *Kilib,* Lubuagan) formerly occupied a place of major importance in Kalinga culture. The ritual activities involving headhunting were as elaborate as those associated with illness and agriculture described in previous chapters. In recent years, with the diffusion of Western technology and ideas, virtually all of the rituals connected with headhunting have lapsed or have been reinterpreted. Headhunting or head-taking has occurred only sporadically of late years, but private vengeance involving either killings or woundings is common and will be discussed in greater detail later in this chapter. The following description of former headhunting and ritual practices is from information obtained from old men who had either participated in the activity as young men or were in their boyhood when headhunting was a live activity. While the version given here comes from the region of Poswoy, northern Kalinga, a check of the data with informants from other regions of northern Kalinga and Lubuagan indicates that practices were similar in these two areas of the present Kalinga Subprovince.

Headhunting parties were formerly organized to avenge an attack by enemy headhunters or to seek revenge for the loss of a relative or a prominent person by death in the region (*see* Chapter II). Parties also went out after regional festivities such as a wedding or a kontad celebration. On these occasions there was considerable drinking, and veteran headhunters boasted of their successful exploits, taunting and goading younger men to assert their manhood by bringing heads. Fired by these talks and their courage reinforced by wine, young men got together and began preparations for further expeditions. As with all important undertakings, the careful observation of omens was important before invading an enemy region for heads. The warriors armed with spears, headaxes, and shields stole into enemy territory, carefully avoiding pit falls, traps and warning devices formerly set up by all villages for protection. Open encounter with the enemy was avoided if possible. If a lone man, child, or woman, no matter of what age, could be located, the war party considered itself fortunate. The warriors swooped down on the defenseless victim, quickly severed the head, or if the cries of the victim drew pursuers before the head could be taken, only the hand or fingers might be taken. The invaders quickly fled, with the enemy usually in hot pursuit at their heels. A pursuing party rarely followed an invading group into the latter's region. When a headhunting party was out, its regional members kept watch for its return, and pursuers would be at a distinct disadvantage in a clash between the two groups. Moreover villages were formerly stockaded and short bamboo sticks with sharpened points were planted along the trails approaching a village to impede rapid travel. Along some of the trails were deadfalls in the form of an overhanging or leaning heavy log to be tripped by a string strung across the trail and thus kill a stranger or warn the village of his approach. Some villages also dug pits on the trails. These pits contained sharpened bamboos at the bottom and were ready to catch and maim or kill the unwary stranger. Only the members of the region knew the location of such traps and warning devices. It was thus hazardous for a pursuing enemy group to follow a party of headhunters all the way home. A small headhunting party cautiously entering an enemy region was usually successful in avoiding traps, but a pursuing party was at a disadvantage because its enemy was prepared to meet it. Moreover, the fleeing party often led pursuers purposely into the traps and thus added to its laurels.

A returning headhunting party which had been successful in its invasion of an enemy region shouted a series of piercing cries about a half mile from the first town or hamlet of its home region. These cries were answered by the *ayaya* call of the women, an eerie staccato cry made by quick movements of the tongue against the upper teeth. This peculiar call was made only on the occasion of festivities honoring the return of a victorious headhunting party. The first cries alerted nearby villages where the women immediately took up the cry, thus disseminating the news throughout the region.

The returning headhunters proceeded to the village from which the leader had come or from which most of the party had been drawn. Here excitement and shouts of joy greeted the warriors, and the *potol,* or evidence of the kill, was examined. Preparations for the rituals and festivities also began at once. One end of a bamboo stalk about six to ten feet in length and about three inches in diameter was fashioned into a basket by stripping the sides. The bamboo stalk called *sakólang,* was then taken to the outskirts of the village and planted near the sacred shrine, podayán (*see* Chapter III). The basket-like receptacle was lined with hibiscus flowers, and the potol (head or heads, hands or fingers) placed inside. While this was going on, relatives of the warriors set out jars of wine, and others tended to the butchering of pigs and the preparation of food. The medium and her helpers meanwhile performed the *sagáng* ceremony. The chants of this headhunting ceremony were no longer remembered by my informants, but the medium was said to petition sangasang, the guardian of the village, to bestow long life on the warriors. During the ceremony she removed the potol from the sakólang and placed it on top of the sacred rocks (bayóg) which form part of the sacred shrine. Later, upon completing her chants in the shrine, the medium returned the potol to the sakólang to remain during the rest of the festivities which went on for two days.

In the frenzied excitement of the initial meeting of regional members and the returning warriors, the skull cap might be removed from the severed heads and some of the brains and basi mixed together. The mixture was then drunk by the warriors to make them courageous and successful.[2] The severed heads, hands, or fingers remained in the sakólang during the festivities, however, and later the potol was boiled and the bones and broken bits of the skull passed around to the participant warriors as trophies. Most prized was the lower jaw which served as the handle of the chief musical instrument of the Kalinga, the gansa. Having participated in a headhunting expedition also entitled a warrior to a tattoo, *dakag*. A man need not have killed an enemy, merely having been present with a party that had killed gave him the right to be tattooed. We have noted elsewhere that most Kalinga men who now have tattoos received them as the result of having killed Japanese soldiers during the closing periods of World War II. Women were reported to have the privilege of being tattooed whenever any male relative had received his tattoo. Since all regional members are considered related, a woman is always able to find some tattooed male relative who gives her the right to be tattooed.

From the reports of informants, a headhunting feast appears to resemble a modern peace-pact celebration in broad outline, although the latter never reaches the frenzied and orgiastic proportions of the head-hunting rites of other days. Men and women sat or squatted about a central area where varied types of activities were performed. Most common on the program was one of the dances described in Chapter IV. The dances were periodically interrupted by the singing of war songs, *as-assay* and *kalommatik*. Occasionally too, men who had participated in head-hunting expeditions gave a pantomimic demonstration of how they had killed and severed heads. The warriors re-enacted the headhunting scene by leaping and prancing around, brandishing spears, shields and headaxes as if they were fighting with an enemy warrior. As the pitch of excitement increased and the large quantities of wine they had drunk began to take effect, old headhunting veterans moved into the circle to relate their war exploits. These were related in a stylized chant while the narrator postured grotesquely. Words were improvised, but how carefully and appropriately a warrior chose his words and how cleverly he rhymed them marked him as a master of the art. Some of the old headhunters goaded the young men to hunt for heads and spoke of those who did not dare to engage in the practice as despicable weaklings.

The reasons for and functions of headhunting among the mountain people of northern Luzon have been generally attributed to religious factors, most specifically to fertility concepts (Worcester 1912:875; Folk-mar MS 1906; Barton 1949:236). With the Kalinga, at least, fertility concepts involving the miraculous increase of crops and human life as an associated aspect of headhunting appear to be absent except that there is widespread belief that the taking of the life of an enemy may cure childlessness in one's wife or female relative. Barrenness may be dispelled by bringing death to a non-regional member by any method, however, not necessarily by the expediency of headhunting. The belief is the basis for the admonition given to all travelers to refuse food offered by a childless woman, lest the unwary traveler be poisoned to help rid the woman of her barrenness. The association of headhunting practices with agricultural activities was denied by my informants and no ritual activities were reported to have been associated with rice fields or swiddens either before or following a headhunting expedition. The reasons given for participating in a headhunting venture were the following: 1) to retaliate an attack by enemy headhunters; 2) to "even the score" when a man has lost a close relative either by natural death or as the result of an accident; 3) to gain prestige and renown.

The final reason given above was the one most often cited by the Kalinga themselves for the existence of headhunting. The respect and esteem in which the headhunter is held even at present confirms these assertions, and the behavior formerly associated with headhunting activities further underscores the prestige factor. Thus successful headhunters were welcomed upon their return from a headhunting expedition with an elaborate celebration and their headhunting achievements were recounted at subsequent festivities. The prestige rewards of headhunting undoubtedly kept the practice alive during the Spanish period despite the efforts of civil and religious authorities to put an end to it. These valued prestige byproducts of headhunting also brought about the temporary revival of the practice during the general unrest following the overthrow of Spanish rule at the turn of the century and again at the end of the Japanese occupation period in 1944–1945. Indeed, headhunting still occurs occasionally in remote areas, as it did briefly in the spring of 1960 in the Natonin area of eastern Kalinga (*see* note 12, Chapter IV). So ingrained is the esteem accorded a headhunter that the glorification of older men who have taken heads has been made a part of the program celebrating interregional peace pacts at present. These performances are given as the final act of the peace-pact celebration. On this occasion men who have killed or taken heads in past times boast proudly of their exploits.

A Kalinga man formerly sought status by an illustrious headhunting record, and it was indeed about the only avenue open to him for distinction. This is particularly true in the north where shifting cultivation of rice did not permit the accumulation of wealth which was an alternative to power and influence among the ethnic groups in the south. Even in Lubuagan, techniques of irrigated rice farming had diffused quite early so that it was possible to amass wealth in rice fields. Elsewhere we have noted the beginnings of important descent groups in Lubuagan and the rise of aristocratic families or kadangyan, who were distinguished from others because of greater wealth. Among both the Southern and Northern Kalinga, status was achieved primarily by personal efforts, but the road to power and influence was more available in Lubuagan, for example, to a man who already belonged to a highly ranked family. Among the Northern Kalinga, class distinctions were apparently non-existent in the past and even at present they are lightly drawn. But a brave, even a ruthless man could take heads, kill and wound and eventually work up the status ladder. A record of many killings made such a man feared and respected and earned him the title of mangngol or "brave warrior." People were afraid of such men, but they were also proud to be identified with them, for a regional population enjoyed high status and security if it could count among its members men of mangngol rank. Besides a distinguished headhunting record, a man enjoyed status if he could increase his family's heirloom collection of Chinese jars, plates, and beads. In order to accumulate these possessions in large numbers it was almost essential to have mangngol status, for such men could purchase such precious items from others for lesser amounts than others might be expected to pay, simply because they were powerful and feared. Also since such men had avenged again and again the losses and injuries suffered by co-regionists, the latter felt indebted to these distinguished warriors and usually gave them what they asked. Early observers among the Kalinga reported that such men were highly feared and respected. An account of a journey into the northern Kalinga country by Worcester in 1905 describes an encounter with headhunting Kalinga. Worcester in an interesting account credits a man of mangngol status by the name of Bakidan with saving the lives of his party. We quote a few excerpts:

It was fortunate indeed for us that we made friends with Bakidan. On the following day we continued our journey down the valley. Our baggage was carried by women, children and a few old and more or less decrepit warriors who obviously felt deeply insulted at being required to render such a menial service, and were decidedly resentful toward Bakidan for having ordered them to do it.

Before we started Bakidan warned us that the Kalingas were queer people, and in consequence it would be well for us very quietly to go around certain of their settlements. Others we would visit. Their inhabitants would be sure to invite us to stay and enjoy their hospitality. He would second every such invitation. We were to pay no attention to his words, but were to note whether or not he sat down. If he did, we might accept the invitation. Otherwise we must plead an urgent engagement farther down the valley and move on.

Things came out exactly as he had foretold. In several villages we heard noises decidedly suggestive of head-*cañaos* [head feasts], and discreetly circled these places. We declined all invitations seconded by Bakidan when he did not seat himself, and rested comfortably for a time in several villages where he did. Toward noon we walked straight into an ambush laid for us in the *runo* grass, discovering it only when Bakidan began to deliver a forceful oration in which he set forth the fact that he had a right to stroll down his own valley with a party of friends without being annoyed by having his fellow tribesmen hide beside the trail and prepare to throw lances.

Bakidan who was himself a famous warrior, told these men that they might kill us if they saw fit to do so, but must kill him first. Apparently, rather ashamed of themselves, they came out on to the trail and slunk off to their town. Bakidan, greatly disgusted, suggested that we follow them and lunch in their village, just to show that we were not afraid of them, and we did this . . .

The people of his village received us in a most friendly spirit, and after attending a bit of a *cañao* [feast] organized in our honour, and doing our best to entertain the crowd with a few simple experiments in physics, and some sleight-of-hand tricks, we retired, as we supposed, for a peaceful night's rest. No such good fortune awaited us. We were aroused in the middle of the night by a fearful din only to find our hut surrounded by a great circle of armed men. The people who had attempted to ambush us earlier in the day had repented of their action in letting us pass through unharmed, had gathered a strong force of fighting men, had surrounded our house and were now vociferously demanding to be allowed to take our heads . . . Bakidan was our only advocate. He still insisted that any one who wished to kill us must kill him first. His reputation stood him in good stead, and no one tackled the job.

While a leader like Bakidan instills fear among all who know his reputation, any group is also afraid of the retaliation from a leader's kindred should harm come to him. It is thus not only the mangngol who is feared but all of his relatives who are indebted to him in many different ways. It is instructive to sketch briefly the development of a mangngol to see how he achieves power and influence.

An ambitious young man accompanied experienced warriors on his first headhunting expedition. In his first encounter with the enemy he guarded against panic, watched the behavior of seasoned headhunters, and learned to be calm and collected. He also carefully observed the proper wielding of the spear, headaxe, and shield. If his party took a head in his first headhunting venture, even if he himself did not take part in the kill, he was entitled to his tattoo. In later headhunting trips he would venture more boldly and sooner or later, if he was lucky, he too would kill. As he matured, learned his art to greater perfection, and fortune permitted, he added to his victims. More and more the regional population became aware of the young man and watched him in headhunting feasts as he performed pantomimic reenactments of his feats and boasted of the numbers he had slain. Feeling his power, he might even kill within his region to avenge a killing or wounding, even though such a case might have been resolved amicably among people who know each other and whose kindreds overlap. Disdainfully in regional festivals he taunted his co-regionists for not matching his headhunting record and as he began to speak up in the informal councils, co-regionists began to consult him in their troubles and asked him to settle disputes. Thus he became an "arbiter" as well. His home became a gathering place for relatives and friends, and as a man of influence in keeping with Kalinga values, he was hospitable and generous, frequently holding a pa-inom (a feast to entertain friends). As a rising mangngol he had no trouble acquiring one or more dagdagas (mistresses) who helped elevate his prestige. He also began to add to his heirloom possessions, using his power and influence to secure these items. At this point he had arrived at the pinnacle of Kalinga success as it was reckoned in headhunting days some sixty or seventy years ago.

It is essential to emphasize that mangngol status was achieved and could not be passed on to family or relatives. While a mangngol was alive all those associated with him enjoyed the respect and deference shown him, but upon his death, people turned to other powerful and influential men. The important ingredient in mangngol status was a distinguished headhunting and homicide record. The only tangible property which came down to a mangngol's relatives were the heirloom possessions he had acquired, but these were usually quickly dissipated by the surviving kin to curry the favor of other men of mangngol rank. The sons of a mangngol were no better equipped than others in the region to achieve the rank of a courageous warrior, for bravery, headhunting skills, and a distinguished war record could not be inherited.

With the disappearance of headhunting, the avenue to power and influence has been rechanneled and now men may achieve status by wealth and political activity. A man may also derive some degree of importance and influence through positions achieved by specialized training and schooling, such as that of municipal clerk or school teacher. Nevertheless the rewards to be derived from headhunting have not altogether disappeared. There are sporadic occurrences of headhunting and at the end of the Japanese occupation when Japanese soldiers could be hunted with impunity, young men had a heyday, rooting out Japanese soldiers from hiding places, luring them into homes with promise of food and then falling upon them and hacking up their bodies. Most of the skull fragments and jaw bones possessed by the Kalinga at present come from this temporary resurgence of headhunting. Thus the attraction of headhunting or head-taking has not disappeared — it is only that the penalty for homicide is high and the practice is inconvenient and impractical because wage work, schooling, and other recent changes make traveling imperative through former enemy regions. To some extent, private vengeance through killing or woundings, whether within the region or without, satisfies the old headhunting craze. But vengeance is also prompted by a desire to uphold kinship pride, and some individuals engage in it against their will to satisfy the constant urging of relatives to avenge when one of their members has been killed or injured. While weregilds are usually paid in these cases, the kinship group, operating in an older set of values, is rarely satisfied unless blood is drawn. Minor cases of woundings or injuries are sometimes resolved by token woundings, where the individual who committed the act, whether intentional or not, submits himself (or provides a substitute) to be wounded or injured in the same manner and in the same place. Yet there are individuals who are feared, distrusted, and admired also, because they will not let a killing or injury be resolved other than by vengeance. This is particularly true of individuals in the Lubuagan region and other densely populated regions in the south where killings and woundings are usually resolved by counter killings or enormous weregild payments are demanded with the threat of vengeance — and even when paid, do not always avert retaliation among such regional populations. Barton (1949:231–252) provides numerous examples of killings and woundings for which weregild payments were accepted and the settlement thus made violated by retaliation. Desire to uphold kinship pride may be involved in cases of retaliation even when weregilds are accepted, but personal prestige factors also motivate many avengers.

The Kalinga, as most of the people in any society, are not introspective about their culture; they do not attempt to seek other than obvious reasons for a custom. It is apparent, however, that headhunting among the Kalinga served other purposes besides vengeance, retaliation, and prestige. The practice undoubtedly provided the psychological need to release aggression and also served to foster and maintain regional solidarity. Older informants speak with nostalgia about the pleasurable excitement in preparing for and setting out on a headhunting raid, shared in no less intensity by kinfolk and neighbors at home. Headhunting forays of the enemy might even have been welcomed as a break to long, tedious hours of work in the fields and the routine performance of daily tasks. An enemy raid provided diversion, danger also; but it was a pleasurable tingling of excitement for everybody and always the possibility for men to kill or wound and thus achieve or add to their laurels.

Headhunting also served another important function, that of maintaining territorial space. Vayda (1961) points out that psychological and group cohesion factors have generally received greater emphasis than ecological factors in explaining headhunting and primitive warfare and argues that the latter may be of greater importance. Among the Kalinga, the maintenance of regional boundaries is certainly a byproduct of the headhunting complex even though the people themselves cannot explicitly provide such a reason. The Kalinga do not, however, regard the land base itself as in need of defense. There is no competition for swidden land, and among the Northern Kalinga, at least, encroachers on irrigated rice fields are not a pressing problem or of concern, and we believe less so in the past when regional populations were smaller. Thus the constant fear of enemy headhunters among the Kalinga in the past does not appear to arise out of strictly ecological, economic or political concerns, but concern for personal physical safety. And naturally enough, this is the reason given for the defensive measures the Kalinga take; rather than that they fear territorial conquest. Nevertheless, it is clear that the headhunting complex has kept regional boundaries intact.

While the Kalinga occasionally participated in retaliatory and defensive group skirmishes distinguished from headhunting, large scale warfare was unknown. Thus an alternative method for maintaining territorial boundaries employed by modern nations existed only in embryonic form among the Kalinga. Of the two devices, headhunting is to be preferred from the standpoint of the loss of lives and the destruction of property. Head-taking involved small groups of warriors who had to sneak stealthily into an enemy region, strike suddenly and then flee as soon as an alarm was sounded. Such techniques do not take a large toll of lives on either side and there is no destruction of enemy's land, crops or possessions. It was not possible to determine the number of heads lost by a regional group to the enemy during the course of a year. Old men who had a reputation for being headhunters boasted of taking ten or more enemy heads, but when asked about the number lost to their own regional population their estimates became highly conservative. In Bolo in the region of Salegseg an old warrior considered a half-dozen heads lost to the enemy during the course of a year, a reasonable estimate at the height of the head-taking period in his boyhood. He was quick to add, however, that enemy regions lost considerable more, a remark that can probably be discounted as boasting.

Former headhunters report that headhunting activities rarely disrupted routine farming and household activities for long periods. Headhunters did not attack a village unless it was completely unattended, they sought their prey in lone workers in the swiddens or rice fields or on the trail. The victims of the headhunter were disproportionately high in old, infirm men and women. Women from middle-age down and children away from home were always in the company of a few men in their prime, but old men and women in their crass independence usually went about alone refusing the protection offered them by men in their prime. A headhunter achieved distinction regardless of how or whom he killed and beheaded and the boasting recitals frequently mention old men and women as victims.

Warfare

Headhunting is distinguished from warfare or battle (*baloknit,* Lubuagan; *botad,* Mabaca dialect, northern Kalinga). We have noted above that headhunting involved a small party of men, indeed often a lone warrior. Kalinga warfare or battle includes all of a region's available manpower pitted against another such group from an enemy region. Battle is triggered off by some insult, injury, or perhaps a series of killings emanating from another region. Encounters of this kind are always announced, the challengers move up to the regional boundary and from a hill or slope overlooking one of the settlements they shout a challenge. The shouting amounts to declaration of war, the enemy, having been warned, assembles its warriors along the boundary line. The groups facing each other taunt and insult each other, and hurl rocks; then with spears drawn and shields ready to fend off the opponents' spear thrusts, they begin to move closer. When the group is within spear-throwing range, the real battle gets under way. The challenged group has the option to make peace by agreeing to pay indemnities or make other reparations. However, since a life taken can only be satisfied by substituting another life, a group which has been challenged to war over a killing or a series of killings usually decides to fight it out. Such pitched battles could take a large number of lives if fought to the last man, but the Kalinga usually stop after a few men from each side have been mortally wounded and others injured. The side which has fared worse in the encounter initiates the truce, its leaders calling attention to the larger number they have suffered in dead or injured or both. A peace is then effected, indemnities and reparations being made and the the affair ended by drinking and feasting. Matías Calumnag, head teacher at Pantikian (Balbalan municipal district) Elementary School, a native of the Mabaca region but married into the region of Banao, believes that the establishment of peace following a battle was the predecessor of the modern Kalinga peace pact.[3] But the peace-pact institution itself has promoted warfare of this type by discouraging headhunting and private revenge. Battles of the botad type are of frequent occurrence in recent years among Kalinga regions having peace pacts with one another. Barton makes a number of references to such battles (1949:154, 236), and the epilogue of Barton's book (1949) contains an excerpt from the Baguio Midland Courier for October 26,

1947, reporting a war narrowly averted between the regions of Mabong-tot and Mangali. Judge Tanding B. Odiem of Tinglayan, Kalinga in an unpublished paper makes reference to a number of "tribal wars" in recent years and describes a Tinglayan-Sumadel encounter.[4] While both Calum-nag and Judge Odiem indicate the positive attributes of the peace-pact system, it is clear that the peace pacts by emphasizing regional responsi-bility for offenses also obligate the region to act as a unit to right wrongs when all possibilities for a peaceful solution to troubles between two regions have been exhausted. Formerly headhunting and private revenge resolved such conflicts — the principle of collective responsibility pro-tected the anonymity of the headhunter or private avenger. The latter, in Kalinga belief, was performing a service for his kindred and region. While vengeance from the enemy region was almost sure to come, the successful avenger himself was no more nor no less in danger of his life than anyone else in his region. At present, as headhunting has been legally outlawed and also prohibited by the peace pact, an instance of homicide demands finding the actual killer. Since the kind of anonymity that formerly pro-tected the headhunter and avenger has been removed, individuals are not so ready to seek private vengeance. Furthermore, modern conditions have devalued the prestige factor in headhunting, and it is now possible to achieve distinction by ways other than killing. Yet feuds between regions are deeply rooted and not easily forgotten. Peace-pact celebrations and interregional visiting which invariably involve excessive drinking, trigger habitual Kalinga boasting and taunting patterns which in turn fan the flames of old feuds and often lead to the rupture of peace-pact alliances. Individuals hesitate to take private vengeance and the offended region may decide to act as a unit by challenging the offending region to war. The affair may not go beyond simply a rattling of headaxes, spears, and shields, but, at least, pride has been assuaged. And if there is a battle with some lives lost and others injured, it is unlikely that individuals will be sought out to be jailed for in such encounters the whole regional popu-lation is involved. If the rather ineffective Philippine constabulary comes to investigate, regional populations give confusing and misleading infor-mation thus protecting the identity of leaders and usually no arrests are made. Thus the threat of interregional warfare is everpresent and occas-ionally flares up in temporary scuffles. A deterrent to this kind of warfare in recent years has come, however, from the possibility of really bloody encounters through the use of modern firearms. While the possession of modern weapons by mountain natives is prohibited by Philippine law, many have acquired rifles and pistols illegally through trade with low-landers. And although rifles are used mainly for hunting, Kalingas are not adverse to using them in interregional warfare. In both of the recent aborted warfare encounters, Mabongtot-Mangali and Tinglayan-Sumadel, each group possessed firearms and was prepared to use them. Peacepact holders intervened and averted war, but it was not so much the statemenship of the pact-holders that brought about a rather uneasy peace, but the prospect of a bloody, annihilating battle with modern weapons.

While headhunting has virtually disappeared, private revenge in the form of killings and woundings is common. From reports received during the field research period, it is no exaggeration to say that in each region two to three killings and some dozen woundings annually can be attributed to the vengeance motive. Such acts of vengeance are always explained as "payments" for previous killings or woundings of a member or members of the avenger's kinship group. These "payments" may be for "debts" of long standing between two kindreds or they may be vengeance for a killing or injury which took place moments before.

Even fairly minor injuries, cuts, or wounds, if inflicted by another, must be settled to the satisfaction of the injured party's kindred. Whether the injury was intentionally or accidentally inflicted is of little importance; all injuries caused by the instrumentality of another person must be settled or explained. If the injury was caused by a member of the same kindred, an explanation of the facts to an older male, kin to both individuals involved, is the initial step. The male relative then talks to the immediate families of the two people involved and settles the problem amicably by providing a token gift from the family of the individual responsible for the act to the family of the injured party. Among the Northern Kalinga, intraregional troubles are usually handled in the same manner as injuries or disputes that arise between two immediate families of the same kindred. This is because the whole regional unit is conceived to be a single kindred. When populations are dense and there are many overlapping kindreds, as in Lubuagan and other regions of the south, intraregional difficulties are often resolved by resort to vengeance. In all intraregional troubles, however, the immediate move of regional leaders is to explore the possibility of settling the problem peaceably and quietly. This ideal does not always succeed, however, for hot-headed individuals may take up bolo, headaxe, or spear and strike a member of the offending party's kindred before investigation and settlement are made. The role of the regional leader is important in settling intraregional disputes and, for the latter part of the nineteenth century to the present, in interregional problems as well, via the peace pact. Before the spread of the peace pacts, however, interregional troubles could be satisfied only by resorting to headhunting practices. The existence of a peace pact between two regions does not, of course, insure that troubles or disputes will be resolved peaceably.

When there is trouble between two regions, pact-holders try to get together immediately to settle the problem before individuals from the injured party's region take vengeance and compound the difficulties. Travel outside the region is postponed or reduced strictly to the essential minimum in order to avoid the possibility of individuals from the two regions encountering one another. But meetings do occur, and vengeance is often taken despite efforts at prevention. On my initial trip to the northern Kalinga country, my hosts in Lubuagan insisted that I take as a guide a youth of the extended family. Since Lubuagan had peace pacts with Salegseg and Mabaca, where I was bound, it was felt that the youth was perfectly safe. On the Dangwa truck we learned that two school boys, one from Salegseg and the other from Lubuagan, had "boxed" each other, that is, had a fist fight. One of the boys had received a bloody nose. The information was confused. No one knew which one of the boys had started the fight or which one had gotten the worse of the encounter, but my young companion was panic-stricken. He was safe on the truck, a public transportation vehicle, for by a kind of tacit agreement among the mountain tribes no one is permitted to resort to vengeance while riding a public conveyance. My companion was afraid, however, of what might happen to him when we arrived at the end of the truck route in Salegseg. I suggested that he ride back to Lubuagan on the truck, but he had, of course, to spend part of an afternoon and night in Salegseg, for the truck did not return to Lubuagan until the following day. Besides he felt that he ought to fulfill his obligation of being my companion and carrier for another long day of hiking over a tortuous trail to Mabaca still ahead of us. But his fears suddenly disappeared at Salegseg when more accurate news was received and it was learned that the Salegseg boy had started the fight and the Lubuagan boy had gotten the worst of it. It was the Salegseg population which would now be afraid and apprehensive until satisfactory settlement could be made between the two regions. Retaliation was most unlikely from my companion who was timid by temperament and among strangers — he was happy to let some one else "even the score."

The vengeance pattern places workers and students in locations away from their home regions in a difficult position. News of troubles which involve two different regions travels to individuals of the two regions who may be friends and are living far away from home. The one whose regional member was killed or wounded by a member of his friend's kindred is put into the awkward and unpleasant position of having to kill or wound his friend in order to live up to kinship expectations. The vengeance system thus can prolong the distrust and fear of one another among Kalinga of different regions who are working or pursuing an education together. Many Kalinga today would like to place friendship ties above kinship responsibilities, but an individual can never be completely certain of the reaction of a friend when a member of his own kinship group has wronged a member of his friend's kindred, because the kinship tie is the most important bond of the Kalinga, indeed of the Filipinos generally. It is undoubtedly the factor which explains the instability of political parties and the paucity and ineffectiveness of extra-kinship institutions throughout the Philippines (compare Lande 1958: 174–207).

The Peace-Pact Institution

The Kalinga peace-pact institution *(Bodong),* is obviously a response to recent historical developments. The former regional isolationism of the Kalinga was broken by Western cultural penetration, particularly by creating opportunities for trade and travel. The earliest dates on which peace pacts were actually established occur around the turn of the century *(see* peace-pact lists).[5] Negotiations for such pacts very likely began earlier, however, possibly with the opening of the Spanish military "road" or trail from Abra over the Cordillera Central into the Saltan and Chico valleys during the latter part of the nineteenth century. As interregional travel and trade became more common during the first and second decades of the present century the number of peace pacts increased. Indeed, new pacts are still being made as travel continues into relatively more isolated areas.

Given the traditional animosity between regions, the headhunting practices, and the vengeance system, measures to safeguard the interregional traveler had to be taken when extensive traveling became feasible. The Kalinga's answer to this problem was the peace pact which is simply a more formal adjudication system already employed to deal with intraregional, intra-kindred problems. The peace-pact system is, therefore, not something revolutionarily new. The Kalinga, like other mountain peoples of northern Luzon have a complex legal system, obviously very old, to handle local regional problems.[6] This body of procedures was simply incorporated into the peace-pact system and now these "laws" are called upon to resolve interregional problems as well. The peace-pact meetings or celebrations, for example, resemble the lounging sessions of regional leaders during a kontad, wedding or funeral ceremony. Peace-pact meetings give an opportunity for local leaders to exhibit oratorical skill before a wider audience and to be instrumental in settling the problems of a larger population.

The peace-pact system may have been suggested by the trading partnerships widespread throughout the Philippines and in Borneo as

Delegates from Poswoy are en route to Dalupa for a transfer celebration of the peace pact between the two regions. Oratorical matching of wits helps leadership qualities to emerge, and compensates for the competitive challenge of headhunting in the past.

reported by Barton (1949:144–145) but it is primarily a response to changes brought about by Western contact and influence and not simply a device indicative of the arrival of the Kalinga at a point in social evolution where "territorial units are dominating kinship groups" (*ibid.* p. 137). Particular historical, economic, ecological or other circumstances must be sought to explain the change from one type of social organization into another. It is no accident, therefore, that the peace-pact system arose among the Kalinga who were in an area where Western influences first penetrated the restricted and regionally bounded mountain populations. Peace pacts are most numerous among the Kalinga of the Chico and Saltan river valleys, and the pacts between Kalinga and peoples in Abra are more extensive than with any other non-Kalinga people. This is, of course, precisely the area through which ran the newly constructed or vastly improved Spanish trail which opened up travel and trade opportunities into one of the most isolated areas of northern Luzon.

It has undoubtedly occurred to the reader to wonder how the Kalinga secured their rather large stores of Chinese beads, plates, jars, gongs, and iron objects, if we assume that extensive trade and travel did not come until after the mid-nineteenth century. An answer to this question will refer us back to the historical chapter where we postulated sparse populations three hundred years ago in the mountains, and noted the movement of large numbers of lowland and foothill peoples who experienced Spanish oppression.[7] Before this time, it is our belief that fairly extensive relations existed with Chinese traders in the lowland areas. Hence Chinese manufactured items were accumulated. Many of these items were undoubtedly carried by the refugees into the mountains, others could have come through the limited trading partnership system, and it is acknowledged by the Kalinga themselves that many of these items have come in the recent American period from Christian Tinguians who had abandoned their own attachment to these items.[8]

The effect of the peace-pact system on interregional relations among the Kalinga as well as the impact of the system on other mountain peoples needs a fuller discussion. We will return to this significant and interesting subject later on but at present there is need to discuss the mechanics of the peace-pact institution in more detail and also to describe the social and ceremonial activities which are an integral part of the peace-pact system.

We have noted considerable variation in the practices of the Kalinga cultural and social sub-systems already described. This variation is observable not only between Northern and Southern Kalinga, but also from region to region within the two subcultural divisions. The developments of regional autonomy and the animosity between regions have undoubtedly produced these differences. The peace-pact institution, since it is an interregional peace mechanism, attempts to ameliorate rather than intensify differences. Its avowed purpose is to find solutions to interregional troubles by ways other than those traditionally employed in a blood feud system.

Within each region, fairly satisfactory and consistent methods of arbitration and compromise, by appeal to an intricate body of custom laws, have long existed. The "arbiter" in the home region was the successful headhunter, acknowledged as a leader because he was feared and respected. In the south, family connection and property have also been associated with the role of the arbiter, but the additional attributes of a brave warrior were also requisite. In recent years as headhunting has become illegal and inconvenient or impractical, the tendency has been everywhere to stress wealth, an aggressive personality, and forceful speech habits as traits of the arbiter. The former characteristics have not completely disappeared; it is still considered proper if the situation warrants it, for a regional leader to kill an offender of custom law (or a member of his kindred) who refuses to abide by the decisions mutually agreed upon by a group of regional leaders. These arbiters do not meet as a formal body, but an offense or crime is discussed informally in the frequent festivals or ceremonial occasions where regional leaders are wont to discuss the affairs of the region. Through long discussion a kind of unanimous decision about a matter is reached and one of the arbiters makes the pronouncement on the offender's family.

The regional pattern of adjudicating wrongs sketched above has been transferred virtually "intact" to the peace-pact system. In broad outline, Kalinga regional adjudication systems are much the same, but there are differences among the "laws" from region to region which become greater with distance. These differences bring headaches to the interregional leaders who must work them into a coherent and mutually agreed-upon set of provisions which is the central feature of the peace pact. But decisions are reached as evidenced by the expansion of the peace-pact system in recent years.

Modesta Abawag, pact holder from Asiga for Allangigan, begins the steps of the ceremonial dance, the *salidsid*, which is an important feature of every peace pact meeting in the north.

A peace pact is initiated by two individuals from different regions, and each one of the individuals holds the peace pact for his particular kinship group, although its provisions are binding on the whole region.[9] The procedure in instituting a peace pact can be conveniently illustrated by a hypothetical case. In this fictitious account we have attempted to reproduce as faithfully as we can the social environment and emotional atmosphere in which a peace pact is born. We have followed its development step by step to the ratification of the pact and the celebration following. We have introduced a number of incidents which frequently occur in specific cases in the establishment of a pact between two regions, but it is unlikely that all of the incidents we have presented here will ever occur in any one of them.

Let us suppose that Juanito from region A has met Emilio from region B in Lubuagan where both have come to trade.[10] No peace pact exists between regions A and B. Let us suppose, also, that the Lubuagan pact-holder for region A also holds the one for region B. Thus he is hosting both Juanito and Emilio. Commonly a pact-holder has two pacts, even as many as four, although beyond this number is considered too much of a hardship for any one person.

In our hypothetical case there are a number of visitors from regions A and B and so the Lubuagan peace-pact holder decides to give a palanos (or pa-inom), a friendship feast, to honor his guests, to display his generosity and to uphold his prestige. A palanos is open to all of a host's kindred and many of these come, as well as some of the prominent men of the region who have a standing invitation to all such feasts. Pigs are butchered and wine flows freely. Juanito and Emilio find themselves squatting next to each other at meal time and become acquainted. Later they come together again over cups of wine and begin to exchange information about the character of one another's region. Both know, of course, that no peace pact exists between their regions, for all adult Kalinga, especially traders and travelers, know all the peace pacts held by their region. They are also aware of the status of these pacts, that is, whether they have been broken, reinstituted or in the process of being reestablished. This information is vital for one's life is in danger should he be in a region with which his own region has no pact or in a region which has just broken its peace pact with his own.

Let us suppose that a peace pact was never instituted between A and B. This would not be the case today if both regions are in the Kalinga Subprovince, for these regions all have or have had peace pacts with one another for many years, although new ones are still being made outside of the subprovince of Kalinga. But if we assume that this is a new pact, we can present all of the important steps that lead to a formally instituted pact between the two regions.

As the wine brings about good feeling between Juanito and Emilio they begin to discuss trade opportunities. Juanito learns that Chinese beads and jars bring handsome prices in region B, and Emilio is amazed at how cheaply carabaos may be bought in region A. The idea of a peace pact with themselves as pact-holders occurs to them at once and in the morning before leaving they decide to talk over the matter with their respective regional leaders as soon as they return home.

At home, Juanito meets with partial disappointment for the lakays or regional leaders do not consider him forceful enough to be a pact-holder. The lakays had found an opportunity to discuss the matter of a peace pact between the two regions at a koli-as for old Capitán X who had died a year previously (*see* description of koli-as, Chapter III). The koli-as drew all the important regional leaders together for Capitán X had been a mangngol and an outstanding arbiter.[11] The lakays, as they lounged around a fire outside the former dwelling of Capitán X had discussed the matter far into the night and had reached a decision only in the evening of the second day. They reviewed all of the past grievances between region A and B and were particularly incensed over the killing of Capitán Y by a man from region B in 1930 at Lubuagan.[12] Lubuagan had met its peace-pact obligations to region A by immediately bringing the body of Capitán Y to his family in region A and sending as well a pig for the funeral feast. Lubuagan, too, had at once sent a stern warning to region B's peace-pact holder for Lubuagan, indicating that the peace pact between Lubuagan and region B was in serious danger of rupture for a man with whom Lubuagan had a peace pact had been killed on Lubuagan soil. It is said that region B made an immediate and handsome restitution to Lubuagan, but ignored region A. Since no peace pact existed between A and B the only recourse would have been a counter killing by region B. Indeed several attempts had been made and a youth from region A almost succeeded in 1950 in "evening the score." The youth had knifed an old woman from region B in the market at Baguio. The woman had almost died, but since she lived, the old score remained unsettled. The youth was unfortunately caught in the act and is still serving a sentence for attempted homicide.

So the lakays of region A were very much concerned that a forceful man who would have the fear and respect of both regions should hold the pact for region B. The pact-holder must, of course, come from Juanito's kindred (excluding spouses in this case, *see* special definition of kindred, Chapter II) for Juanito had initiated the matter. In their deliberations the regional leaders finally decided that Juanito's first cousin, Balniwit, a son of Juanito's mother's sister had the requisite courage. "For, did he not immediately avenge his first cousin Pedro's spear wound in the thigh inflicted by a man from region X by cutting a gash in the arm of a youth from region X he had met in Tabuk? He was a man who acted quickly and fearlessly. Besides, he was already a pact-holder for region Y, a tough region which always insisted on a heavy *dosa* (weregild) from other regions, but Balniwit was feared and respected there and region Y did not try to pull any fast ones on region A."

The next day Balniwit's spear was dispatched to Emilio in region B. The spear was accepted by Emilio himself; apparently he had been found to possess the requisite characteristics of a pact-holder by his own regional leaders. In turn Emilio sent his spear to Balniwit and so the preliminary stage, a period of truce called *sipat* or *alasiw* was established between the two regions.[13]

With spears exchanged indicating that each region had reviewed its past grievances with the other, the next step in the peace-pact procedure is called the *simsim* or *singlip,* "the tasting." This is an actual meeting of the leaders from the two regions. Where the meeting takes place depends on the initiative exercised by the proposed peace-pact-holders. It is not a big affair, the Lubuagan region is said to butcher only a pig for the occasion, but Poswoy informants boast that they always kill a carabao for the event. The simsim or singlip is a kind of Kalinga pow wow where all the grievances discussed by each group separately are brought out for review by the interregional delegation. If the assembled group appear to find a basis for settling these differences, a date is set for the next meeting or stage in the establishment of a peace pact called the *lonok* or *inom.* This is a big affair where the issues discussed in the simsim or singlip are reviewed and eventually a set of provisions drawn. At present these provisions are usually written either in Ilocano or English or in both languages and the set of regulations is designated the *pagta.* The *pagta,* the "laws" of the bodong (peace pact) are to be strictly observed by both regional members.

Let us return again to our hypothetical case:

> Upon receiving Emilio's spear Balniwit has immediately dispatched a messenger to region B inviting Emilio and his regional leaders to the simsim or singlip in region A. In the meantime Balniwit has contacted the members of his kindred and asked them to contribute food and wine. The meeting is arranged, as is customary, in Balniwit's own hamlet and residence. To impress his visitors, but also his co-regionists, Balniwit has butchered a carabao, arranged for entertainment in the form of a few renditions of dangngo, ogayam and salidomay (*see* Appendix, "songs of the Kalinga") and has also provided for gong players to furnish music for the dances.
>
> Emilio and his co-regionists arrive early on the morning of the first of two days set for the meeting. They are immediately taken to Balniwit's residence, where they are given wine while preparation for food and entertainment get underway. Soon the gong players start thumping and dancing begins in front of the residence in a cleared circular area around which stand the regional guests. The visitors from region B are grouped near Balniwit's house and they are asked to begin the dancing. Emilio receives the ayob (a piece of cloth) while Balniwit's wife has been given a scarf — both are invitations to dance. Then follow the other male visitors, all of them being matched with region A women. A few women, some of them wives, others relatives of the visitors have also come and these also dance. The gongs play for about an hour. Then the prominent men from region A deliver speeches of welcome while some chant ading and dangngo, praising the visitors. Some of the visitors, too, deliver speeches, complimenting region B for its generous hospitality and fine entertainment. Again the gongs strike up, stopping in about two hours to allow time for the serving of meals on banana leaves spread out on the ground. When everyone has eaten, the gongs play again for about an hour and then stop for

the serious discussions to begin. An old man from region B in a faded gee-string rises and speaks in a barely audible, raspy voice. He extends a welcome to the visitors calling them honorable and distinguished guests and praises them for their wisdom and humanitarianism in agreeing to come and help to settle differences between the two regions. He goes on in this vein for about thirty minutes and then gradually moves to citing incidences fostered or perpetrated by region B against his region. He begins with minor offenses: stealing, insults, school fights at Lubuagan, and ends by calling attention to the most grievous of the crimes, the murder of Capitán Y. The old man started out calmly, but ends up shaking with emotion. A middle-aged man in patched tan shorts also from region B speaks from a squatting position on top of a terrace rock wall. He too praises the intelligence and wisdom of the visitors and moves gradually to the recitation of grievances and like the old man ends up with the murder of Capitán Y. The next speaker is a visitor, incongruous in an old faded corduroy sports jacket and gee-string. His voice is loud and controlled and it is immediately clear that here is a man experienced in oratorical renditions. Chewing betel he carefully times his most effective remarks with scarlet spittings of betel juice. The visitor speaks for about an hour and a half in praise and flattery, but the final fifteen minutes are devoted to a pointed and remarkably convincing defense of his region, waiving all responsibility of his region in Capitán Y's death. As the visitor finishes a young man in a torn shirt and tattered shorts staggers into the open circle, muttering half-coherent belligerent remarks. He is a shiftless drunkard from region A and well known as a trouble-maker. Balniwit acts quickly and leads the drunk out of the cleared area and at the same time orders the musicians to start playing. Thus a tense moment portending unpleasant consequences is averted by Balniwit's quick thinking and action. In the gaiety of the dancing all is forgotten and when the discussions resume after about an hour, the speaker who answers the visitor's remarks has had a chance to think over his own reply. This speaker is a school-trained man in his early thirties, a well organized and emphatic speaker, an example of the younger generation with political ambitions who often use peace-pact meetings to influence audiences and gather a following. His remarks, delivered in a clear, controlled voice point out the need to settle past grievances to the satisfaction of all concerned and emphasize the importance for the Kalinga to work together and so to reap the benefits that a modern Philippine nation could offer to a united people.

The discussions went on far into the night. As Balniwit sensed a lull in enthusiasm or noted a ruffling of tempers he would call on the gong players to provide music and thus offer distraction. In the morning all the issues having been aired and reviewed and a tentative basis reached for their solution the date for the final stage of the peace pact is set. This final meeting is the lonok or inom when the pagta or "law" of the bodong between region A and B will be formally drawn and then ratified.

Balniwit once again scored diplomatic victory by offering his home for the lonok celebration. He had cleverly asked prominent co-regionists to make appropriate invitational speeches. Overwhelmed by the suddenness of these invitations and perhaps a bit apprehensive that their own region might find it inconvenient to entertain such a large group, the visiting delegation consented to come again to region A for the lonok.

Peace-pact celebrations whether renewals, transfers or simply "warm ups," occur during the dry season from March through May. During this time work in swiddens and fields is at a minimum, the trails are relatively dry and people have the time to travel and to enjoy the interregional celebrations. It is unlikely, however, that a region will be able to spare the time or to afford to give more than one peace-pact feast a year for these festivals are time-consuming and costly. Thus it is not realistic to assume that the lonok Balniwit had committed his region to celebrate will be given the same year. Since a lonok is a big affair to which come not only the people from the two regions involved, but also guests from other regions as well, a region acting as host will want to prepare many weeks ahead of the event.

The description of our hypothetical case may be resumed on the eve of the lonok.

Balniwit had put his whole kindred to work in preparing for the celebration. Some of his relatives had brought large vases of wine, others have prepared sweet cakes of *dikit* rice, and others have furnished rice, coffee, and sugar. Balniwit himself had provided two carabaos and three pigs for the feast. Male relatives had worked for more than a week constructing a large pavilion from bamboo poles. Within this structure the main activities of the lonok would take place: the review of cases, the drafting of the pagta, the dances, and other forms of entertainment. Beyond the dance pavilion, leading off from an arbor serving as a temporary kitchen, was a long elevated platform underneath a canopy of bamboo poles. This was the dining area — the meals are served on top of the platform out of reach of roaming pigs and dogs. But most impressive of all, thought Balniwit, was a gate archway which he had had constructed at the entrance of his hamlet. On the archway his son had transcribed the words: "Long Live the Peace," "God Bless Us," "Welcome and Mabuhay."[14] On one end the boy had also drawn a Kalinga headaxe and shield.

Balniwit did not neglect plans for entertainment. He had engaged several orchestras and had organized a number of skits. Women and children were told to practice a version of the salidomay they had sung recently at a *dolnat* (peace-pact warm-up) where visitors from region Z had been honored by flowery words incorporated into the chorus. For the lonok, region B would be substituted and the song sung at an auspicious moment at the height of the celebration. Chanters of dangngo and ogayam were also alerted and asked to make especially flattering improvisations in these chants for their guests. Although olalim popular in region B was not a favorite in region A, a man from Sumadel recently married into the region and now a citizen of the region had been asked to sing a rendition of the song. Finally, Balniwit requested his daughter to repeat the recitation of a poem she had recently recited upon completion of the sixth grade in the central school at Salegseg. The poem was about Lincoln, "O Captain, My Captain!" and while Balniwit did not understand the words and had never heard of Lincoln, he had been impressed by his daughter's elaborate flourishing hand movements. Pride and strong emotion assailed him as he heard his daughter utter the words, "O Captain, My Captain!" with typical pan montane accent on the final syllable). These designations were, of course, applied among the Kalinga to men of prominence and while no one as yet had addressed Balniwit as "Captain," he felt that as he gained wealth, prestige and influence as an arbiter, people would so address him. Yes, it would be most appropriate for his daughter to repeat her recital of "O Captain, My Captain!"

We have attempted in the foregoing hypothetical account to present incidences which were observed in a number of peace-pact celebrations and which are typical, but which did not all occur in any one specific case. The value of a hypothetical illustration is that a number of typical happenings, observed at different times and places, can be brought together. The method also makes it possible to bring in information not observed or which is not possible to observe. Thus the meeting of Juanito and Emilio was hypothetical even in the report of my informant: "this is the way a peace pact can begin." It is, of course, impossible bodily to follow Juanito and Emilio as they returned to their respective regions and hamlets seeking out their prominent men to support their desire for a peace pact between the two regions. Finally the hypothetical situation can be used to capture thoughts and emotional reactions of the subjects themselves. This is an unconventional approach, but the mental operations of a subject (as representative of his group) are extremely important in securing a rounded picture of a celebration such as a peace-pact meeting.

If we assume that some three hundred to five hundred people attended the lonok, so carefully organized by Balniwit, we have a good notion of the numbers characteristic of these affairs. The progression of events in the lonok follows an order similar to that of the simsim or singlib already presented in our hypothetical case. A lonok is a two-night affair, however. It begins with the arrival of guests early one morning, goes through that day and night, all of the next day and night, and ends about mid-morning of the third day. There are other important differences. The first day and night are devoted to social activities — dancing, singing, and the presentation of skits and plays by children. The serious discussions do not begin until the second day, when the provisions of the pact are worked out.

Pact-holders do not ordinarily take part in these discussions although they may listen occasionally in the role of neutral observers. The visiting pact-holder has the responsibility of watching the behavior of his compatriots to see that they do not do anything to break the good relations between the two groups. The host pact-holder's responsibilities are considerably more involved; he not only has the job of keeping his co-regionists in check, which is much more difficult since there are many more people from his region attending the event, but he is also responsible for everything running smoothly. He must see that there is plenty of wine and food, that important guests receive the special attention they deserve, and most important of all, that his co-regionists behave themselves. Neglect of any one of these duties will deflate his reputation as a pact-holder and will lower the status of his kinship group and region. If guests are not given deferential treatment, or if a prominent individual is insulted, the incident may bring about the rupture of the pact — certainly it will be one of the cases to be brought up for litigation in a future pact meeting. The Kalinga are extremely sensitive about slights and insults and demand reparation when they occur.

Entertainment is not prohibited during the pagta period of a pact meeting. The host pact-holder observes the "lawmakers" and if they seem tired, or if heated arguments are under way, he may call for an entertainment diversion. So, periodically, these discussions are interrupted by gong music, by short skits presented by children, and a variety of other types of entertainment. In these interludes, a visitor may suddenly arise and give a spontaneous oration, or the pact-holder himself may deliver a speech of admonition. Often a distinguished visitor is asked to speak. If the speaker speaks in English or Ilocano, an interpreter immediately arises and translates the speech into Kalinga.

The proceedings during the pagta and the events following may be briefly summarized by reference to a pact meeting between Asiga and Allangígan I attended in April of 1960. The event took place at Allangígan, Pinokpok municipal district. The "lawmakers" sat in chairs (rather unusual in other parts of Kalinga) and discussed the provisions to be incorporated into the pagta. The host pact-holder occasionally came to sit and watch, but most of the time he was supervising the distribution of wine, the preparation of food and a host of other tasks. If he noted a lull in the discussions he often suggested a break for entertainment which might be dancing, speeches by visitors, or skits presented by children. A rather interesting play was performed during one of these interruptions by the children of a former Ilocano school teacher, now a retired farmer in a nearby hamlet. The children put on a skit on the life of José Rizal, the Philippine national hero. The part of Rizal was played by the eldest daughter, a teen-age girl who wore slacks, a man's shirt, and a black hat for the part. The Kalinga audience was extremely responsive and applauded the performance loudly. I later learned that the play was a stock performance given frequently in Philippine high schools. The incident is noted here to illustrate the varied kinds of entertainment given in peace-pact celebrations and also to indicate Kalinga identification with

Immediately after the provisions of a peace pact are accepted, the pact-holders and their wives form a double line and drink from a Chinese plate of wine, in a ceremony called *totem,* or "drinking the pact."

the general Philippine culture as evidenced by their understanding and enthusiastic reception of the play.[15]

In the morning the pagta sessions went on in the manner sketched above. There was a break at midday for meals, eaten off platforms of the type described in our hypothetical account of the lonok. In the late afternoon it was announced that the laws of the pagta had been drawn to the satisfaction of all the prominent leaders. I was told that later these provisions would be included in the pagta portion of the written pact and signed (or marked with an X) by the pact-holders and the prominent men who had participated in the discussions. (*See* peace pact Documents in Appendix.)

Immediately upon announcement that the provisions were accepted, the pact-holders and their wives formed a double line facing each other. They were given a Chinese plate of wine from which all drank in turn until the wine was consumed. Two rice-pounding mortars were then inverted and on each of the mortars a dish of wine was set and two individuals at a time, one from Asiga and one from Allangigan, took turns in drinking the wine. Each person had to drink all the wine without picking up the dish. The dishes were refilled as soon as they were emptied and another pair crouched over the mortar to drink. This wine drinking rite in the lonok is called the totom. This went on until all had drunk, where-upon the gongs played and dancing was resumed. The important part of the peace pact was finished and some people left, but the majority remained for the dancing and entertainment which continued until well past midnight. Toward morning, the pokaw, or palpaliwat began. These are the boasting sessions of men who have a headhunting record. The boasts are chanted in a halting voice and made to rhyme. How cleverly a boaster chooses his words and how cleverly he rhymes them reflect credit on him. While the audience seems to enjoy these affairs and the performers have some status among youths, most of the young prominent leaders in the regions I have visited do not participate in the event. It is my belief that as headhunting and killings lose their prestige value, as is happening rapidly, these boasting sessions will disappear.

The pokaw sessions terminated the Asiga-Allangigan peace-pact celebration and by mid-morning of the third day only a few people remained. The Asiga people received gifts of food and items of clothing and departed happily for home. It had been a grand affair and there was time for a few more such celebrations before the heavy rains began. The dry season is presently a gay season for the Kalinga; formerly it was the time for headhunting, but Western contact and influences have brought about important changes, some good, some bad. The peace-pact system is considered a good thing by the Kalinga.

If a pact is being newly established, the first step, the exchange of spears, is initiated by two individuals who hope to benefit personally from the arrangement. The advantages that such individuals might hope to enjoy, for example, would be trading privileges, but there may be other benefits as well. The two individuals who initiate the arrangement ordinarily become the pact-holders, but each individual's regional leaders have the authority to choose another person to hold the pact, one they feel to be the most qualified. The person they choose must, however, come from the same descent group as the initiator of the pact.

Once a pact has been established and then broken, the new pact-holder (should the original pact-holder have died or resigned, voluntarily or through pressure from regional leaders) is drawn from the descent group of the original holder. Thus the initial holder of a pact becomes the head of a descent group since all subsequent holders of the pact must be drawn from his bilateral descendents. So far, these descent groups have shallow roots, they go back no more than three or four generations, and of course new pacts are still being initiated with towns or regions outside the Kalinga Subprovince. Peace pacts, the Kalingas say, are inherited like property — but the regional leaders pass the holding of the pact along to an individual of the descent group they feel most qualified to hold the pact. Women may also hold pacts but they do not perform the tasks that are associated with them and a husband or a near relative must act for them. A husband who performs the duties of pact-holder for his wife does not "own" the pact, hence he cannot pass on the pact to his own kindred. One of his children by his pact-holder wife may, of course, inherit it and be the pact-holder with approval of regional leaders, but if he marries again, his children by his second wife and their descendents have no right to the pact.

Let us briefly review the three types of Kalinga peace-pact events or stages, two of which have already been discussed and described. The first of these is the simsim or singlip. This meeting takes place during the truce period sipat or alasiw and is for the purpose of exploring the possibilities of a pact between the two regions. If the past grievances between the regions are not too grave, if they are resolvable, then the regional delegates set a date for the next meeting. This is the lonok or inom where the provisions or "laws" of the peace pact are discussed and worked out into the pagta. The third event or stage is called the dolnat. This is a renewal of the pact and is celebrated if trouble develops between two regions having a pact, or if several years have elapsed since the last meeting. A dolnat is also held if the pact has been transferred from one pact-holder to another, either through death and subsequent inheritance or because the present pact-holder desires to relieve himself of the responsibility. The dolnat resembles the lonok in all essential features, indeed in the Mabaca-Salegseg area the lonok is simply the final stage of the initial pact that has progressed from the prior stages of sipat and simsim. Subsequent pact celebrations are simply referred to as dolnat, unless there is a cut or rupture of the pact *(nagpas)* in which event the three stages (sipat-simsimlonok) must be repeated. In some areas, for example, the Limos-Pinokpok area (Pinokpok Municipal District), the terms lonok, inom and dolnat appear to be used interchangeably, both for the final stages in the establishment of a peace pact and the subsequent renewal celebrations.

The peace-pact activities may be conducted in one location for the whole period of the celebration, or the first day and night may be held in one village and the activities moved to another village for part of the second day and the final night. Such moves are made if two important towns jointly hold a pact, as the case of a peace-pact transfer celebration which I attended in Dalupa and Ableg, both of which towns jointly hold the pact with Poswoy.

A move from one town or village during the course of a peace-pact celebration is also made if the peace-pact holder lives in one village, but has important and influential relatives in another town. The practice of having the celebration in two towns or hamlets permits relatives to share the duties of furnishing food and the facilities for entertainment. Peace-pact celebrations are costly and the task of putting them on is difficult and demanding, hence such duties and responsibilities are often shared by two towns or hamlets.

In its journey from the home region, the visiting peace-pact delegation is preceded by a group of young men playing the bamboo clappers (patangkog). Patangkog players also precede the peace-pact group when the latter moves as a body from one town to another, as was the case in the peace-pact transfer celebration between Poswoy and Dalupa-Ableg cited above. These devices are used to dispel bad omens and to invite good fortune. A regional party about to depart on its journey to participate in any one of the four steps or stages establishing a peace pact will observe all of the omens which foretell good or evil consequences. If the omens are not favorable, the party will send word ahead indicating that the trip must be postponed. The postponement is usually only for a day and while there may be a few false starts, eventually the omens will predict a successful journey and the group then proceeds, with the patangkog players in the lead.

The Provisions of the Peace Pact

The body of provisions or pagta of the peace pact clearly indicates the application of intraregional adjudication procedures to interregional problems. The differences which may be observed in peace-pact provisions from one area to another reflect regional and areal variations in custom laws. Close geographical regions employ a large number of designations for custom-law procedures in the deliberations during the pagta discussions as well as in the written version of the pagta. On the other hand, peace pacts between regions lying at considerable distance from one another try to discuss the "laws" in more general terms and the body of provisions contained in the pagta are similarly phrased in general terms. Compare, for example, the two peace-pact documents included in Appendix V.

The provisions or pagta of the Lubuagan-Penarrubia pact avoid the use of specific Kalinga terms for indemnities and fines such as *boto, dosa, molta,* and other similar designations. This is understandable since Penarrubia is a community in Abra whose inhabitants are Iloconized Tinguians and the Kalinga language and terms of litigation might be unintelligible. The pact between Asiga and Allangigan, however, is one between Kalinga of the same general subcultural area, hence the use (in the pagta) of the typical north Kalinga designations employed in intraregional discussions and settlements.

Some of the terms of litigation and their meanings used in intraregional adjudication procedures are listed below. These designations are now commonly employed in peace-pact discussions and deliberations, as well. The terms listed here are specifically from the region of Poswoy, but cognate forms exist in other regions of the Kalinga Subprovince.

boto	A payment to those helping to arbitrate or settle a dispute. In the peace pact, boto is a fine payable to both peace-pact holders.
dalagdag	A counter injury inflicted by one who has been injured or wounded. It may be specified by regional leaders to settle a case of accidental injury.
dosa	Indemnity or weregild to be paid to the relatives of an injured party.
kigad	A sign, usually of knotted runo leaves — marking a regional boundary line alongside a trail.
pasoksok	A bribe made by a thief or offender to one who has caught the culprit in the act of committing a crime with the understanding that the offense will not be reported. The term is also used for a gift of money given to an influential individual to curry favor — like giving money to a judge to dismiss a case.
pasolot or *pasarot*	The return of a stolen article together with another item equal in value.
molta	A fine when the case is settled informally. It defrays the expenses of a feast celebrated to bring the principals of a dispute and their kindreds together.
soldak	(Lubuagan *bakdoy*) The declaration of a neutral zone or truce between two regions at war with one another by a third, uninvolved party.

The body of the provisions contained in the pagta reflect pan-montane principles of kinship and blood feud. For example, in many pacts a killing is not negotiable by fines, but the provisions prescribe satisfaction by "payment with another life." Thus in our sample pact (*see* Appendix) between Lubuagan and Penarrubia, murder and poisoning must be "paid with life." In such pacts the pact-holder from the murderer's region must kill the murderer or some one from the murderer's kindred to keep the pact in force and prevent war or vengeance. Our other sample case, the pact between Asiga and Allangigan, is typical of north Kalinga pacts. Here it is possible to negotiate a killing by payment of boto and dosa. The Lubuagan-Penarrubia case illustrates the old vengeance pattern of "evening the score" while the settlement of homicide by fines appears to be a concession to modern pressures to bring down the incidence of killings and woundings. All regions hold to the traditional view that the kindred is collectively responsible for the act, and conversely that the kindred must share in the weregild and fines when one of its members has been murdered or wounded. Further, accidental homicide or injury is rarely

Prominent men, and arbiters of the peace renewal celebration between Asiga and Allangigan, argue some violations of the pact before final settlement.

differentiated from intentional killing or wounding. Kindreds bring pressure for satisfaction no matter how an infraction may have been brought about as long as it can somehow be related to another region or kindred. In minor accidental injuries, inflicted by another, the practice of token woundings (dalagdag) is a technique by which payments of vengeance are avoided, but this is not very common. All of these practices are, of course, features of the kinship principle and the blood feud which are deeply imbedded in Kalinga thinking and which find expression in the peace-pact provisions.

Despite the fact that the northern Kalinga regions incorporate a provision to settle homicide with a dosa, kindreds are rarely satisfied with simply being paid off and often retaliate by a counter-killing or wounding. Homicide more than any other act brings about the rupture of a pact, and the pact-holder does not always have the courage to take a life from his own region to satisfy the provisions in those pacts which give him such a license.

Compromise and concessions are constantly being made in working out the provisions of a pact. The Dalupa-Ableg region objects to a provision for boto, that is, a payment to both peace-pact holders for certain crimes, but Poswoy in its pacts with northern Kalinga regions regularly puts in such a provision. In the pact with Dalupa-Ableg, however, Poswoy acceded to Dalupa-Ableg and omitted any reference to a boto in the pagta of the pact. Adjustments are made, therefore, to fit regional and areal subcultural differences.

Kalinga peace-pact documents we have examined all have the following general pattern:

1. A statement giving the names of the peace-pact holders and their pledge to uphold the provisions of the pact.
2. The specification of the boundaries of the region and/or towns to be covered by the pact.
3. The pagta proper, listing the "laws" or provisions of the pact. Among these the most common are:

    a. *Killing and Wounding* — Specification is made as to whether inter-regional killings and woundings should be settled by payment of fines and indemnities (dosa) or only by counter-killings and token woundings (dalagdag). This provision also includes payment of a boto, if any, and indicates the amount. The amount of the dosa is not ordinarily made in this provision, but is left open for discussion and settlement between the two pact-holders after the act has taken place.

    b. *Stealing* — Ordinarily this provision provides for return of the stolen item with another article of equal value (pasalot or pasarot), or if the stolen item cannot be returned, by a payment twice its value. In some pacts the amount demanded is triple the value of the article; in this case, one third goes to the pact-holder and the rest to the person from whom the article was stolen. Payment of this type made to the pact-holder is not considered boto as boto are situations conceived to be offenses against the peace pact itself, hence both pact-holders receive a payment. The payment which a peace-pact holder receives in adjucating a case of stealing is a "collector's fee."

    c. *Lost Articles* — This provision is sometimes made a part of the article for stealing. The provision provides for the protection of a visitor's property. If an article is lost and is not found during the immediate search which has been initiated by the pact-holder, the visitor is compensated by money or gifts worth twice the value of the article lost. The compensation is made from a collection made by the pact-holder among his co-regionists.[16]

    d. *Hospitality* — Hospitality is one of the most important provisions of the peace pact and is included in all the pacts. It guarantees the following accommodations and benefits:
    1. A generous welcome to the visitor
    2. The best of lodging and food
    3. Assistance to those who are traders
    4. Help in the collection of debts (if this is the object of the visit)

In addition to these main acts, others are usually included to make the visitor as comfortable as possible.

e. *Death, Illness, and Accidents* — This provision assures visitors immediate attention and the best accommodations available in the region in the case of an unfortunate mishap. The provision usually specifies acts as follows: If the visitor is injured or becomes ill, he will be treated according to his wishes or the customs of his region; in the event of death, the body will be wrapped in blankets and quickly dispatched to his home region with some money or a pig to help in the funeral expenses.

f. *Courting Married and Unmarried Women* — Most pacts stipulate the payment of a fine or boto by a man who courts or attempts to court a married woman.[17] A husband who will kill or injure the lover, his wife, or both, is not censured. But, such a rule does not apply to a jealous wife who might take vengeance on her husband or his mistress. A wife who kills or wounds either her husband or his mistress becomes subject to the provisions and penalties that govern killings and woundings.

Most pacts under this category or under a specific provision also include a statement which indicates that concubinage is sanctioned as long as the woman enters into the arrangement freely and voluntarily.

The provision about courting an unmarried woman usually states simply that the visitor must make the fact known to the pact-holder for his region.

g. *Respect of Neutrality* — A provision to respect the neutrality (soldak or bakdoy) of a region is often incorporated into the pact. This means that if regions A and B have a pact and B is at war with C, members of C must not be harmed by members of B on A's territory. Since most pacts carry this provision, a visitor caught in a region which has just broken its pact with his own may seek refuge in an adjacent region. For a man caught in this predicament, however, the best thing to do is to run to the home of the pact-holder for his region who is obligated to protect him and to have him conducted home safely.

4. *Residence* — Most pacts include a provision which requires that in interregional marriages the regional affiliation of the couple be specifically established. If residence is in a location other than the home region of either one of the couple, protection is facilitated if the couple and their children become "citizens" of only one region. If the couple decides to establish their residence in the home region of one or the other, the "alien" spouse must change his or her "citizenship."

"Dual citizenship" is discouraged for it presents difficulties in enforcing the pact, although the individual who holds it is in an advantageous position. Such an individual receives double protection; should one region of which he is a "citizen" break its pact with another, he is still covered by the second's pact. But an individual with a "double citizenship" presents too much of a headache to the two pact-holders responsible for him and he is pressured to choose one and drop the other.

5. *Inclusion or exclusion from the pact* — A statement indicating those members of a region to be included or excluded from a pact is an

important part of the peace-pact document. Students or wage workers usually carry the provisions of the pact wherever they are studying or working, but a colony of a region, such as those of Mabaca in Tabuk, might be excluded. The reason for this exclusion is that a population which is so far removed from the parent region cannot be protected adequately, nor can its members be watched carefully enough to prevent them from breaking the pact. In some pacts, regional members who are government law enforcement officers are specifically exempt from some of the provisions of a pact. Thus a police officer who kills a member of another region is not liable (nor is his kindred) to the provision which sanctions a counter-killing, or imposes fines and penalties for homicide.

6. The final part of the peace-pact document lists as witnesses of the pact, the signatures, thumb prints or X marks of the peace-pact holders. Underneath the two signatures, arranged in two columns, there are the signatures or marks of some of the prominent men of the two regions. These are the men who have engaged in the discussions and deliberations which have resolved the past grievances and which have resulted in compiling the articles or provisions contained in the pagta.

In addition to the general provisions listed above, there are more particular ones in specific pacts. Thus, in a pact between Lubuagan and Sallapadan (Abra), a provision instructs each pact-holder when acting as host to visitors from the other region to keep dogs from barking, to keep down impolite noises of regional members while eating, to prevent the rattling of pots and pans in the kitchen, and to control the tempers of men and women in the house. The pact also has a provision directing the pact-holder to see that drunkards do not annoy any visiting members from the other region and authorizes the pact-holder to punish such troublemakers. Some regions also put in a provision for collecting indemnities from a region which has killed or wounded a recent guest. For example, during the period of my research, a lowlander on his way to the Limos region (Pinokpok Municipal District) was fed and lodged in Alingag (Salegseg region, Balbalan) and then proceeded to Limos, where he was killed. Salegseg has registered a complaint and a claim for indemnities against Limos for having killed a guest "whose stomach still contained the food served him as a guest of the Salegseg people." A visitor in northern Kalinga remains the guest of the region where he has last eaten, hence the region where he is subsequently killed is obligated to pay indemnities to the region where the victim was a guest.

It is clear from the above account that the Kalinga peace-pact system is based on ideas and adjudication procedures already present in the endogamous regional populations. These intraregional, intra-kindred techniques for resolving local problems were simply transferred to settle interregional difficulties when mobility became an essential part of Kalinga life. In the transfer, it is apparent the adjudication processes and the character of the pact meetings themselves adhered closely to traditional concepts and practices revolving around the key principles of kinship and the blood feud. While the pacts were made between regions or communities, they are still conceived as pacts between kindreds (*see* Chapter II). Also, retaliation for homicide by killing or counter-wounding is still sanctioned in most of the pacts. The pact-holder carries on in only slightly modified form the characteristics of the courageous warrior or mangngol of headhunting days. Headhunting has almost completely receded into the past and the modern pact-holder need not have a headhunting record, but like the mangngol he must be courageous and, if circumstances demand it and in order to keep the peace, he must be willing to kill a member of his own kindred. A weak man cannot be a pact-holder, and regional leaders make sure they appoint a strong man as a pact-holder, but always the choice is made from the nearest kin of the initial holder's bilateral descendents.

The peace-pact system is thus not a radically new thing to the Kalinga, and because its organization and procedures are familiar, the institution has spread rapidly. A glance at the four peace-pact lists included in the Appendix shows how widespread the pacts are from a geographical point of view. The pacts are most numerous in the subprovince of Kalinga, but they spill over the boundaries into Abra, the Cagayan Valley and into the adjacent subprovinces of Bontoc and Apayao. Regional populations in the central area, that is, those in the municipal districts of Tinglayan, Lubuagan, Tanudan, and Balbalan rarely have less than fifty pacts with other regions and communities. Pacts are sometimes broken, but so important are they for providing physical (and psychological) security that negotiations for renewal are immediately initiated. The Kalinga peace-pact institution serves a highly valued social function, however, as well as a safety one. It permits ambitious men to achieve status and distinction beyond regional and community boundaries as wise counselors and arbiters. For the regional populations at large, peace-pact meetings provide social interaction and recreation on a grand scale.

The theoretical question of an emerging Kalinga state which interested the first serious student of the Kalinga is important to consider further. R. F. Barton in his exemplary study of Kalinga custom law, (1949), conceived the idea of the Kalinga as a society in transition from kinship units to larger units where territorality was more important than kinship. Barton's basis for this belief rested on the rigidly bounded territorial unit or region (in the central area) and the interregional peace-pact system.

Analysis of the kindred or kinship circle and the territorial region of the Kalinga in both Lubuagan and northern areas illustrates conclu-

Members of the host region at any peace-pact meeting are expected to spend considerable time and energy in providing feasts and entertainment. The pacts themselves contain precise rules for courtesy to visitors.

sively that the territorial unit instead of being a "progressive principle from which the state rises" (Barton 1949:137) is simply a carry over from an earlier period when kinship group and territorial region were equated. The region has nothing to do with the evolution of a higher or more complex political order. Given the headhunting complex, the Kalinga simply realized they must stay within the bounds of a specific geographical region; to venture outside the region meant certain death. Organization within the region was loose and amorphous. At present in Kalinga, especially in the north where conditions aproximate past conditions most closely, households are loosely grouped into hamlets. A dozen or so such hamlets, in turn, form specific regions whose geographical boundaries are rigidly defined. Regional populations are still essentially endogamous. There is no central authority, no single position of leadership for the region as a whole. A few influential leaders, men who cultivate more land than others, who have more pigs and carabaos and who can speak eloquently, are sought by the regional population to settle disputes. These are the men, too, who on social and religious occasions make speeches of admonition and proper conduct. Such men also vie for positions as peace-pact holders and compete for municipal offices.

The development of the peace-pact system among the Kalinga, rather than elsewhere in northern Luzon, has been the result of specific historical factors, as we have noted. Contact with Western cultural influences and opportunities for trade and travel first came into the northern Kalinga area over the Spanish trail. To take advantage of these new developments, a device which would safeguard travel across endogamous regional population units hostile to one another had to be developed. The answer was the peace-pact institution. Once established, the system spread rapidly, for it served a crucial need to the Kalinga now suddenly on the move — yet still distrustful of one another.

The Kalinga regional units and the peace-pact system do not, therefore, indicate a society at the threshold of state organization. The regional units are survivals of endogamous units, not unlike band organizations elsewhere in the world, and the peace-pact system is a device brought about by modern conditions. The Kalinga regional population group was, and still is, essentially a kinship unit while the peace-pact system operates on the kinship principle and the related concepts of the blood feud.

Evidence for at least a partial departure from dependence on the kinship group exists in northern Luzon, but it is found among the densely populated areas of the central part of the Mountain Province rather than among the marginal Kalinga. The ward organization of Sagada, (Eggan 1960), and Bontoc, (Jenks 1905), indicates an organization which overrides the kinship group. Eggan, (1960:28), describes the Sagada ward as follows:

> ... Each ward is a geographical unit and possesses a paved ceremonial platform (or platforms) with an attached men's sleeping hut ... Formerly each also had one or more girls' sleeping dormitories — or widow's houses — used for courtship purposes ... The ward is a political and ceremonial unit. Its older male members make up an informal council ... which settles disputes within its jurisdiction and organizes and carries out the rituals and ceremonies essential for ward and village welfare ... The ward also provides a "school" in which boys are informally trained for participation in ward and village activities ...

Bontoc ward divisions, associated structures, and their functions, are similar to those described by Eggan for Sagada, (Jenks 1905). The wards are not, however, politically independent units, but tied into the village organization both at Sagada and Bontoc. Sagada and Bontoc thus exhibit an organization which appears to be well along the road to independence from the kinship group.

If more effective and dependable food resources and a more efficient technology and larger population densities are equated with more complex socio-political institutions, it is understandable that such correlations should occur in the Bontoc and Sagada areas. Here irrigated rice terraces have made possible larger and more dependable rice yields, and populations have attained a density that is highest in the Mountain Province. Kalinga populations, even the relatively more densely populated area of southern Kalinga, do not approach the densities found in Sagada and Bontoc.[18] The growing of rice in irrigated terraces everywhere among the Kalinga is a recent phenomenon and the technique has not reached the effectiveness achieved among the former peoples. It is not surprising, therefore, that the nonkinship ward organization which appears to be a device to integrate larger populations is not found among the Kalinga.

As interregional hostilities subside, regional boundaries are beginning to become blurred and the rigidly endogamous nature of regional populations is beginning to disappear with increasing marriages across regions and with non-Kalinga. These developments are the result, however, of Spanish and American contact and of influence from the modern Philippine nation. The peace-pact institution is important in this process, not as an assertion of Kalinga nationalism, but as a device to end fear, suspicion, and reprisals across kindred, community, and regional lines. The institution's continuing spread and popularity is, however, mainly a response to its associated social and recreational functions. Everyone has a good time at peace-pact celebrations, and men have an opportunity to try out oratorical skills and talents as arbiters.

Notes to Chapter 5

1. Intraregional killings and woundings which occur in the Lubuagan region have been explained as a recent phenomenon, the result of increased populations and the confusion brought about by overlapping kindreds, *(see* Chapter II).
2. This practice is also reported by Worcester (1912: Vol. 23:877) for the Northern Kalinga and by Barton (1949:237) for Lubuagan.
3. This report is contained in a twenty-eight page typed manuscript entitled: "History and Cultural Life of the Town of Balbalan" written by Mr. Matías Calumnag and kindly lent to me by the author.
4. The paper is entitled: "The Workings of the Bodong System of the Kalingas." A copy of the paper was secured for me through the courtesy of the Reverend Carl Lutz of the Lutheran Philippine Mission, Tinglayan, Kalinga.
5. The initiating and celebration dates are of course approximations given by Kalinga pact-holders, hence there are numerous discrepancies when the four lists are compared one to another. Nevertheless, it is significant that all the dates are within the present century.

6. Barton (1949) describes in some detail the intricate legal system of the Lubu-agan Kalinga. His study of Ifugao Law (1919) also illustrates the complex legal system of another northern Luzon mountain people.

7. Keesing views the bulk of the population in the mountains of northern Luzon as post-Spanish; the result, primarily, of lowland peoples retreating from Spanish oppression (Keesing 1962:304; 334–336).

8. Christian lowlanders do not consider the beads, plates, jars, gongs, and other items of Chinese manufacture collected by the mountain peoples as precious or valuable. Indeed, lowlanders believe that the possession of these articles stamps one as pagan. They are not, however, adverse to selling them to the "Igorotes" (pagan mountain folk), in return for food and other utilitarian objects.

9. A peace-pact holder's kinship group is a descent group since only those relatives descending bilaterally from the original pact-holder have the right to hold such a position. At present, all adults know the original holders, hence peace-pact descent groups have shallow roots of no more than two or three generations.

10. To illustrate some of the differences between northern and southern Kalinga practices and attitudes associated with the peace-pact system, we are assuming in this hypothetical case that region A is in northern Kalinga and region B somewhere in the Lubuagan municipal district.

11. We introduced a koli-as feast (in our hypothetical case) because regional leaders are often influenced on such an occasion by the accomplishments of the deceased. If this were a true case, as indeed it could well have been, the fact that Capitan X was a brave warrior would have had exactly the kind of effect it did on the lakays — that of choosing a forceful, strong-willed man for a pact-holder.

12. Cases of many years standing sometimes become the basis of discussion, arbi-tration, and settlement. At the dolnat (occasion celebrating the renewal of a pact) I attended between Dalupa-Ableg and Poswoy, the discussion revolved around a man from Poswoy who had been killed by people from Guinaang (another region in Dalupa-Ableg territory) some forty years previously. The affair had been settled between Poswoy and Guinaang, but Dalupa-Ableg apparently had not made restitution to Poswoy, as is customary in such cases. From the beginning of the discussions it was rumored that Dalupa-Ableg was to be assessed a fine of five pesos, and indeed, had already agreed to pay it. Yet, perhaps there was no other problem to settle, so the discussion of this case went on among the regional leaders for more than ten hours. I was told that if peace-pact arbiters have no case to settle they will invent one, "for, after all, the peace-pact celebration must go on and the discussions are the central feature of the peace-pact meetings."

13. Two or three different terms exist for important events or stages in the estab-lishment operation of a peace pact. Most of these designations were terms which identified procedures in interregional litigation and now refer to similar types of operations in the interregional peace-pact system. Since the terms have originated in different areas of the Kalinga Subprovince among Kalinga speaking variant dialectical versions of the language, the items are not always the same, but all Kalinga recognize them as simply legitimate alternative designations.

14. *Mabuhay* means "welcome" in Tagalog.

15. The Northern Kalinga appear to be further along the acculturation path; hence this reference to Kalinga identification with the dominant Philippine culture may not hold for other areas of the Kalinga Subprovince.

16. It apparently does not occur to the Kalinga to lie about losing an article or to increase the value of a lost item with the intention of profiting from the decep-tion. The good relations between two regions are such an important desideratum

that personal gain at the expense of endangering the pact is not considered. It must be remembered that an individual who endangers a pact is also accountable to his own regional pact-holder.

17. Our sample case, the pact between Asiga and Allangigan is not clear on this point. The provision stipulates a boto of forty dollars to be paid to the lover. If the husband kills both his wife and her lover there is no boto, but when he kills only one [of them], then there is. It is not clear who pays the boto if the husband does not kill both of them — I suppose the surviving wife (with her kindred's assistance), or her lover if he is not the one killed, would pay the fine.

18. Population figures for villages of Bontoc and Sagada municipalities reveal a range from four hundred to four thousand; those of the municipality of Balbalan in north Kalinga from about ten to one hundred fifty. Ifugao has higher densities of population for the subprovince, but if we consider area and settlement conditions, Bontoc and Sagada are more densely populated. Ifugao has dispersed hamlets, but distances between hamlets are not as great as in Bontoc subprovince. Crucial factors in the development of non-kinship political systems appear to be dense populations in highly concentrated areas.

Outgoing personalities and forceful characters rise to positions of leadership in Kalinga communities through the mechanism of the peace pact. Pangngat Suyam (above) has been the holder of four Lubuagan region pacts. Awanon (below), pact holder from Poswoy for Dalupa-Ableg region, exemplifies the full participation of women in the intercommunity negotiations of the Kalinga.

6. | Conclusions

THE AREAL LIMITS of what have been described as Kalinga social and cultural characteristics are not possible to determine precisely. These characteristics are not restricted to the Kalinga Subprovince, but grade into neighboring areas populated by peoples bearing different ethnic designations. The ethnic groups presently named within the boundaries of the Mountain Province are Ibaloy, Kankanay, Bontoc, Ifugao, Kalinga, and the Isneg or Apayao. Ibaloy and Kankanay are included in the Benguet Subprovince while the other names are designations for the remaining four subprovinces. None of these groups are distinct social and cultural entities. What we have in the Mountain Province is a population which becomes increasingly different with distance from any local group. Regional populations interconnected by kinship ties exhibit the highest degree of homogeneity, and prominent geographical features delimit a second level of relatedness. There are no sharp cultural breaks in the boundary area between any two named ethnic groups, although considerable detailed differences are evident in the areal extremities of such groups. Vanoverbergh in an analysis of dress and adornment styles in the Mountain Province first noted the unity and chain-type relatedness of these people. We quote from his conclusions to that study (1929:240–241):

> The various so-called non-Christian tribes of the Mountain Province of Luzon, while differing one from the other in numerous details, are *actually essentially one.* [Italics in the original.] Whether they were originally one or have become so in the course of time is another question.
> In the present paper we have confined our attention to dress and adornment, and for the present we shall draw our inference of unity from this

[*239*]

field alone. We could however as easily follow the same line of inference and reach the same conclusion by reviewing and discussing their dialects, their sacrifices, and so forth. All this evidence combined constitutes almost overwhelming proof for the unity of these peoples.

It is true that, if we compare, e.g., an Ibaloy woman with a South Kalinga woman, the fundamental identity or similarity of dress appears far from obvious. It is otherwise however if we proceed step by step from one group to the neighboring one. We may either start from the centrally located Bontoc Igorot and proceed north and south, or else start from the extreme north and south and proceed toward the center.

The temporal cultural factor — like the areal one — is difficult to characterize, because the Kalinga, as other ethnic groups, have a shallow history as a distinct group.[1] It has become necessary, therefore in different places and particularly in the historical part of this study, to refer broadly and in general to the "mountain peoples" and/or the "mountain populations." It is not until the beginning of the present century that the Kalinga emerge as a distinctive ethnic entity. Formerly the only discrete social units in the area of the present Kalinga Subprovince were the local, regional populations. These were endogamous units of closely related kin, and while cultural similarities existed over adjacent regions and areas, relations between regional populations were antagonistic, marked by frequent interregional headtaking forays. The division of the Mountain Province into subprovinces with ethnic designations for these units and particularly the treatment of the subprovinces as separate administrative units brought about ethnic consciousness in varying degrees.[2] Among the Kalinga where this consciousness appears to be strongest, identity as a distinct people was heightened by the peace-pact system. The latter, as we have noted, came in with the development of trade and travel opportunities toward the end of the last century.

The ethnic consciousness of the Kalinga is an important ingredient in contemporary Kalinga culture, and we will return to the subject later. At present we need to consider the problem of the original populations in the mountains to get a better comprehension of the present situation. Our interpretation of the historical data on northern Luzon and the ethnographies of the ethnic groups now recognized in the Mountain Province lead us to suggest an original, fairly uniform, population in the mountains. The constant references in the early historical records to the retreat of lowland peoples into the mountains in the wake of Spanish control indicate that much of the mountain populations came in during the period of initial Spanish contact, i.e., some three hundred years ago.[3] Lowland cultures, whether along the western and northern coastal strip of Luzon, the Cagayan Valley, or southward in the Pangasinan area, do not appear to have differed greatly when the Spanish arrived. It is important to remember that the high population densities in the Philippines are recent phenomena, the spectacular rises occurring in the present century. At any rate, the descriptions to be found in the early missionary reports of lowland peoples living adjacent to the mountains appear to be remarkably alike. Undoubtedly easy transportation by ocean and/or rivers provided continuous contacts and permitted the operation of a continuous process of cultural leveling. While dialects and separate languages surely existed, there is no reason to believe that they were more numerous or more divergent than today. Vocabularies of the languages spoken in northern Luzon at present are replete with numerous cognates so that some communication is possible across different languages. These conditions undoubtedly also existed in the past and, as at present, one language was probably known to all and thus served as lingua franca.

The late Felix Keesing, on the basis of extensive ethno-historical research, has presented a number of plausible hypotheses for the derivation of contemporary mountain groups from lowland areas (Keesing 1962, *see* especially pp. 317–343). Keesing's postulations are convincing, and without reproducing exhaustively his interpretations, we may report briefly that the refugees appear to have fled to mountain locations nearest their original lowland homes. The present distribution of the population in the Mountain Province suggests that the refugees settled in single family units or in groups of related families. These nuclei, in the course of the years and with increased population, developed into the contemporary local or regional units consisting of a single large village or most commonly of a group of related villages. Populations hemmed in by prominent geographical features and pursuing the same subsistence practices delimited a larger area of social and cultural relatedness, but as elsewhere in the Philippines, the local or regional group remained the self-conscious unit. Members of the local group are linked by ties of kindred, loyalty, responsibilities, and privileges. This was and is the unit which feuded and took heads from other such units. Some trade certainly went on, but compared to lowland areas, such trade was undoubtedly restricted.

The threat of Spanish control, the demand for payment of tribute, and the liability to recruitment for labor, served to isolate the mountains from lowland populations, while feuding and headhunting separated local groups from one another. Adjustments to differing ecological conditions that were considerably more varied than those in lowland regions triggered a process of differentiation. If the isolation had persisted for a long period, significant cultural differences might have resulted, but the time span, two hundred or three hundred years at most, was not long enough to produce drastic changes. A reverse trend came in the late nineteenth century with the construction of roads and trails, and the reversal has been accelerated by American control, beginning early in this century and continuing to the present.

We have postulated an original, fairly uniform population in the mountains, derived primarily from lowland areas in post-Spanish times. This population, in its adjustment to varying ecological conditions and to population increases across a period of some three hundred years, has developed local characteristics, but the common cultural base has not been obliterated. In the central area, in response to local environmental and demographic conditions, there developed a more technologically and socially complex culture based on the cultivation of rice grown on irrigated terraces. Primary among the diffused items emanating from this area are the terraced farming techniques themselves, but equally important are the non-agricultural aspects. Among the Kalinga we have indicated the social and religious complexes which appear to be associated with ecological and subsistence factors. It seems appropriate here to reiterate these complexes and relate them more specifically to probable causal factors.

The ecological conditions and subsistence patterns are more varied in the mountains than in the lowland areas of northern Luzon, and it is apparent that cultural variations correlate with these differences. Three primary subsistence patterns are evident among the mountain peoples. South of the Bontoc area, root crops and rice grown in irrigated terraces are dominant. Among the Southern Kalinga, rice grown in swiddens and irrigated rice in terraces vie with one another, with the latter appearing to be replacing the former at present. North of the Southern Kalinga, dry rice is dominant, with the invasion of irrigated rice terraces so recent that the newness of this farming technique is everywhere remarked upon. Mountain peoples also rely on subsidiary crops, primarily sugar cane, tropical fruits, and vegetables, domesticated animals (water buffalos, pigs and chickens), and to a lesser extent on products of hunting — deer, wild pig, wild chickens, and birds. Initially the mountain populations may have drawn more heavily on fruits, vegetables, and wild life, but primary emphasis on one of the three subsistence patterns undoubtedly soon became established. The historical record and the contemporary distribution of subsistence patterns indicates conclusively that irrigated rice-terrace farming, which allows for the highest densities of population, arose in the central area. Terracing is equally intensive and complex in both the Ifugao and Bontoc areas, and it is not possible in our present state of knowledge to establish the priority of either area for its development. We have thought it best from our Kalinga perspective to refer to this region simply as the "central area." From this central area, diffusion also moved southward. But the nature of this diffusion is not clear, and we have decided to concern ourselves only with changes among the Kalinga, particularly among the Northern Kalinga.

Organizations and structures absent or only suggestively present elsewhere among the mountain peoples are found in the Lepanto-Sagada-Bontoc region of the central area. This is the ward complex and associated with it are a men's council, a "dormitory" for men, another similar structure for women, and a paved lounging platform or platforms.[4] The ward is a territorial division of a village or community. It is not a kinship unit. The ward complex (*ato, dapay* Eggan 1954, Keesing 1954, Scott 1958c) functions as a kind of school for boys and its older male members form an informal council which settles disputes and supervises rituals and activities for the welfare of the community.

The ward as a non-kinship unit, assuming ceremonial and governmental functions in behalf of the community, occurs only in the Lepanto-Sagada-Bontoc area. Northward from Bontoc the ward system fades out in the Tinglayan district of Kalinga.[5] Lubuagan and the northern Kalinga are organized solely or primarily along kinship lines.

The crucial factor in the development of a political organization overriding the kinship principle appears to have been the large village or town aggregations. The ward system in its essential features is also absent among the Ifugao, although people are intensive cultivators of rice in irrigated terraces; indeed their terraces are even more spectacular than those of the Lepanto-Sagada-Bontoc groups. The settlement pattern among the Ifugao is one of dispersed hamlets and there are no large villages. Prominent physical features such as rivers and valleys do, however, define and delimit self-conscious population units among the Ifugao. These population units do not exhibit extra-kinship integration, but they are bound by religious ritual far more closely than other local groups in the Mountain Province. Ifugao religious practitioners appear to be priests in the anthropological sense; they are elaborately organized and perform complex rituals connected with the cultivation of rice. In the Mayawyaw rice rituals the head priest performs rituals for the welfare of the entire Mayawyaw Valley (Lambrecht 1932–51, 4: 154–155). Ifugao genius thus seems to have been directed to a complex development of the priesthood, and to ritual control rather than to the political integration of large villages or towns.

Other group interests and responsibilities in the central area as well as elsewhere in the Mountain Province are the concern of kinship organizations. Two types recently delineated by Eggan (Eggan 1959) are evident in the Mountain Province — the bilateral descent group and the personal kindred. The former appears to be primarily restricted to the central area of irrigated rice terraces. Descent groups are the descendants in both lines of particular ancestors. Among the Ifugao, genealogies as much as ten generations back can be provided by certain priests, and these are employed "to keep track of economic and other transactions and also for maintaining proper relationships with the ancestors of the Skyworld" (Eggan MS 1959). Descent groups have also been reported for the Lepanto-Sagada-Bontoc regions. In Sagada the descent groups are named and "have rights to cultivate certain hillsides first cleared and planted by a particular ancestor, and stands of pine trees are similarly owned and exploited by the direct descendants, who appoint a 'warden' to regulate the gathering and use of wood" (Eggan 1960).

Descent groups of the kind reported in the central area are absent in the north, but at least three important family lines are recognized in Lubuagan. An individual descendant from one of these family lines is charged with particular areas of Lubuagan rice terraces and settles disputes that arise in connection with them. The existence in Lubuagan of an aristocratic class, the *kadangyan,* (but not in northern Kalinga) may also be cited as the possible beginning of descent groups based on wealth, influence, and prestige. Initiators of specific peace pacts also established descent groups, for only from the latter may a future peace-pact holder be selected. These family lines all have shallow roots, however, and do not go back more than two or three generations.

The rise of descent groups and their continued existence would seem to require fairly stable economic conditions, the existence of valued property, and the presence of influential offices or positions which can be passed on to descendants. Irrigated rice fields which fulfill the criteria of economic stability and valuable property are new among the Kalinga. Swiddens have a temporary existence, important only for a few productive years, rarely more than two or three. While the descendants of a man who had initially cleared a swidden plot have priority rights to the plot, permission for others to reuse it is freely given. The work involved in making a new swidden is no greater than clearing and planting an old one. The sparse populations in the north apparently did not provide excessive competition for swidden land among a local population. The only highly valued property — heirloom possessions of Chinese manufacture: plates, jars, gongs, etc. — changes hands fairly frequently. Such property was given to curry the favor of a mangngol or brave warrior. We have noted that the mangngol was feared and yet respected and esteemed, for he provided protection and also settled disputes. Individuals and families who wanted to remain on the good side of a mangngol periodically gave him gifts, primarily of valued heirlooms. There were no positions to be inherited; the influential position of mangngol was achieved by courage, skill and luck in headhunting ventures. It is under-standable, therefore, that descent groups correlate with those areas which have a more stable economy, valued possessions in permanent rice fields, and positions which are inheritable.

The important social unit among the Kalinga is the personal kindred or kinship circle. These units are found everywhere among the mountain peoples and indeed are important organizations throughout the Philip-pines. The number of relatives included in the kindred vary; in some areas the kindred is limited to relatives bounded by second cousins, grandpar-ents, and grandchildren; in other areas the limits are extended farther to include third cousins, great grandparents, and great grandchildren. Among the Kalinga, spouses of the members of the kindred are also considered members of the unit. The kindred is thought to be the proper exogamic unit for any individual, but actually, rigid marriage restrictions apply only through first cousins. In native conception, kindred members have the responsibility to assist one another in difficulties, especially with respect to revenge and the payment of weregilds. The kindred or kinship circle is a discrete unit only in terms of a single individual, and thus, except for siblings, is never the same for any two individuals. In the north where the kinship circle is equated with the territorial region, the kinship circle does in fact exhibit discreteness. The concept of the kindred as an exogam-ous unit is qualified in these areas, and marriage is condoned freely with second counsins and beyond. The outer limits of the kinship circle are also extended to include all residents of the region. Since the population until recently was sparse in the north Kalinga areas, it is possible that relationships within the third-cousin degree were maintained within the boundaries of the territorial region. Such population units were thus actually demes (compare Murdock 1949 pp. 62–63).

As a rigidly delimited geographical entity, the region is most char-acteristic of the middle Chico and the Upper Saltan and Mabaca River Kalinga (*see* Chapter V). These units were formerly strictly endogamous and even at present regional populations exhibit distinctive dialectical and subcultural characteristics. The Kalinga recognize some sixty territorial regions in what is now the subprovince of Kalinga. Size of regions vary, since they are obviously related to geographical features, population size, the suitability of the terrain for dry rice farming, and the availability of fruits, vegetables, and wild game. Up to about sixty years ago, the regional unit provided all the subsistence and social needs of the local group; mobility was then largely confined to the region, except for simple trade via the trading partnerships and occasional headhunting expeditions into enemy regions. The diffusion of irrigated rice terraces and increased popu-lations has brought changes. In the south, where population increases have been especially marked, the equation of the kinship circle or kindred with region has been disrupted. Regional populations among the Southern Kalinga are at present characterized by a series of overlapping kinship circles. Regional cohesiveness so marked in the north is much weaker in the south, but still stronger than elsewhere in the Mountain Province.

Analysis of the kindred and the territorial region of the Kalinga in Lubuagan and in the northern areas illustrates conclusively that the territorial unit instead of being a "progressive principle from which the state rises" (Barton 1949:137) is simply a carry-over from an earlier period when kinship group and territorial region were equated. The region has nothing to do with the evolution of a higher or more complex political order. Given the head-taking complex, the Kalinga simply realized that they must stay within the bounds of a specific geographical region; to venture outside the region meant certain death in the hands of the enemy.[6] Organization within the region was loose and amorphous. In the northern Kalinga area where conditions approximated past conditions most closely, households are loosely grouped into hamlets. A dozen or so such hamlets in turn form specific regions whose geographical boundaries are rigidly defined. Regional populations are still essentially endogamous. There is no central authority, no single position of leadership for the region as a whole. A few influential leaders — men who cultivate more land than others, who have more pigs and carabaos, and who can speak eloquently — these are sought by the regional population to settle disputes. These are the men, too, who on social and religious occasions when the population of a region are together, make speeches of admonition and proper conduct. Such men also vie for positions as peace-pact holders and compete for municipal offices. Kalinga regional or territorial consciousness thus seems to be directly related to the earlier headhunting complex and fear of venturing away from one's closely related and trusted relatives.

Modern influences and introductions such as the peace-pact institution, the creation of subprovinces with ethnic designations, and other similar developments have also brought about a consciousness of the peoples within the Kalinga Subprovince as a distinct people. This notion of Kalinga identity has spread so quickly in the subprovince that only among the very old, and only in places far removed from the central Kalinga areas of the Middle Chico and Upper Saltan River valleys, is one likely to find the lack of Kalinga ethnic consciousness. Frequent interactions of Kalinga from different regions and areas, particularly in connection with peace-pact celebrations, have set off a process of cultural leveling.

This has been a reversal of the process of cultural differentiation which continued until friendly relations were established with Christian lowland populations and American administrators toward the end of the nineteenth century. Marriages between formerly endogamous regions are also beginning to take place with attendant cultural exchanges. Today the Kalinga are aware of being a distinct people, and while such identity has some political overtones, it is unlikely that this ethnic consciousness will develop into a nationalistic movement.[7] The Kalinga have much in common with other mountain peoples in northern Luzon, and through wage work and schools where they are comingled with other mountain peoples, they are now beginning to recognize a common destiny with them. Kalinga concerns and interests thus go beyond the subprovince to the Mountain Province and from thence to the Philippine nation and the world.

Social and cultural expressions among the mountain peoples appear to reflect the variant ecological situations or else are the result of historical changes. In the central area the cultivation of rice on irrigated terraces appears to have produced the most complex social and cultural conditions. Northward the advance of irrigated rice terraces has been replacing or supplementing dry rice and the socio-cultural expressions along this continuum are the primary concern of this study. The diffusion of irrigated rice terraces has not completed its northward migration and the Apayao area remains an area of swidden farming. Since the late nineteenth century and continuing through the contemporary period, historical circumstances and population increases have also influenced and are continuing to modify the socio-cultural picture.

The ward system as a non-kinship complex is limited to the central area where it is associated with large village or town aggregations. The bilateral descent groups appear to have a wider distribution, as strongly or perhaps even more strongly represented among the Ifugao with their hamlet settlement patterns, as in the large villages or towns of the Lepanto-Sagada-Bontoc regions. Descent groups are associated with rice grown on irrigated terraces, but the crucial factors for the emergence of this social unit we believe to be valuable inheritable property and status positions which can be passed on to one's descendants. Such social units are directly related to the existence of propertied families or a nascent aristocracy among the mountain peoples. The kindred or kinship circle is important throughout, but it is the primary social unit in the dry rice areas. Superimposed on the kindred or overlapping kindreds is the territorial region which seems to occur where scattered hamlet living is the settlement pattern. Regional identity is strongest with the Kalinga, but it is also present among the irrigated terrace farming Ifugao. The crucial factor for regional consciousness may be the settlement pattern which is similar in both groups — dispersed hamlet living.

Religious expressions appear to complement both ecological conditions and the distribution of the social units noted above. The most elaborate priest-type religious practitioners are found among the Ifugao. Religious practitioners here and generally, in the central area, are men. Among the Ifugao, religious ritual is performed for the benefit of a regional unit comprising several villages and is primarily associated with the cultivation of rice. In the Sagada-Bontoc area, religious ritual is likewise connected with the cultivation of wet rice, but it is also associated with community interests and the ward system. Family or bilateral descent groups also appear to receive some attention ritually in the central area, although the nature of this association is not clear in the literature. Everywhere certain stages in the life cycle, particularly early infancy, marriage, and death receive attention, but these life-cycle ceremonies are emphasized in the north, with little or no attention given to rituals associated with the community, the regional population, or with the cultivaion of wet rice. Sickness rites are important throughout but they receive primary emphasis among the dry rice cultivators of north Kalinga and Apayao. Headhunting rituals appear to have been important among all the mountain peoples, but reached especially spectacular and sanguinary proportions among the Kalinga and Isnegs of Apayao. We have noted the reorganization of former headhunting ceremonies in Sagada into rituals emphasizing community welfare, and among the Kalinga, to activities associated with interregional peace-pact celebrations. These reorganizations are, of course, due to recent historical influences primarily Spanish and American.

In the central area, the Ifugao have a profusion of deities with none of them singled out as more important than others. Sagada, Bontoc, and all Kalinga recognize a single benevolent deity or culture hero, but apparently nowhere is this deity directly propitiated or placated. Souls or spirits of the dead and a host of nature spirits, some good, but mostly malevolent, are recognized and the latter placated by sacrifices. Most important in the central area are the spirits of the dead. The attention given to ancestral spirits actually makes the religion of these people a form of ancestor worship. Northward from the central area the emphasis on ancestral spirits seems to diminish along with the decreasing practice of wet rice cultivation and the increasing cultivation of dry rice. The relationship that covers concern over dead ancestors, importance of rice fields and family connections is not merely fortuitous; it is to be expected that where certain family lines are distinguished and where specific ancestors are recognized, the memory of the departed will be venerated. The belief is generally held among mountain peoples that a deceased's situation in the afterworld is improved by sacrifices offered by living relatives. Hence an individual may pass on to a specific son or daughter select plots of rice fields, pigs, and carabaos because he expects that particular offspring to offer sacrifices on his behalf after he is dead. It is the closest departed relatives, usually a parent or grandparent, who send sickness and calamities as punishment because sacrifices are not being performed. As we have pointed out in Chapter IV, there is a close relationship between the amount of property inherited and the amount of sacrifices to be performed to appease the spirit of the relative who had bequeathed so generously. Generosity among the mountain peoples appears always to have a practical goal in relations among the living as well as between the living and the dead.

Among the Kalinga, the attention to ancestral spirits is strongest in the Lubuagan area and becomes less important in the north where placation of malevolent non-ancestral spirits is predominant. In neither the Lubuagan Kalinga nor the north Kalinga do the spirits of the dead receive the attention they are accorded in the central area of the Mountain Province, however. Thus it would appear that concern with non-ancestral spirits among the Kalinga correlates with swidden agriculture and the lack of (or at least the recent absence of) bilateral descent groups. It is important to emphasize, of course, that the absence of valuable inheritable property among swidden farmers and not simply dry rice cultivation *per se* is the crucial factor in the custom that accords less special attention to ancestors.

Rituals over rice are comparatively unimportant in the swidden areas of the north, and those rituals which exist are associated with dry rice. Even in Lubuagan, where wet rice has been important for more than half a century, little ritual is associated with rice grown in terraces. The lack of concern over ritualistic practices connected with wet rice indicates the recency of the diffusion of rice terraces and also illustrates that rice production is not a source of concern or anxiety to these people as compared with the central mountain groups. As we have also noted above (Chapter IV), people ritualize those activities with which they are preoccupied and which present to them pressing anxieties. Illness occupies this central position of concern and anxiety among the Kalinga, and not so long ago headhunting as well. As we might expect, the most elaborate ceremonies revolved around these concerns.

In the central area, the religious practitioners are male, while they are female among the Kalinga. Keesing (1962:317) indicates that early Spanish sources make reference to women sorcerers and doctors throughout northern Luzon. In postulating an Ilocos origin (among other alternatives) of the central area peoples, Keesing (*Ibid.*: 321) suggests that male priesthoods might be "Spanish-inspired" along with "the emergency of their aristocracies of wealth, and elaborated concepts of landed property with a focus on ownership of rice fields." It seems to us that the independent development of irrigated rice terraces alone necessitates an emphasis on ownership of rice fields and the development of regular inheritance patterns, and therefore also provides for the emergence of wealthy families and a nascent aristocracy. It does not seem necessary to postulate Spanish influence for the development of this complex. The shift from an older pattern of women mediums to male shamans or priests is not easy to account for, but the tendency among central mountain peoples to think of the founding ancestors as "fathers" might be an explanation. Thus, the change from women religious practitioners to men would have come with the development of bilateral descent groups which in turn would have resulted, as postulated, with the change to irrigated rice terrace farming.

Other correlations between ecology and socio-cultural conditions are not readily explainable. Scott (1962) in a description of house types in the Cordilleras of northern Luzon, has delineated "two major lines of architectural technique . . . the Southern Strain (including Ifugao, Bontoc and Benguet) and the Northern Strain (Apayao and northern Kalinga), with highland Kalinga proper presenting interesting combinations." It is clear that Scott's southern and northern strains represent the major ecological divisions between irrigated terrace cultivators and swidden farmers, with the "Kalinga proper" representing the area where both techniques of farming are employed. There are no features in the variant house types which would suggest a correlation with the different types of social units noted above. At present, better-to-do families live in larger, lowland-type houses containing two or more rooms with galvanized iron roofs. Such houses have a wide distribution all over the Mountain Province, but do not at present set apart a wealthy class from a poor class, nor do they appear to reflect other social conditions.

Dress and adornment styles from the central area northward conform essentially to the ecological conditions we have noted. Vanoverbergh (1929:181–242) distinguished a number of different dress styles, but recognized the general unity of all Mountain Province cultures, not only with respect to wearing apparel, but also to other characteristics. In the area of our interest Vanoverbergh recognized differences in dress styles between the Ifugao and Bontoc and northward from these central groups he distinguished also the Southern Kalinga from the Northern Kalinga. Thus the ecological differences correspond also to the clusters of variant dress and adornment styles, but these styles apparently have no socio-cultural correlates.

The distribution of a number of other characteristics among the Kalinga reveals the replacement of former traits by the spread of wet rice (compare Keesing 1962:317): The uses of fermented rice wine with, or in place of, an apparently older and more widespread use of sugar-cane wine, and, tobacco replacing betel-chewing in places where terraced wet rice cultivation has become firmly established (but not Ifugao!). In this context we may also mention the octagonal Kalinga house which Scott (1962) has noted is found only in areas of irrigated rice terraces.[8] There is also no obvious connection between these traits and the socio-cultural situation but they are apparently a response to factors generated by the spread of irrigated terraces.

The connection between ecology and socio-cultural conditions is apparent in a number of our examples above, but in other instances the traits found in association with specific types of ecological situations appear to be fortuitous. In still other cases the spread of specific artifacts, usages, and ideas can be attributed to known historical contacts. Thus the Kalinga peace-pact system, as we have noted, was developed as a response to Western contact and influences coincident with the establishment of a trade route from Abra across the Kalinga country to the Cagayan Valley. Christian beliefs, contemporary governmental and political systems, modern technology, schools, hospitals and the like, are, of course, recent introductions. Thus, while social and cultural expressions are closely associated with the ecological setting, historical and modern influences constantly modify their form and content.

Western influences and American control redirected Kalinga culture perhaps more profoundly than the cultures of other peoples in the Mountain Province. The initial contact between Americans and Kalinga was friendly. The Kalinga cooperated with American administrators; native leaders and lieutenant governors during the first two decades of the present century set about the task of organizing and readjusting social usages on a Western model. It is remarkable how quickly and how smoothly changes were brought about. At the turn of the century the populations within the present subprovince of Kalinga were restricted to geographical regions; they were feuding, warring and taking heads across these regional units. Over a period of a half century, a host of changes have taken place: headhunting has virtually stopped; a sense of ethnic oneness has developed; American-type schools have been established; and the Kalinga have become a part of the Philippine local, provincial, and national governmental system fashioned along Spanish and American patterns. The efforts to Christianize the Kalinga may not have developed as rapidly, but it is noteworthy that Belgium and American missionaries have been well received. The changes have come about largely through the efforts of the Kalinga themselves; the number of administrative officials from the outside has been limited. For the early years the only direct contact was maintained by the lieutenant-governor and the occasional visits of the Provincial Governor and the Secretary of the Interior. When accultura-tive developments among the Kalinga are compared to conditions among many North American Indian groups, some explanation for the contrast-ing results is needed. American Indian administration has been con-ducted under an enormous budget and with a complex personnel which has often approached the total American Indian population. The dura-tion of the contact and supervision has varied, but even for tribes in the Western United States, administrative control has gone on for at least twice as long as for the Mountain Province peoples. Yet, except for a few isolated cases, American Indians have not assumed the management of their own affairs; while schooling, health, and other needs have also been poorly met. In many areas there is apathy or passive acceptance of the Indian service and little or no cooperation with the Indian Bureau's admin-istrative officials. To say simply that the Kalinga and other mountain peoples were receptive to Western ideational and technological introduc-tions and cooperated with American administrators and their Philippine successors is not enough. Explanations must be sought in the contact situa-tion, the policies of American administrators, and the nature of the cul-tures under contact in both cases (*see* Spicer 1961:2–6 and 525). This is of course a problem which deserves exhaustive study, but we believe that we can indicate some of the more obvious factors which may account for the acculturative differences.

The contact situation between Americans and Mountain Province peoples throughout the history of American control can be considered favorable, while the relations between White Americans and Indians at different times during the contact period have been definitely unfavorable and even hostile.[9] Some American Indians took up arms against the encroachment of Whites on Indian land; others resisted more passively, but objection was registered in one form or another. The prevailing response pattern observable in most Indian reservations today is a rejec-tion of American culture in varying degrees. In some groups there is a kind of apathetic resignation to American authority which in individual Indians exhibits itself in bitterness and resentment toward Whites gen-erally. Few American Indians as groups have been absorbed or assimi-lated into the dominant American culture.[10] There are, of course, clear-cut historical reasons for these differences: White Americans wanted the resources to be found on Indian land, usually the land itself; in the Philip-pines there were no exploitative motives; Americans were civil servants, at least during the early years of American control. Another important ingredient in this complex is that the Kalinga and other mountain peoples were but part of a greater whole moving into Westernization and national independence. The dominant-subordinate aspect of the contact situation so strong in American Indian-White relations was absent, and while the mountaineer may have at times felt the dominating role of the lowland Filipino administrator, he knew that this person and he himself were both subordinates under American authority. The absence of racial distinctive differences between lowland Filipinos and mountain peoples also made it easier for the latter in more recent times to tread the path of acculturation into a Westernized Philippine culture. With the American Indians and other racially visible people, acceptance into the dominant White American culture is difficult even when the individual is "acculturated."

Turning now to the nature of the contacting cultures, we find again some significant differences between the two cases. Most important for initial consideration is the level of Kalinga socio-cultural integration. While the Kalinga at the time of American contact were living in band-like organizations, we believe that this was in part the reaction of a beleaguered refugee folk whose fears and suspicions had been aroused, not only against Spanish oppressors, but also against their neighbors in the mountains.

Early Spanish reports indicate a peasant-type culture in the lowland areas where customs were much the same and where considerable economic and social interaction went on. In the mountains peasant existence broke down. In part the nature of the rugged mountain terrain lent itself to regional isolationism, while the tradition of head-taking made it convenient to use this technique for maintaining spatial distance from peoples who were not kin and suspected of the most base motives. The rapidity with which the Kalinga were able to adopt a peasant-type world outlook and achieve a sense of ethnic identity appears to demonstrate the premise that regional isolationism was an accommodation to anxiety born out of their refugee experiences. When the threat to personal safety was removed, the Kalinga speedily became the most mobile people in the province via the mechanics of the peace-pact system. Kalinga ethnic consciousness helped to accelerate the acculturative process since the new political order, schools, and the like all promoted interaction on a broader geographical level.

In the New World, north of the Rio Grande, there were no truly peasant-type societies in pre-Columbian times. North American Indian groups were all essentially tribal, concerned primarily with their own separate destinies as territorially delimited units such as bands or villages.[11]

Parallels between American and Kalinga cultures, far more than those between white American and Indian, also undoubtedly facilitated the acculturation of the Kalinga. The Kalinga more than the American Indian, fitted the American or northern European image of the noble savage — the early reports and even an occasional contemporary reference call attention to the Spartan qualities of the magnificently formed Kalinga male warrior (compare Worcester and Hayden, 1930:456; Scott, 1960b:243). Other parallels may be listed: Kalinga society is essentially classless, equalitarian, and individualistic. Family background or other social considerations are unimportant for status and prestige. Division of labor is perhaps geared to giving males more leisure, but this is because of the former need for men to be on the alert for an enemy attack and at present, men do a variety of difficult tasks, hardly less demanding than those done by women. Individualism and equalitarian aspects of Kalinga life have been noted in inheritance practices: men and women retain title to their own property and all children inherit, even children of concubines, and even the rights of the rare servant, whether of his person or his property, are safeguarded.

Another factor which is perhaps the most outstanding parallel to American culture is the drive for individual distinction and prestige. In the Kalinga this trait formerly exhibited itself in the quest for renown as a headhunter and in the mangngol's role as an arbiter of regional troubles and disputes. With the suppression of headhunting, the Kalinga's quest for the satisfaction of personal prestige needs has been directed to positions created by the modern Philippine political and governmental structure and to participation in the popular Kalinga peace-pact system. The Kalinga nominate and elect a variety of officers on the local and municipal levels and follow political activities enthusiastically on all levels of the Philippine political hierarchy. Aspirants to political offices or to non-elective positions in the government are not wanting. The drive for individual achievement and distinction, however, is highlighted in the peace-pact meetings. In these meetings the male Kalinga is given full opportunity to exercise his love for debate and oratory. Proud and haughty aspirants for leadership who in former times might simply have taken spear and headaxe to settle an injury, a killing, or an effrontery from a foreign region, now match oratorical wits with one another. The modern courtroom and the clever lawyer trying an infraction of criminal law are mirrored in the peace-pact arena. The "courtroom" is a small vacant plot in a village or an arbor hastily erected for the occasion. The "jury" is the assembled audience of a large portion of the two regional populations and visitors from other regions having pacts with the two principal regional participants. The Kalinga speaker may appear insignificant in a gee-string or old faded shorts, tattered and torn; but eloquent words and skillful amassing of evidence against the opposing region evoke respect and admiration from co-regionists and opponents alike. There are no formal requirements to practice "law" and no restriction based on class, caste, or occupation. The ability to persuade and to suggest reasonable forms of arbitration which maintain the honor and dignity of the regional populations measure the stature of the Kalinga "arbiter." Such a man now enjoys the status and distinction formerly accorded the renowned headhunter or mangngol.

Variant cultural expressions among the Kalinga and other Mountain Province peoples appear to be a response to regional isolationism borne out of their position as refugees as well as to ecological differences in a mountain environment. In addition, recent historical circumstances have set off other processes which have brought about a sense of ethnic identity and acculturation toward a Western or American model. As the result of the latter changes and developments, the Kalinga together with their neighbors have moved rapidly to a position where they now consider themselves a distinct people, but view their social, political, and economic destiny in common with the modern Philippine nation.

Notes to Chapter 6

1. The meaning of the designation itself is not clear; most Kalinga believe that it is derived from *Kaling a* or *Kalingnga,* translated as "warrior" or "enemy warrior," although the name is now everywhere in the Mountain Province pronounced as *Kaling ga.*

2. Scott, in a recent publication, attributes "tribal" consciousness among the younger generation to the division of the Mountain Province into subprovinces (Scott 1960b:243).

3. Keesing (1962:304) while not denying the possibility of pre-Spanish mountain dwellers, also believes that the contemporary population has descended primarily from refugees who moved into the mountains in post-Spanish times. The supposed antiquity of Mountain Province peoples is based largely on the exaggerated speculations of the time it took to construct the rice terraces, but we now have a number of examples of elaborate terracing in shorttime periods. Keesing *(Ibid.,* pp. 89 and 323) cites the Loo valley terrace system in the headwaters of the Agno River, Benguet, built in two years, and an irrigation ditch in Bontoc which opened up an extensive system of new terraces. We may cite also elaborate terraces in the upper Saltan Valley which are said by Kalinga informants to be no more than forty or fifty years old. Perhaps the strongest evidence of the recency of Mountain Province terraces is the lack of reference to them by pre-nineteenth-century observers. (Keesing, *Ibid.,* pp. 332–323.)

4. While these institutions appear to have parallels elsewhere in Southeast Asia, their complex development in the central area of the Mountain Province in association with irrigated rice terraces and dense populations would seem to favor local development or elaboration of an older complex *(cf.,* Eggan 1954: 331).

5. The "fading out" of the ward complex northward through southern Kalinga, rather than a distinct break at the Bontoc-Kalinga boundary line was established

by information given me by Mr. William Scott of Sagada and Reverend Carl Lutz of the Tinglayan Lutheran Mission.

6. Other reasons for and/or functions of headhunting are discussed in Chapter V.

7. The division of the Mountain Province into five separate provinces corresponding to the present subprovinces was recently proposed. Benquet, Ifugao, and Bontoc did not favor the proposal, but Kalinga and Apayao, through their spokesmen, former Congressman Juan Duyan (Kalinga), and former deputy governor, Camilio Larrowin (Apayao), strongly supported the division *(The Mountaineer,* November 11, 1962).

8. Formerly the octagonal house was apparently the residence of the wealthy (Barton 1949, Plate V), and thus set apart well-to-do families in those areas of the Kalinga Subprovince where rice terraces had diffused. At the present time, well-to-do families live in lowland-style houses with galvanized roofs throughout the Mountain Province. These houses do not, however, indicate a wealthy socio-economic class.

9. Spicer (1962:16) in his book on the impact of Spain, Mexico, and the United States on the Indians of the Southwest, 1533–1960, reports that "probably the easiest generalization to make which would apply to all the Indians of the region is that all offered resistance and at some time fought to maintain their independence of White domination." While this statement is specifically for Indians of the Southwest, it is generally applicable to all Indian groups in the United States as well.

10. See Simpson and Yinger, May, 1957, for a recent analysis of the relations between American Indians and Whites from the initial contact period to contemporary times.

11. The concepts of "tribal" and "peasant" are employed here in the meanings given them in the writings of Redfield and others (see *e.g.* Redfield, 1956; Wagley and Harris, 1955; Wolf, 1955). The tribal society or community is a whole by itself, isolated, self-contained, providing for all of life's needs by itself and having a vertical or "up and down" dimension or relation. The peasant society or community is also a small society but it is not an isolate; it is not complete in itself; it bears not only a side-by-side relation, but also an up-and-down relation to more primitive tribal peoples, on the one hand, and to towns and cities on the other.

Reference Matter

Appendix I

Relationship Terms*

Consanguineal Relations

Second Ascending Generation

á:po   Lubuagan and N. Kalinga reference and address term for grandparents, either male or female. Also used for great-grandparents. Extended in address to siblings and cousins of the grandparents.

a-á:po	grandparents	
á:po lakáy	grandfather (lakáy – man)	
lakáy	mature or old man	Lubuagan
lalakáy	mature or old men	and
á:po bakót	grandmother (bakót - old woman)	N. Kalinga
bakót	old woman	terms
bakbakót	old women	
á:po	ascendants	

First Ascending Generation

amá   father. (si amá – my father, in reference.) Extended vocatively by N. Kalinga to parents' brothers, parents' male cousins and to husbands of father's and mother's sisters.

ína   mother. (si ína – my mother, in reference.) Extended vocatively by N. Kalinga to parents' sisters, parents' female cousins and to wives of father's and mother's brothers.

olitóg   Reference term in Lubuagan for parents' male and female siblings, parents' 1st and 2nd male and female cousins and the spouses of parents' siblings. (si olitógko – my parents' sibling, in reference.) Preferred term of reference in N. Kalinga for parents' male siblings, parents' 1st and 2nd

---

* For comparative purposes Kalinga relational terms are listed here in a manner similar to a list presented by Eggan for Sagada (MS 1959: Table I).

male cousins and the husbands of parents' female siblings. (si olitógko – my father's or mother's brother, in reference).

a-amák — uncles (N. Kalinga).

ka-amá-ak — Alternative term of reference in N. Kalinga for parents' male siblings, 1st and 2nd male cousins and the husbands of father's and mother's sisters.

íkit — Term absent in Lubuagan. In N. Kalinga preferred term of reference for parent's female siblings, parents' 1st and 2nd female cousins and the wives of parents' male siblings. (si íkitko – my father's or mother's sister, in reference.)

i-íkit — aunts (N. Kalinga).

ka-ína-ak — Alternative term of reference in N. Kalinga for parents' female siblings, 1st and 2nd female cousins and the wives of father's and mother's sisters.

Ego's Generation

son-ód — Lubuagan and N. Kalinga reference term for sibling, either brother or sister, also for half-brother or sister having same father, but different mother *see* below for half-brother or sister with same mother, but different father).

kabag-ís — N. Kalinga reference term used only for real siblings. Meaning: "coming from same umbilical cord." Term derived from Ilocano? Does not exist in Lubuagan.

bosát — N. Kalinga alternative term for sibling. Does not exist in Lubuagan.

pangngó — 1st born, oldest brother or sister.

odídi — last born, youngest brother or sister.

gawa-án — in between 1st and last born

pingngí — twins

i-óman — Lubuagan term for half-sister or half-brother having same mother, but different father.

sinóman — N. Kalinga term for half-brother as above.

kapínsan — Lubuagan and N. Kalinga reference and address term for 1st cousin, extended vocatively to second cousin, but not to third.

kapídow — Lubuagan and N. Kalinga reference term for second cousin.

kapítlo — Lubuagan and N. Kalinga reference term for third cousin.

ági — Lubuagan reference term for relative beyond the 4th cousin degree.

wági — N. Kalinga reference term for relative beyond the 4th cousin degree.

First Descending Generation

anák	child, male or female	
a-anák	children	Lubuagan
aggabák	daughter or son of a mistress	and
in-anák	adopted child	N. Kalinga
amon-ákon	nephew or niece. Extended referentially and vocatively to cousins' children.	terms

Second Descending Generation

apó: Lubuagan term for grandchild, male or female; son's or daughter's child. Extended to children of nephews and nieces.

apók   N. Kalinga–grandchild. Applied as above.

a-apó: Lubuagan–grandchildren

a-apók   N. Kalinga–grandchildren

Affinal Relations

katonggang-ák   Lubuagan and N. Kalinga reference and address term for parent-in-law; father-in-law.

malong-ág   Lubuagan address term for father-in-law.

mad-án   Lubuagan address term for mother-in-law.

manog-áng   Lubuagan and N. Kalinga reference term for child-in-law; son-in-law or daughter-in-law. Lubuagan and N. Kalinga use anákko (my son or daughter) vocatively for son-in-law and daughter-in-law.

káyong   N. Kalinga referential term for sister's husband or spouse's brother. Vocatively may say *káyongko* (my brother-in-law) or *son-ódko* (my sibling).

kom-ámang   Lubuagan referential term for all of spouse's relatives except parents' in-law. Vocatively Lubuagan uses *son-ódko* (my sibling) for siblings' spouses and for spouse's siblings' spouses.

ípag   N. Kalinga referential term for brother's wife or spouse's sister. Vocatively may say *ípagko* (my sister-in-law) or *son-ódko* (my sibling).

abílat   N. Kalinga referential term for spouse's sister's husband. Vocatively N. Kalinga address this relative and the wife of spouse's brother simply by name.

asawá   spouse

asawák   my spouse

asawák bakót   my wife (bakót – woman)

asawák lakáy   my husband (lakáy – man)

abílyan   Lubuagan term for parents-in-law, parents of a married couple.

abálan   N. Kalinga term as above.

Collective or Generalizing Terms

mamalóng-ag	N. Kalinga and Lubuagan term for ancestors, "old men."
sin kapo-ón	Lubuagan and N. Kalinga term for "kinship circle" or kindred.
man-ági	Relatives collectively, Lubuagan and N. Kalinga.
tomagotagó	stranger, non-relative (N. Kalinga).
bósol	non-relative, a potential enemy (N. Kalinga and Lubuagan).
man-á:po	grandparent and child
man-amá	father and child
man-ína	mother and child
a-amák	"uncles" (N. Kalinga)
i-ínak	"aunts" (N. Kalinga)
manson-ód	brother and sister, two or more brothers, two or more sisters.
manpínpin	1st cousins
manpídpidow	2nd cousins
a-anák	children
a-apó:, a-apók	grandchildren (1st term, Lubuagan; 2nd, N. Kalinga).
a-amonákon	nephews and nieces, children of 1st cousins
ka-asawá	newly weds
kakatoggáng-ak	parents-in-law.
man-abílyan	Lubuagan term for co-parents-in-law, relationship between parents of a married couple.
man-abálan	N. Kalinga term as above.
kom-ámang	Relatives of spouse except parents-in-law (Lubuagan).

Status Terms

lalakáy	male
baba-í	female
lakáy	man
bakót	woman
lalakáy	old men
bakbakót	old woman
pangngát	Influential and respected leaders in the region. N. Kalinga rarely uses this term, preferring "lakáy" or "capitan."
bagnáng	the wealthy class
kapós	the poor
poyóng	A servant, in Lubuagan. In N. Kalinga a person or family not having a home.
man-ó-odon	"helpers" in N. Kalinga mostly women who care for babies, feed pigs, pound rice, and the like.
dagdagás	mistress, "sweetheart"

Stages in Life Cyle

malnós (N. Kalinga and Lubuagan)	newborn
ma-ímis (N. Kalinga and Lubuagan)	baby begins to smile
mantopák (N. Kalinga)	} child sits alone
om-amoy (Lubuagan)	
manlokgób (N. Kalinga)	child learns to creep
komíyang (N. Kalinga)	} child begins to walk
manadaldálan (Lubuagan)	
manoddák (N. Kalinga and Lubuagan)	child runs around
maba-ón (N. Kalinga and Lubuagan)	child can be sent on errands
mangngkáyyo (N. Kalinga and Lubuagan)	old enough to gather firewood
bibíyo (Lubuagan)	"companion" age when boys go courting
mamabbagó (N. Kalinga)	ages 12–16
bomabaló (Lubuagan)	} young man
babalbaló (N. Kalinga)	
bababagó (N. Kalinga)	mature man (20–30)
bababbalásang (N. Kalinga)	mature woman (20–30)
lomakáy (N. Kalinga)	} middle-aged man (30–60)
momalóng-ág (Lubuagan)	
bomakbakót (N. Kalinga and Lubuagan)	middle-aged woman (30–60)
lakáy (N. Kalinga)	} old man
malmolóng-ág (Lubuagan)	
bakbakót (N. Kalinga and Lubuagan)	old woman
pang-ís (N. Kalinga and Lubuagan)	widower
baló (N. Kalinga and Lubuagan)	widow
basíg (N. Kalinga and Lubuagan)	childless

Appendix II

Important Ceremonies

LIFE CYCLE CEREMONIES

For Two Regions: Lubuagan (South Kalinga) and Poswoy (North Kalinga).

Lubuagan

1. *Makóbin.* A ceremony to induce pregnancy.
2. No special rite for pregnant woman who becomes ill.

3. Nothing comparable.

4. *Manilóm.* A feast when wife becomes pregnant to offset evil consequences and to placate the spirits.
5. *Ngílin.* Restrictions placed on members of the household.
6. *Kontíd.* A series of ceremonies beginning with birth and continuing for one to one and a half years.
7. When child is about four months old, father's relatives give child a special gift — usually a bead necklace. No name for the occasion.

Poswoy

1. No ceremony

2. *Yabyáb.* A sickness rite for a special type of illness to which pregnant women are believed to be susceptible.
3. *Sabbláy.* A sickness rite if both husband and wife become ill.
4. Nothing comparable.

5. Same

6. *Kontád.* Same.

7. *Kawól.* A simple ceremony for teething when child is about four months old. Child is given a bead.

8. *Omóy pasíbit.* When child first utters the name of a relative the child is taken on a formal visit to the relative's home.

8. *Omapó.* First formal visit to any near bilateral relative made by child and parents.

9. *Mamilók.* First time baby is taken to father's parents or father's relatives. Occasion for a feast.

9. *Balón di babát.* Same.

10. *Gabbók.* A ceremony for well-being, performed three or four months after birth.

10. *Gabbók.* Specifically a curing rite performed only if the child becomes ill.

11. *Banát* (a gift) or *mang-abílyan* (literally "becoming in-laws"). This is a marriage arrangement or contract made soon after birth.

11. *Banát* or *mang-abálayan.* Same.

12. Circumcision — about the age of seven.

12. None.

13. *Malógtogaw.* A form of bride service in contracted marriages only. Boy is between twelve and fifteen years old.

13. *Magngótogaw.* Same.

14. *Togtógaw.* The wedding feast.

14. *Pasing-án* or *amóng.* Same.

15. *Posípos.* General curing rite.

15. *Dáwak.* Same.

16. *Bagongngón.* Funeral rites.

16. *Bagongngón.* Same.

17. *Koli-ás.* Mourning period observed by near relatives of the deceased. Varies from about a month for children to a year for an adult.

17. *Koli-ás.* Same.

KONTAD CEREMONIES

Kontád or *Kontíd* is the designation for a series of ceremonies given for a child during its first year or year and a half of development. The series and the specific ceremonies themselves vary from region to region, but the general pattern of these ceremonies is similar throughout the Kalinga country. The series described here is for the region of Poswoy, north Kalinga.

1. *Ológ.* This is the first ceremony, performed a few days after the birth of the child. The special *kontád* medium, *mangkokontád,* butchers a pig and chants special prayers. The ceremony lasts for two days and is primarily to remove the restrictions of the *Ingngíling.* The baby receives a name at this time, usually a name from one of its prominent ancestors.

2. *Pinintalók.* This is the second ceremony of the *kontád* series performed about a month after birth. The *mangkokontád* is again in attendance. A general feast is prepared for members of the kindred in the child's hamlet and those of nearby hamlets. A rooster and a hen are offered as sacrificial victims and a rice cake is cooked with coconut milk. The immediate household members are forbidden to eat gabi leaves, sour fruits, frog, tadpole, and shellfish.

3. *Inambók*. The third ceremony of the *kontád* is performed when the child is about one and a half months old. Rice cake, mixed with coconut oil and moulded round, is an important feature of the prepared feast. A rooster and hen are again the principal sacrificial victims.

4. *Síbit*. This ceremony takes place about three months after birth. A rice cake, as in the ceremony above, is prepared, and leaves are placed around the cake for decoration. The cake is called *Inátata*. A rooster and a hen are again sacrificed.

5. *Binógnay*. This is the fifth ceremony of the *kontád*. The rice cake is omitted on this occasion, but a rooster and a hen are sacrificed.

6. *Kalwásan*. This is the last ceremony of the kontad series and is performed about a year or year and a half after birth. A rice cake is prepared as in the *síbit* above, but only a rooster is sacrificed on this occasion. The mangkokontad cooks the rooster on the bank of a brook near the village and erects a small hut of runo reeds.

Purpose of the Kontád. The *kontád* ceremonies are performed to insure the proper development of the child and to prevent its becoming ill or suffering any kind of misfortune. The series is particularly intended to stave off the influences of malevolent and ancestral spirits whose machinations are believed to be especially effective during this period of a child's growth. Prayers chanted by the medium for boys and girls differ in certain respects. The medium emphasizes good health and good fortune for both, but for boys she petitions the spirits to bestow bravery, talent for playing musical instruments, and for wealth and prosperity. For girls the medium asks the spirits to make a girl industrious, generous, and pleasant in her relations with relatives and friends.

It is important to emphasize that the medium in the *kontád*, as in other ceremonies, attempts to placate rather than petition the spirits. The sacrifices, the lavish feast, the dancing and other forms of entertainment are primarily to buy the favor of the spirits and thus avert illness, death, and other misfortune.

Appendix III

Songs of the Kalinga

1. *Ádi* or *áding*. Sung by men or women as a solo to highlight an auspicious occasion or to praise a prominent individual or an honored visitor. It is popular in festive gatherings such as weddings and peace pacts and is a favored courting song of young men.
2. *As-assáy*. A song to celebrate a victorious headhunting expedition. It is sung as a group song by men who have actually participated in taking a head or heads of the enemy *(see Kalommatik* below).
3. *Ballagoyós*. Man's courting song. It is sung as a solo with improvised flowery words to fit the beauty and personality of the girl being courted.
4. *Dalóng*. A song of the Eastern Kalinga. It is used for courting or for diversion and may be sung as a solo or group song by either sex. It resembles the *ballagoyós* in melody.
5. *Dandan-ág*. A southern Kalinga funeral song sung by men and women upon the death of an old man or woman.
6. *Dangngó*. A man's song of praise sung in large gatherings, particularly a favorite at peace-pact celebrations. A man sings or chants the song incorporating words appropriate to the occasion.
7. *Dangdang-áy*. Women's group song sung in large festive gatherings like weddings and peace-pact celebrations.
8. *Day-óndon*. A lament sung by a woman when her suitor or husband has gone on a long journey.
9. *Gosómbi*. This is a ballad reporting the activities of a number of mythical characters, but particularly about a hero, *Gawán,* and a heroine, *Gammílayan*. It is sung as a solo by a woman during the harvesting of rice *(see* a version of the Gosombi included in this section).
10. *Kalommatík*. Northern Kalinga war song, sung by a group of old men and women upon the return of warriors from a successful head-taking foray. The song precedes an elaborate feast which features dancing and boastful recitals of killings.
11. *Ogáyam*. A northern Kalinga song recounting the auspiciousness of a special occasion such as a peace-pact celebration, wedding, or presence of a distinguished visitor. It is sung by either a man or a woman as a solo.

12. *Olálim.* This is the southern and eastern Kalinga version of *ogáyam;* it differs only in melody.
13. *Pokáw* (northern Kalinga); *Palpalíwat* (Lubuagan). These are the boastful recitals of Kalinga warriors who have participated in killings. They were formerly the central feature of head-taking feasts; at present, they are performed at the end of peace-pact celebrations.
14. *Salidómay* or *diwás.* Pan-montane songs for all festive occasions and for gatherings of young people from the mountain tribes of north Luzon in cities away from home. These songs may be sung by either a man or woman as a solo or by groups of either men or women alone or by mixed groups of both sexes. When young students return home on vacations from Baguio and Manila it is common for them to join in singing one version after another of the salidómay as they ride the jolting Dangwa bus from Baguio to Tabuk.

Appendix IV
Peace Pact Data For Four Regions: Lubuagan, Salegseg, Mabaca and Poswoy

PEACE PACTS OF LUBUAGAN REGION

With Regions or Barrios of:	Former Holder or Holders	Year Pact Initiated	Present Holder and Place (Sitio) of Residence	Last Renewal Date
Tinglayan Municipal District				
1. Tinglayan proper	Basyag — inherited from his father, Banotan	1902	Solan, son of Basyag (Linas)	1948
2. Bangad	Galamoy (dead)	1902	Tawtaw, son of Galaymoy (Tangadan	1948t.
3. Sumadel	Kagaid — inherited from his father (both dead)	1902	Benito Busal, nephew of Kagaid (Mabilong)	none
4. Mallango	Bulayao inherited from father, Tumin	1902	Bulayao (Mabilong)	1959
5. Bilong	Wakas (still alive)	1902	Wakas (Mabilong)	none
6. Dananao	Pataotao — inherited from father	1902	Pataotao (Linas)	none
7. Tulgao	Pataklang — inherited from his father	1902	Pataklang (Mabilong)	none
8. Butbut	Pukao — inherited it from his father but Antonio Canao took over because of controversy	1938	Legaspi Canao, son of Canao (Linas)	1956t.
9. Basao	Manaltag inherited from father, Patangao	1902	Manaltag (Tangadan) transferred to Talipa, niece of Manaltag, in 1960	1960t.
10. Bugnay (usually included with Butbut in peace pacts) Same as Butbut				

Note: t — transferred, but no renewal celebration

With Regions or Barrios of:	Former Holder or Holders	Year Pact Initiated	Present Holder and Place (Sitio) of Residence	Last Renewal Date
Lubuagan Municipal District				
1. Guinaang	Gaiyampo (dead) then Canao (dead)	1900	Legaspi Canao, son of Canao (Linas); pending choice of one child to be holder	none
2. Balatok	Pukao (a woman) inherited from her father	1905	Domingo, her son, has pact (Linas)	1957
3. Tanglag	Ligawon (a woman) inherited from her father, Agoac (dead). Ligawon also dead.	1901	Suyam (temporary holder), husband of Ligawon — must go to descendants of Ligawon, not Suyam (Kimatan)	none
4. Mabungtot	Sindung (a woman) inherited from her father	1902	Sindung (Mabilong) broken, 1957, by a killing	none
5. Puapo Dangtalan	Gaiya-an — inherited from his father	1902	Buliwan, nephew of Gaiya-an	1959
6. Magsilay	Dumalsin (alive) inherited from Gongon (dead)	1902	Salangoy, nephew of Dumalsin	1956
7. Kagalwan	Carino Alunday (selected by pangngats)	1949	Carino Alunday (Podpod) broken, 1957 — "politics"	1949
8. Dalupa-Ableg	Pact ruptured 1940 by Lubuagan after the wounding and death of one of its citizens.	1901	Reinstated by Magwaki, the brother of the man slain by Dalupa people (Tiwod)	1948
Balbalan Municipal District				
1. Poswoy	Pukao (a woman) inherited from her father	1920	Pukao (Linas)	none
2. Balenciagao	Iway — inherited from his father	1900	Went to nephew, Martin Cobsin, in 1945	1945
3. Pantikian	Palangya — inherited from his father. Then to Max Duguiang, cousin of Palangya	1901	Max Duguiang (Linas) broken, 1957 — "politics"	none
4. Salegseg	Palangya — inherited from his father	1902	Max Duguiang	none
5. Balbalasang (two holders)	Puminglot inherited from his father Palangya — inherited from his father	1900	Puminglot; (Uma) Sang-a, son of Palangya (Gaang)	1946
6. Buaya	Pallayok — inherited from his father	1902	Max Duguiang, son of Pallayok (Linas)	none
7. Mabaca	Madalum (dead)	1905	Omosao, the son of Madalum (Tangadan)	1950
8. Daongagan	Ngaiyaan — inherited from his father	1938	Alilong, the son of Ngaiya-an (Dangoy)	1946
9. Balbalan proper	Canao (selected by pangngants of Lubuagan) (dead)	1953	Legaspi Canao, son of Canao (Linas) broken in 1957 for same reason as #3 above	none

With Regions or Barrios of:	Former Holder or Holders	Year Pact Initiated	Present Holder and Place (Sitio) of Residence	Last Renewal Date
Pinukpuk Municipal District				
1. Limos	Duguiang — inherited from his father	1905	Duguiang (Linas)	none
2. Asiga	Bakuli (dead)	1905	Sagasag, son-in-law of Bakuli; wife, Ma-ora, temporary holder (since Sagasag's death)	1956
3. Magaogao	Galamoy (dead)	1936	Sang-a, son of Galamoy (Tang-adan)	none
4. Guilayon	Pulitod — inherited from his father	1905	Macwis, son of Pulitod (Dangoy)	1958
5. Pinukpuk proper	Longod — inherited from his father	1905	Longod (Kimatan)	none
Tabuk Municipal District				
1. Maganao	Pulitod — inherited from his father	1905	Pulitod (Podpod)	none
2. Gobgob	Sikdawat (selected by pangngats)	1948	Sikdawat (Tabbangao)	none
3. Kalakad	Maladalon (selected by pangngats)	1908	Amangao, son-in-law of Maladalon (Linas) temporary holder	none
4. Lyulyu	Salapao — inherited from his father	1952	Salapao (Dangoy)	none
5. Malbong	Lungayat — inherited from his father	1902	Lungayat (Linas)	none
6. Amlao	Liyaban (selected by pangngats)	1958	Liyaban (Linas)	none
7. Naneng	Likadang — inherited pact from his father	1902	Likadang (Songbob) broken, 1953, because of stealing animals and failure to entertain	none
Tanudan Municipal District				
1. Lubo	Agowac — inherited pact from his father	1901	Salbang, son-in-law of Agowac, temporary holder (Mabilong)	none
2. Dakalan	Uyam	1905	Emilio, son of Uyam	none
3. Mang-ali	Pulitod — inherited pact from father	1905	Pulitod (Podpod)	none
4. Taloktok	Addum — inherited pact from father	1904	Eway, son-in-law of Addum (Linas) temporary holder	1960
5. Pang-ol	Banutan — selected by pangngats, went to Bulanao.	1910	Omao, nephew of Bulanao	none

With Regions or Barrios of:	Former Holder or Holders	Year Pact Initiated	Present Holder and Place (Sitio) of Residence	Last Renewal Date
Bontoc — Subprovince				
1. Sadanga	Suyam — selected by pangngats	1949	Suyam (Kimatan)	1949
2. Balwang	Long-od — selected by pangngats	1902	Long-od (Kimatan)	none
3. Botwagan	Chaplain — inherited pact from his father	1902	Chaplain (Podpod)	none
4. Saklit	Balingog — inherited pact from his father	1902	Balingog (Kimatan)	none
5. Manducayan	Dumaging inherited from father, Wansi	1902	Dumaging (Dugnac)	none
6. Bontoc proper	Wakas — selected by pangngats	1936	Wakas (Tang-adan)	none
7. Tokukan	Buung (dead)	1902	Odok, nephew of Buung.	none
Ifugao — Subprovince				
1. Banaui	Manaltag — selected by pangngats	1956	Manaltag (Tang-adan)	none
Apayao — Subprovince				
1. Kabugao	Pikut — selected by pangngats	1927	Washington, son of Pikut (Ga-ang)	none
2. Kalitkitan	Iuag — inherited pact from father	1927	Cobsin, son of Iuag (Kimatan)	none
Abra — Province				
1. Abang	Suyam — inherited it from his uncle	1956	Suyam (Kimatan)	1956
2. Salpadan	Suyam — inherited pact from father	1930	Suyam (Kimatan)	1956
3. Penarrubia	Saklag — selected by pangngats	1956	Saklag (Linas)	none
4. Lamao	Pingit — selected by pangngats	1932	Pingit (Kimatan)	none
5. Licuan	Max Duguiang	1932	Max Duguiang (Linas)	none
6. Lacub	Suma-al (dead)	1932	None, selecting among brothers for holder	none
7. Buneg	Max Duguiang	1932	Max Duguiang (Linas)	none
8. Gubang	Antonio Canao (dead)	1932	Legaspi Canao, son of Antonio Canao (Linas)	

PEACE PACTS OF THE SALEGSEG REGION

With Regions or Barrios of:	Former Holder or Holders	Year Pact Initiated	Present Holder and Place (Sitio) of Residence	Last Renewal Date
Tinglayan Municipality				
1. Tinglayan proper	a) Tayama, b) Diyan	1934	John Buyag, son of Diyan (Ballantoy)	1937
2. Botbot-Bugnay	Cammagay	1916	Lingayo, son of Cammagay (Ubel)	1959
3. Basao	Salingbay	1917	Pedro Angid (Alingag)	1958
4. Tulgao	Layogan	1932	Marcelo Banasan (Alingag)	1957
5. Dananao	Gumatay	1929	Santiago Bon-as (Pusa)	1955
6. Bangad	Manadac and Pattal	1924	Jose Canao (Alingag)	1958
7. Sumadel	Sagudang	1918	Bal-enay (Ubel)	1959
Lubuagan Municipality				
1. Lubuagan	Langayan	1901	Lourdes Galoma Falgui (Alingag)	1946
2. Mabongtot	Magayam	1928	Lunes Idday (Alingag)	1938
3. Tanglag	Sagao	1917	Pio Guimbot (Bolo)	1960
4. Uma	Tangdol	1925	Bogas Lingbawan (Dusoc)	1961
5. Balatoc	Baluden	1930	James Maglia (Alingag)	1934
6. Guinaang	Donglayan	1916	Amadeo Palangdao (Nawoy)	none
7. Ableg	Dalingay	1905	Isidoro Manao (Liglig)	1934
8. Magsilay	a) Duslay, b) Massagan	1902	Jackson Simangon (Bolo)	1936
9. Cagalwan	Gunayon	1912	Juan Alunday (Nawoy)	1930
Balbalan Municipality (Salegseg belongs to this Municipality)				
1. Balinciagao	Madday	1908	Layogan (Liglig)	1934
2. Balbalan	Sangdaan	1910	Tawagon (Ubel)	1932
3. Daoangan	Cosagon	1906	Basco Mamawag (Nawoy)	1924
4. Poswoy	Gunnawa	1902	Tomas Balingao (Bolo)	1952
5. Buaya	Abayao Anniban	1910	Alunday (Nawoy)	1958
6. Manat (includes Mabnawag, Buluan & Tawang)	Tangi	1914	Ligway Panabang (Pépé)	1960
7. Mabaca	Balatao Tangdol	1904	Luis Tangdol (Gawaan)	1932
8. Pantikian	George Bongaoen Salingbay	1934	Roberto Uggas (Alingag)	1943

With Regions or Barrios of:	Former Holder or Holders	Year Pact Initiated	Present Holder and Place (Sitio) of Residence	Last Renewal Date
Pinukpuk Municipality				
1. Magaogao	Mangliwan	1914	Lawagan Balangcad (Bolo)	1936
2. Dugpa (some of this tribe are scattered but they carry the pact provisions)	Dusagan Ating	1908	Bassat Dusagan (Dusoc)	1938
3. Mananeg		1910	Gongon, then Victor Balansi (Dusoc)	1921
4. Pinukpuk proper	Dumacyon	1915	Eleno Tangdol (Gawaan)	1924
5. Apatan	Lioagan	1916	Edita Balicao (Alingag)	1958
6. Allaguia	Ammogao	1911	Labbutan (Kilayon)	1932
7. Ballayangon	Manao	1915	Lammawan (Liglig)	1931
8. Ammacian	Baliling	1918	Danguiwan Baclod (Bolo)	1936
9. Wagod	a) Sagmayao, b) Bogacon	1924	Simeon Bogacon (Bolo)	1937
10. Aciga	a) Dannang, b) Bulaay	1920	Ramon Aggalao (Gawaan)	1957
11. Matucad	Lumiwan	1920	Lammawon (Dusoc)	1934
Tabuk Municipality				
1. Amlao (including Biga but not Pacatalig)	Duslay	1906	Balansi (Alingag)	none
2. Caladcad	Danao	1909	Roldan Tamdog (Alingag)	none
3. Tabog	Daogas	1920	Lawagan (Nawoy)	1954
4. Pingao, Gubgob and Tuga	Mangwag	1919	Pedro Calumnag (Liglig)	none
5. Guilayon	Daowan	1915	Fernando Tawagan (Gawaan)	1954
6. Naneng	a) Malaggan, b) Tabbagon	1935	Dugnayan Manadao (Alingag)	1961
7. Malbong	a) Maggay, b) Tabbagon	1919	Marcos Gongon	1934
8. Gamonang tribe Malig Sokbot	Banasan	1914	Peter Banganan (Liglig)	none
9. Magnao	Ipan	1915	Bawan (Liglig)	1931

With Regions or Barrios of:	Former Holder or Holders	Year Pact Initiated	Present Holder and Place (Sitio) of Residence	Last Renewal Date
Tanudan Municipality				
1. Lubo	Lummiwan	1912	Fruto Gunnawa (Pusa)	1931
2. Mangali	Taya	1910	Emmanuel Calangao (Alingag)	1957
3. Dacalan	Tawacnig	1910	Victor Laginday (Pusa)	none
4. Taloctoc	a) Binoloc, b) Anggaco	1916	Limay Anggaco Gupaal (Nawoy)	1937
Bontoc Subprovince				
1. Sadanga Municipality				
a. Sadanga proper	Gongon	1931	Benito Daoayan (Dusoc)	1932
b. Bolwang	Calagui	1930	Alfonso Sagalon (Pusa)	none
c. Betwagan	Malasi	1958	Malasi Bunagan (Alingag)	none
2. Natonin Municipality				
a. Natonin proper	Condaya	1928	Lubuangon (Ligayan)	none
b. Maducayong		1930		none
Apayao Subprovince				
1. Conner Apayao				
a. Sacpel	Domayag	1928	Buyogan Coloy (Alingag)	1936
b. Carikitan	Danguiwan	1926	Delfin Gumnad (Balantoy)	none
c. Calapog	Gumatay	1920	Cassiano Pattal (Ubel)	1926
d. Balolawag	a) Labutan, b) Gayudan	1918	Alfredo Tangdol (Pusa)	1948
e. Nagwagan	Siddayao	1920	Madoyacan (Bolo)	1929
f. Talifugo (Eyackbab)	Battawang	1920	Calixto Maglia (Ubel)	none
g. Tonog-Dagara	a) Tangui, b) Lubuangon	1918	Lammawon (Liglig)	none
2. Kabugao, Apayao				
a. Kabugao proper		1934	Lingayo (Ubel)	none

With Regions or Barrios of:	Former Holder or Holders	Year Pact Initiated	Present Holder and Place (Sitio) of Residence	Last Renewal Date
Abra Province				
1. Bangilo		1910	Alberto Layugan (Liglig)	1955
2. Danag	Dumacyon	1910	Jose Malannag (Alingag)	1962
3. Sallapadan	Lumiwan	1914	Pablo Lugao (Dusoc)	none
4. Botloc	Cosidon	1912	Pedro Manadao (Alingag)	1942
5. Baay	Manadao	1916	Daoayan Dalwog (Nawoy)	none
6. Colyong, San Juan Mun.	Mangwag	1915	Malatag (Bolo)	none
7. Baccoc, Lagangilang Mun.	Gunnawa	1921	Apaling (Ubel)	none
8. Licwan & Lacub Mun.	Balicao	1924	Maria Ande (Alingag)	none
9. Buneg Mun.	Sangdaan Dumacyon	1918	Eleno Tangdol (Gawaan)	none
10. Mataragan	Tangi	1912	Ligwan Panabang (Pepe)	none
11. Gacab, Malibcong, including Balbalasang, Talallang & Secsecan	Banganan	1931	Camilo Bogya (Alingag)	1937
Cagayan Province				
1. Tuao, Cagayan				
a. Balacnit	Gannaban	1936	a) Madoyacan, (Bolo) b) Anaclito Lamipao (Alingag)	1957
b. Tuao (Abot & Bayumbayan)		1947	Lingbawan (Dusoc)	none

PEACE PACTS OF THE MABACA REGION

With Regions or Barrios of:	Former Holder or Holders	Year Pact Initiated	Present Holder and Place (Sitio) of Residence	Last Renewal Date
Tinglayan Municipality				
1. Bangad	James Bagsao	1935	James Bagsao (Canao)	1947
2. Tinglayan proper	Roberto Ganagan	1958	Roberto Ganagan (Canao)	none
3. Butbut	Victor Camadog	1958	Victor Camadog (Canao)	1960
4. Sumadel	Pablo Basian	1937	Eugenio Bagsao (Canao)	1962
Lubuagan Municipality				
1. Lubuagan proper	Camalao (dead)	1905	Maria Kegan, granddaughter (Canao)	1938
2. Ableg	Akilno Daggay	1933	Akilno Daggay (Agudong)	1934
3. Guinaang	Siknawan (dead)	1930	Margarita M. Banatao (her niece) (Tappo)	1948
4. Tanglag	Sagaok	1931	Sagaok (Canao)	1944
5. Cagalwan	Cabanag	1926	Cabanag (Amasian)	1935
6. Uma	Andres Palangdao	1960	Andres Palangdao	none
7. Balatoc	Ambit (dead)	1938	Alingay (her niece) (Canao)	none
8. Magsilay	Sikaawan (dead)	1925	Margarita M. Banatao (Tappo)	1960
9. Mabangtot	Luna Anggaboy	1957	Luna Anggaboy (Bocay)	none
Balbalan Municipality				
1. Buaya	Pedro Awili	1920	Pedro Awili (Balala)	1955
2. Salegseg	Maximo Gaayon	1904	Maximo Gaayon (Agudong)	1947
3. Balbalasang and Pantikian	Bitagong	1921	Bitagong (Bayuwong)	1922
4. Balinciagao	Pedro Dangilan	1960	Adriano Sagao (Canao)	none
5. Balbalan proper	Roberto Tombali	1940	Roberto Tombali (Bayuwong)	none
6. Daoangan	Flora Kigan	1929	Flora Kigan (Canao)	1936
7. Poswoy Ababaan	Tungdo (dead)	1923	Juan Tungdo (son) (Madalit)	1960
8. Tawang and Bassao	Lumawig		Lumawig (Bayuwong)	1944

With Regions or Barrios of:	Former Holder or Holders	Year Pact Initiated	Present Holder and Place (Sitio) of Residence	Last Renewal Date
Pinukpuk Municipality				
1. Pinukpuk proper	Cabannag	1926	Cabannag (Ammacian)	1936
2. Ammacian	Manangbao (dead)	1923	Josephine Siagan (her granddaughter) (Canao)	1935
3. Wagod	Juan Gulayon	1922	Juan Gulayon (Ammacian)	1926
4. Asiga	Danao (dead)	1925	Emilio Abawag (his nephew) inherited it (Canao)	1956
5. Matucad	Otan (dead)	1934	Lino Taway (his grandson) inherited it (Tappo)	1946
6. Limos	Bitagong	1933	Bitagong (Bayuwong)	1936
7. Ballayangon	Luna Anggaboy	1943	Luna Anggaboy (Bayuwong)	none
8. Calbayan	Mathew Buliig	1947	Mathew Buliig (Madalit)	none
9. Limos	Bading	1932	Bading (Pasnaan)	none
10. Sappil	Balumaag (dead)	1926	Alingai (her daughter) inherited it (Canao)	1954
11. Magaogao	Lorenzo Macasing	1949	Lorenzo Macasing (Balala)	none
Tanudan Municipality				
1. Mangali	Camalao (dead)	1935	Maria Kigan (her granddaughter) inherited it (Canao)	1955
2. Lubo	Bawagan	1935	Bawagan (Canao)	1936
3. Pangol	Roberto Tombali	1956	Roberto Tombali (Bayuwong)	none
4. Taloctoc	Banawa (dead)	1932	Gunawa (her granddaughter) inherited it (Agudong)	1954
Tabuk Municipality				
1. Naneng	Kulaban	1935	Kulaban (Canao)	1938
2. Malbong	Bangit (dead)	1931	Pedro Bangit (his son) inherited it (Canao)	1935
3. Amlao	Balunggay	1931	Balunggai (Canao)	1950
4. Gilayon	Ramon Manangbao (dead)	1946	Antonio Canao (his grandson) inherited it (Balala)	none
5. Tubog	Tomas Bangawan	1948	Tomas Bangawan (Canao)	none

With Regions or Barrios of:	Former Holder or Holders	Year Pact Initiated	Present Holder and Place (Sitio) of Residence	Last Renewal Date
Bontoc Subprovince				
1. Samoki	Marcelo Banatao	1939	Marcelo Banatao (Tappo)	none
2. Mainit	Magay	1960	Magay (Masait)	none
Apayao Subprovince				
1. Nabuangan	Langayan	1931	Langayan (Balala)	1948
2. Calapog	Kilobong (dead)	1933	Rita Palangdao (her granddaughter) inherited it (Canao)	1948
3. Calapog	Baluyan	1933	Baluyan (Ammacian)	1955
4. Akbob	Tubban (dead)	1931	Pablo Bayudan (his grandson) inherited it (Bayuwong)	none
5. Lallayug	Pedro Bulayao	1943	Pedro Bulayao (Canao)	none
6. Mawanan	Juan Biyao	1946	Juan Biyao (Madalit)	none
Cagayan Province				
1. Balaknit	Leon Bayubay (dead)	1925	Fred Tangbawan (his nephew) inherited it (Canao)	none
2. Tuao	Baluyan	1957	Baluyan (Ammacian)	none
Abra Province				
1. Bangilo	Bawagan	1936	Bawagan (Canao)	none
2. Matalagan	Danao (dead)	1934	Martin Abawag (his nephew) inherited it (Canao)	1950
3. Bunig	Alekgu (dead)	1960	Rosa Ganapan (her daughter) inherited it (Canao)	none
4. Lacub	Bugawit (dead)	1960	Andres Palangdao (his son) (Canao)	none
5. Salapadan	Tuban (dead)	1947	Alingay Buliig (her granddaughter) inherited it (Madalit)	none

PEACE PACTS OF POSWOY REGION

With Regions or Barrios of:	Former Holder or Holders	Initiated Year Pact	Present Holder and Place (Sitio) of Residence	Renewal Last Date
Tinglayan Municipality				
1. Botbot-Bugnay	Laging Danao	1960	Tabugay Laging (Tukod)	none
2. Tinglayan	Pablo Banson	1959	Pablo Banson (Pasiñgan)	none
3. Tulgao	Pedro Cosidon	1949	Pedro Cosidon (Pulay)	none
4. Sumadel	Mariano Obal	1957	Andres Baguingan (Lubluba)	none
5. Basao	Pedro Daoayan	1959	Pedro Daoayan (Polay)	none
Tanudan Municipality				
1. Lubo	Manadao	1928	Lugad Layugan (Lisbong)	1960
2. Tanudan	a) Waldiwadan b) Unagan Dayac c) Dagmay Balutoc	1925	Eyal Gumacdang (Angod)	1951
3. Gaang	Alberto Gaano	1940	Jr. Gaano (Tucod) (dead) (successor not yet designated)	1959
Balbalan Municipality				
1. Balinciagao	a) Canao b) Bangonan Awingan	1909	Carmen Awingan (Buacon)	1949
2. Balbalan proper (Gobang)	Agaton Calwing	1941	Blas Calwing (Capas) (dead — new pact holder not yet selected)	1956
3. Banao-Pantikian Balbalasang	a) Palleon b) Gumacas	1918	Ebon Dalyagan (Pulay)	1951
4. Salegseg	Manao	1904	Digay Anniban (Pasingan)	1958
5. Buaya	a) Battawang b) Banawa c) Balasi	1906	Emilia B. Dugyawe (Cacalawan)	1949
6. Mabaca	Buyogan	1917	Francisco Balinte (Buacon)	1960
7. Nambucayan	a) Canao b) Dagwat	1928	Cannay Dagwat (Dugong)	1939
8. Bonnong	a) Gaowon b) Lumnay	1920	Daligding (Buacon)	1935
9. Baay-Limos	Pasingan	1916	T. Sawadan (Lunas)	1960
10. Bassao	a) Dumnay b) Balaoing	1943	Osias Gumannao (Capas)	1954
11. Magnao	a) Bogas b) Balasi		Siwagan Balasi (Cacalawan)	none
12. Allaguia-Limos	Sangdaan	1921	Isabel Layog (Butol)	1959

With Regions or Barrios of:	Former Holder or Holders	Year Pact Initiated	Present Holder and Place (Sitio) of Residence	Last Renewal Date
Pinokpok Municipality				
1. Aciga	a) Singay Guibasan b) Lumatac	1917	Luis Balladao (Lisbong)	1954
2. Ammacian	Juanita Bannas	1920	Tomboli Balanso (Capas)	1959
3. Wagod	a) Manadao b) Lummay Gallasic	1918	Matilde Daligdig (Buacon)	1947
4. Pinokpok proper	a) Bulayang b) Tawacneg c) Lugayan Balcanao	1930	Veronica Balcanao (Lalladog)	none
5. Ballayangen	Pasado Dagwat	1926	Terso B. Dagwat (Dugong)	1958
6. Magaogao	Agsiwan Malangay	1924	Maria Cullangan (Lubluba)	1947
7. Mananig	Sangdaan	1929	Osias Layog (Butol)	1949
8. Dugpa Builayon	Juanita Bannas	1920	Tomasa Balanso (Capas)	1942
9. Allangigan	a) Amnanay Gangngat b) Cambali Tandingan	1923	Pepita Tandingan (Capas)	1940
Lubuagan Municipality				
1. Lubuagan	a) Sannadan b) Ongod	1920	Ernesto Baligod (Butol)	1941
2. Balatoc	Dalwines	1960	Baddongon Eddamag (son-in-law) (Capas)	none
3. Tanglag	Mamanao	1939	Candida Dungguiis (Capas)	1946
4. Kagalwan	a) Waldiwadan b) Alamban Awing	1919	Ramona Dammog (Capas)	1949
5. Ableg Dalupa	Aowanon Balanso	1937	Gamay (Butol)	none
6. Guinaang	a) Toddao b) Baggay	1923	Mariano Bawit (son-in-law) (Cacalawan)	1960
7. Bulen-Magsilay	a) Aguiwanas b) Doyac	1921	Camilo Doyac (Butol)	1948
Tabuk Municipality				
1. Naneng	Bannas	1903	Lasi Taggay (Buacon)	1946
Apayao Subprovince				
1. Daga	a) Juanita b) Biana Taclawan	1931	Ceferino Taclawan (Pugo)	1945
2. Nabuangan	a) Cangilgan b) Gannocat c) Gumabay	1938	Daline Gumabay (Mamaga)	1940
3. Calapog	Gayudan	1922	Lumnay Wali (Benac)	1940
4. Sappel	a) Egsot b) Biana Taclawan	1922	Ceferino Taclawan (Pugo)	1949

With Regions or Barrios of:	Former Holder or Holders	Year Pact Initiated	Present Holder and Place (Sitio) of Residence	Last Renewal Date
Bontoc Subprovince				
1. Tukukan	Gannisi	1952	Gannisi (Lisbong)	none
2. Betwagan	Malaggan	1947	Malaggan (Seklang)	none
Abra Province				
1. Bangilo	a) Aggayaban b) Capitan Dawaton	1918	Dawaton, Jose (Capas)	1939
2. Gacab	Binang Dugayon	1958	Dugayon (Secklang)	none
3. Danac	Temoteo Sawadan	1959	Temoteo Sawadan (Lunas)	none
4. Matalagan	a) Sinowan b) Manao c) Tawacnig	1926	Gattongay Tawacnig (Lalladog)	1957
Cagayan Province				
1. Balacnit	Tombaga	1930	Maiyao Dumog (Pasingan)	1956
2. Abbot Tuao	Cacnay Banatao	1935	Cacnay Banatao (Pugo)	1960
3. Bagumbayan	a) Annawan a) Paula Balutoc	1935	Caridad Balutoc (Buacon)	none

Peace-Pact Document
Lubuagan and Penarrubia (Abra-Tinguian)*

REPUBLIC OF THE PHILIPPINES
MOUNTAIN PROVINCE
MUNICIPAL DISTRICT OF LUBUGAN

PEACE PACT AGREEMENT

WE, SACLAG and FRED OMNAS, both of legal ages, married and resident of Lubuagan, Kalinga, Mountain Province and Penarrubia, Abra respectively, do hereby bind ourselves and our people in a Peace Pact, (Bodong).

That, We, SACLAG AND FRED OMNAS, Peace-Pact holders and legal representatives of our people, pledge to respect, and uphold the principles of the bodong, maintain, defend its integrity and shall with our lives, properties and parties protect and enforce the provision (Pagta) as provided approved by our people against any violation thereof.

SCOPE

TERRITORIAL JURISDICTION
    a — LUBUAGAN
The Town of Lubuagan, covered by the bodong are: Linas, Kimatan, Songbob, Tiwod, Gongogong, Dugnac, Mabeling, Manangol, Duyaas, Balii, Gotgotong, Tabangao, Gaang, Dangoy, and Agsiang.
    b — Boundaries
North — Cagaluan gate, Dinacan, Balngabang, Palontoc, Daydayop
West — From Daydayop, Tiking to Mosgot.
South — From Mosgot to Eucan down to Canlitong.
East — From Canlitong to Tawang, Goday, Dadsadog, Wait, Malsawa, to Pugo to Cagaluan gate.
    a — Penarrubia, Abra
The towns of Penarrubia covered by this Bodong are: Penarrubia Poblacion, Domayco, Gannao, Pogui-it, Namarabar, Reyang proper and Gravelinas.
    b — Boundaries
North — Domayco
South — Pogui-it and Namarabar
East — Gannao
West — Reyang

PROVISIONS — (PAGTA)

1. Crimes:
    A — All crimes ranging from murder down to slight physical injuries shall be punished according to their nature. Life taken shall be paid for with life, bloodshed to be paid for blood and slight ones to be settled by amicable settlement by the Peace-Pact holders with their town leaders.
    B — Poisoning: Poisoning shall have the same weight as of murder and shall be paid with life.

---

* This document has not been changed or edited from the original.

C — Stealing — Theft and Robberies:

These crimes shall be punished severely. The penalty shall be: For any article, animals or belonging stolen, the kind or value shall be paid back tripled, one part goes to the Peace-Pact holder of the offended party and the two-thirds goes to the owner of the property stolen. Small things of less value, shall be decided between the two Peace-Pact holders.

D — Rape: Rape shall be dealt with and punished severely. Living together as concubines with love and mutual understanding by both parties shall not be the duty of the Bodong.

E — Hospitality: All visitors, traders, etc., shall be entertained, guided, fed and sheltered during his or her stay and mission. All protection and respect should be due him.

F — All traders, visitors, tourists and others shall before disposing or going on a buy or sale, present to all his or her belongings be shown to the host for security to avoid any expected troubles. If possible the Peace-Pact holder should be informed or approached before any transaction is made.

G — Lost and Found: All properties lost within the house after it had been presented to the host shall be redeemed. Lost properties or belongings outside, on the roads, street or on the way are not redeemable.

H — Death, sickness and accidents:

Any incidents, accidents, sickness or death occurred within the bodong jurisdiction shall at once be notified to the Peace-Pact holders concerned and shall by all means helped in the returned home of the patient concerned.

1. Residence —

Couples from Abra and Lubuagan married must choose their residence and their chosen residence shall be their inclusion in the Peace-Pact jurisdiction.

2. All travelers and students moving and studying outside the territorial scope of the Bodong herein concerned shall carry the terms of provisions of the Peace-Pact where they are.

3. Under these provisions, the Peace-Pact holders shall as representatives of their people be vigilant and well informed of their peoples conduct and shall be ready to fulfill their duties immediately whenever violation thereof occurs.

IN WITNESS to the foregoing Provisions of this Peace-Pact, we hereunto set our signatures (thumb mark) with other Prominent leaders of our town as co-signers this 24th day of April 1956, at Lubuagan, Kalinga, Mountain Province.

1.   **FRED OMNAS**   SACLAG His Mark

     Peace-Pact holder for Penarrubia   *Peace-Pact Holder for Lubuagan*

2.   GALLAMOY His Mark

     Prominent man of Penarrubia   *Prominent man of Lubuagan*

Peace Pact Document
*Asiga (Aciga) and Allangigan**

PAGTA OF THE BODONG OF ACIGA AND ALLANGIGAN AT THE CLOSE OF THE SONGOT AND DOLNAT HELD AT THE HOUSE OF MR. ANDRES ABAWAG, GUMACAD ACIGA, PINUKPUK, MT. PROV., ON MAY 18, 1959.

———

KNOW ALL MEN BY THIS PRESENTS:

That people of barrios Aciga and Allangigan, Municipality of Pinukpuk, Mountain Province, during the occasion cited above, through their chosen representatives whose signatures appear below, by mutual agreement hereby constitute and adopt the following rules and regulations or Pagta for themselves and their posterities to be binding upon them until and before the same shall be amended, revoked, or altered by themselves.

1. The respective territories over which each party shall have jurisdiction over the people who reside therein shall be:

(a) ASIGA: Starting from the East Southward, Botac to Napolayan at the road, to Mount Amtong, down to Cananad Creek, up to Mount Gueoguewan, shooting to Siyot, down to School site, Crossing the Cul-uwan River, to Sulot, up to Tangob Mountain, straight line to Towo, then to Andasi Brook, to Cocogcogon, Powag, to Guingoy, up to Tuwang Mountain, to Mount Palpalayon, to Lipoy, to Abbengdod Brook, then to Pannongan Brook, to Innowangan Brook, to Sabangan Bigan down to Umot, then to Basitao, to Tucac, to Cili, down Cal-uwan River, to Buwi to Podpodan, from Podpodan to Botac.

(b) ALLANGIGAN: South-Eastward from Solong Pilpil-ac to Dalaggan, up to Botod Sanganga, to Abbalong, to Owed, then to Ngilin, then to Mount Catagnodan, then to Capitan, to Sabangan Callaggan, following the Mananig River to Mount Pinogo down to Guimbawan, to Maboyoc Brook, to Polag, to Mount Silpit, to Alimboyogan, to Caniguing, down Mananig River to Layog, up to Ulon to Nabolagotan, down Saltan River, Crossing said River to Pinac-engan, to Pata, straight to Pacawong, following Saltan River to Sabangan Tabagan, then to Pingao, to Malbagui Brook down to Kibog, Crossing Saltan to Sabangan Pilpil-ac.

2. PAGTA:

(a) KILLING:If any of both party kills one person of the other party, it will be considered (BOTO) of which the killer will give the amount of ₱40.00 FORTY PESOS to be given to Peace Holders of both sides, regardless of fines (Doza).

* This document has not been changed or edited from the original.

(b) ACAO: Stealing big or valuable properties like cattles is (BOTO), (₱40.00) FORTY PESOS be taken from the person concerned to be given to Peace Holders of both sides. An additional of the equivalent of the property stolen be given to owner as (pasorot) and the stealer hosts the Public of what is enough for them.

(c) COURTING A MARRIED WOMAN: When a man from any of the two party courts a married woman of the other party it is (BOTO) for (₱40.00 Forty Pesos be collected from the man to be distributed to Peace Holders of both side, regardless of (molta) or Daladag. When the husband kills the wife and the man no Boto, but when he kills only one then there is Boto.

(d) COURTING SINGLE WOMAN: No Boto to be considered but the man must pay unto the woman's parents the amount of (₱5.00) FIVE PESOS to let it be known. When the woman gives birth a (patawid) of one carabao be given, but if the woman will have a bad luck for said birth the man be responsible for all the funeral expenses.

(e) BOXING: When one person from any of the two party boxes a man from the other party there will be no Boto, but a fine of five pesos (₱5.00) be given to the one injured or more depending upon the injury. This includes all employees. But when they settle it between themselves without the Knowledge of the Peace Holders then it be a valid settlement.

(f) IMMORAL ACTIONS: None

3. EXPENSES: For the Pass [past] days —

(a) Aciga) by Bosig

1.	Three (3) pigs worth	₱240.00
2.	Five (5) jars wine	50.00
3.	Decots two (2) Cas.	100.00
4.	Rice ten (10) Cas.	250.00

(b) Allangaiagn — by Calwing

1.	One male carabao	₱150.00
2.	One pig	80.00
3.	One pig (Tinago)	60.00
4.	Wine ten (10) jars	100.00
5.	Rice ten (10) Cas.	250.00

(c) PRESENT EXPENSES: (a) Asiga — Dolnat

1.	One carabao (aralor)	₱200.00
2.	One Pig	50.00
3.	Six Cas. Rice	150.00
4.	One pig	15.00
5.	Five big jars of wine	50.00
6.	Five gosi wine	25.00

7.	Four gtas. Coffee	12.00
8.	8 gats. sugar	8.00
9.	One can kerosene	5.00

BALUTOC ISAL
(Peace-Pact Holder for Asiga)

EYADAN GA-AYON
(Peace-Pact Holder for Allangigan)

WIT. TO MARKS:

EX. VICE MAYOR MANGWAG
(Prominent man for Asiga)

DENNA
(Ex Councilor Allangigan)

EDUARDO MEWAG
(Ex Mayor for Aciga)

ELUS MALAGA
(Prominent man for Ballayangen)

IDDOBA DUGAS
(Ex Mayor Aciga)

MANUEL CULANGAN
(Ex Councilor Ballayangen)

BITANGA
(Ex Mayor for Aciga)

MIGUEL SAGUDING
(Barrio Coun. Limos)

FERMIN DENNA
(Municipal District Clerk)

Bibliography

Bibliography

ANDERSON, BARBARA. "Report on Some Lexico-Statistical Counts on Languages of the Mountain Province, Philippines." Unpublished Paper, University of Chicago, 1960.
ANNUAL REPORTS of the Philippine Commission. Vol. 2. 1908.

BARTON, R. F. *Ifugao Law* (University of California "Publications in American Archaeology and Ethnology" 15.) 1919.
————. *The Religion of the Ifugaos.* "Memoir 65, American Anthropological Association." 219 pp. 1946.
————. *The Mythology of the Ifugaos.* "Memoirs of the American Folklore Society," Vol. 46. Philadelphia: American Folklore Society, 1955.
————. *The Kalingas, Their Institutions and Custom Law.* Chicago: University of Chicago Press, 1949.
BEFU, HARUMI. "Patrilineal Descent and Personal Kindred in Japan." *American Anthropologist,* 65:1328–1341. 1963.
BEYER, H. O. *The Non-Christian People of the Philippines.* "Census of the Philippines:" 1918. 2:907–57.
BLAIR, EMMA H. and James A. Robertson (Eds). *The Philippine Islands. 1493–1803.* 54 vols. Cleveland. 1903–09.
BUZETA, MANUEL. *Diccionario geografico estadistico, historico, de las Islas Filipinas.* 2 vols. Madrid. 1850–51.

CATHOLIC Directory of the Philippines. Manila: Catholic Trade School. 1960.
COLE, F. C. "Traditions of the Tinguian," *Anthropological Series.* Field Museum of Natural History, Chicago, Vol. 14, No. 1, Publication 180, pp. 1–226.
————. "The Tinguian." *Anthropological Series.* Field Museum of Natural History. Vol. 12, No. 1, Chicago. 1922.
CONKLIN, HAROLD C. *Hanunó Agriculture: A report on an integral system of shifting cultivation in the Philippines.* Rome: FAO. 1957.
————. "The Study of Shifting Cultivation." *Current Anthropology,* 1961. 2:27–61.

COULT, ALLAN D. "Role allocation, position structuring, and ambilineal descent." *American Anthropologist,* 66:29–40. 1964.

DAVENPORT, WILLIAM. "Nounilinear descent and descent groups." *American Anthropologist,* 1959. 61:557–572.

EGGAN, FRED. "Some aspects of culture change in the northern Philippines." *American Anthropologist.* 1941. 43:11–18.
————. "Some social institutions in the Mountain Province and their significance for historical and comparative studies." *Journal of East Asiatic Studies.* University of Manila. 3:329–335, 1954.
————. "The Sagada Igorots of Northern Luzon." in *Social Structure in Southeast Asia.* G. P. Murdock, ed. "Viking Fund Publications in Anthropology," No. 29. Chicago: Quadrangle Books, 1960.
————. "Ceremonial Organization and Re-organization in Sagada." Unpublished Manuscript, 1959.

FIRTH, RAYMOND. "A Note on Descent Groups in Polynesia." *Man.* 57:4–8. 1957.
FOLKMAR, D. "Social institutions of the Tinglayan Igorot." Original manuscript in the H. O. Beyer Collection, Manila. Typescript copies in the University of Chicago Philippines Studies Center. 1906.
FOX, ROBERT. *The Calatagan Excavations.* "Philippine Studies." 7:325–390. 1959.
FRAKE, CHARLES O. "Malayo-Polynesian Land Tenure." *American Anthropologist.* 58:170–173. 1956.
FREEMAN, J. D. "On the Concept of Kindred." *Journal of the Royal Anthropological Institute.* 91:192–220. 1961.

GIESER, C. RICHARD. "The Phonemes of Kalinga." *Oceania Linguistic Monographs* (eds. A. Capell and S. Wurm.) No. 3, pp. 10–23. Australia: University of Sidney. 1958.
GOODENOUGH, WARD H. "A Problem in Malayo-Polynesian Social Organization." *American Anthropologist.* 57:71–83. 1955.
————. "Reply to Frake." *American Anthropologist.* 58:173–75. 1956.
————. "Review of Social Structure in Southeast Asia." G. P. Murdock (ed.). *American Anthropologist.* 63:1341–47. 1961.

JENKS, A. E. *The Bontoc Igorot.* "Philippine Islands Ethnological Survey Publications." Vol. 1. Manila. 1905.

KEESING, F. M. and MARIA KEESING. *Taming Philippine Headhunters: A Study of Government and of Cultural Change in Northern Luzon.* London: George Allen and Unwin, Ltd. 1934.
————. *The Ethnohistory of Northern Luzon.* Stanford: Stanford University Press. 1962.
————. "The Isneg: Shifting Cultivators of the Northern Philippines." *Southwestern Journal of Anthropology.* 18:1–19. 1962.

LAMBRECHT, F. "Genealogical Trees of Mayawyaw." *Journal of East Asiatic Studies.* 2:21–27. 1953.

————. "Genealogical Tree of Kiangan." *Journal of East Asiatic Studies.* 3:366–69. 1954.

LANDE, CARL HERMAN. *Politics in the Philippines.* Ph.D. Thesis. Department of Government, Harvard University, Cambridge, Mass., pp. 1–387. 1958.

LEACH, EDMUND R. "On Certain Unconsidered Aspects of Double Descent Systems." *Man.* 62:130–34. 1962.

LEANO, ISABEL WALINGCHAN. *The Ibaloys of Takdian: Their Social, Economic, and Religious Life.* (Mimeographed.) Graduate School, the Philippine Women's University, Manila. 1958.

LOWIE, ROBERT H. *Indians of the Plains* ("American Museum of Natural History, Anthropological Handbooks," No. 1.) New York: McGraw-Hill Book Co., Inc. 1954.

MINTZ, SIDNEY W. and ERIC R. WOLF. "An Analysis of Ritual Co-Parenthood (Compadrazgo)," *Southwestern Journal of Anthropology,* Vol. 6, pp. 341–368. 1950.

MOSS, CLAUDE RUSSELL. "Nabaloi Laws and Rituals, Kankanoi Ceremonies." *University of California Publications in American Archaeology and Ethnology.* Vol. 15, Nos. 3 and 4. pp. 207–384. 1920.

MOUNTAINEER, The: Voice of the North. A Sunday newspaper published by the D.T.C. printing press, Trinidad, Benguet Province. November 11, 1962.

MURDOCK, GEORGE P. *Social Structure.* New York: Macmillan Co. 1949.

————. *Social Structure in Southeast Asia.* "Viking Fund Publications in Anthropology," No. 29. Chicago. Quadrangle Books. 1960.

NADEL, S. F. *The Nuba.* London: Oxford University Press, 1947.

REDFIELD, ROBERT. *Peasant Society and Culture.* Chicago: University of Chicago Press. 1956.

SCHADENBERG, ALEX. "Contributions to the Knowledge of the Banao People and of the Guinanes, Gran Cordillera Central, Island of Luzon, Philippines." Translated by the University of Chicago Philippines Studies Center from the *Transactions of the Berlin Anthropological Society.* Feb. 19, 1887.

————. "A Contribution to the Knowledge of the Tribes Living in the Interior of Northern Luzon." Translated by the University of Chicago Philippine Studies Center from *Zeitschrift für Ethnologie.* Vol. 21, pp. 674–682. 1889.

SCHEERER, OTTO. "Kalinga Texts from the Balbalasang-Ginaang Group." *Philippine Journal of Science.* 19:175–206. 1921.

SCOTT, WILLIAM H. ND. Field Notes on the Kalinga and Other Mountain Province Peoples.
————. "Economic and Material Culture of the Kalingas of Madukayan." *Southwestern Journal of Anthropology.* 14:318–337. 1958a.
————. "A Preliminary report on upland rice in northern Luzon." *Southwestern Journal of Anthropology.* 14:87–105. 1958b.
————. "Boyhood in Sagada."*Anthropological Quarterly.* 31:61–93. 1958c.
————. "The Apo-Díos Concept in Northern Luzon." *Philippine Studies.* 8:772–73. 1960a.
————. "The Word Igorot." *Philippine Studies.* 8:234–248. 1960b.
————. "Cordillera Architecture of Northern Luzon." "Folklore Studies." *Journal of Far Eastern Folklore.* Tokyo: 1962. 21:186–220.
SIMPSON and YINGER (eds.) "American Indians and American Life," *The Annals,* May 1957.
SPICER, EDWARD H. (ed.) *Perspectives in American Indian Culture Change.* Chicago: University of Chicago Press. 1961.
————. *Cycles of Conquest.* The University of Arizona Press, 1962.
SPIER, LESLIE. "The Distribution of Kinship Systems in North America," *University of Washington Publications in Anthropology,* Vol. 1, No. 2, pp. 71–88.

TAFT COMMISSION REPORT. Washington, D.C. 1900.
THOMAS, DAVID and Healey. "Some Philippine Language Sub-groupings: A Lexico-statistical Study." *Anthropological Linguistics.* Vol. 4. No. 9: 21–33. 1962.

VANOVERBERGH, M. *Dress and Adornment in the Mountain Province of Luzon, Philippine Islands.* "Publication of the Catholic Anthropological Conference." Vol. 3. pp. 1–80. 1941.
————. *The Isneg Farmer.* "Publications of the Catholic Anthropological Conference." Vol. 3. pp. 1–80. 1941.
VAYDA, ANDREW P. "Expansion and Warfare Among Swidden Agriculturists." *American Anthropologist.* 63:346–358. 1961.

WAGLEY, CHARLES and MARVIN HARRIS. "A Typology of Latin-American SubCultures." *American Anthropologist.* 57:428–51. 1955.
WILSON, LAWRENCE L. *The Skyland of the Philippines.* Manila: Benipayo Press. (2nd ed.). 1956.
————. "Sapao, Lt. Governor Hale of Kalinga." *Journal of East Asiatic Studies.* 5:1–38. 1957.
WOLF, ERIC R. "Types of Latin-American Peasantry: A Preliminary Discussion." *American Anthropologist.* 57:452–71. 1955.
WORCESTER, DEAN C. "Headhunters of Northern Luzon." *National Geographic.* 32:833–930. 1912.
————. "The Non-Christian Tribes of the Philippines." *National Geographic.* 24:1157–1256. 1913.
————. and Hayden R. *The Philippines Past and Present.* 2 vols. New York, 1930.

Index